Reevaluating Eisenhower

Reevaluating Eisenhower

American Foreign Policy in the 1950s

Richard A. Melanson
David Mayers

UNIVERSITY OF ILLINOIS PRESS
Urbana and Chicago

Illini Books edition, 1989

© 1987 by the Board of Trustees of the University of Illinois
Manufactured in the United States of America
1 2 3 4 5 C P 5 4 3 2 1

This book is printed on acid-free paper.

Library of Congress Cataloging-in-Publication Data

Melanson, Richard A.
  Reevaluating Eisenhower.

  Includes bibliographies.
   1. United States—Foreign relations—1953–1961.
2. Eisenhower, Dwight D. (Dwight David), 1890–1969.
I. Mayers, David.   II. Title.
E835.M38   1987   327.73   86–4363
ISBN 0-252-01340-9 (cloth : alk. paper)
ISBN 0-252-06067-9 (paper : alk. paper)

To the memory of Professor James Leake,
an inspired scholar
and admirer of Eisenhower

Contents

Preface

Within the past decade, many scholars have developed a renewed interest in the social, political, and foreign policies of the United States during the administration of President Dwight D. Eisenhower. Significant, even provocative, works dealing with cold-war diplomacy and Eisenhower's understanding of presidential leadership have resulted from their labors. Still, a definitive evaluation has yet to arise among historians and political scientists about the Eisenhower years, particularly regarding foreign affairs. In this volume a number of both established and younger scholars combine their efforts in order to investigate, debate, and analyze in greater detail than hitherto the foreign policy of the Eisenhower-Dulles era.

Until recently, most academic critics have been quite severe in their judgments of Eisenhower and have accepted the popular image of the war hero whose winning manner hardly substituted for vigorous leadership in international relations. According to such wisdom, John Foster Dulles ran foreign policy while Eisenhower passed an inordinate amount of time on the greens of the Augusta National. In his second term, Eisenhower appeared to practice all the habits of a caretaker president. Diplomacy drifted, and, on those occasions when the president chose to speak on foreign political issues, his garbled syntax seemed to reflect a muddled mind. Except for his ruminations in 1961 about the pernicious influence of a "military-industrial complex," Eisenhower certainly did not bequeath any memorable phrases to the nation comparable to his successor's series of heroic epigraphs.

As he was undistinguished in speech, so, too, was Eisenhower ineffective in coping with crucial issues; his critics—especially those of the Kennedy period—complained that his legacy in foreign policy and national security was positively dreary. His personal allegiance and that of his advisors generally to conservative fiscal policies and to a balanced budget led him to resist those requests from the Pentagon aimed at substantially increasing allocations for the Navy, Army, and Air Force. As a consequence, conventional forces ranging from armored divisions to counterinsurgency teams were reduced, and the United States placed an unhealthy reliance upon nuclear weapons.

This so-called "New Look" may have produced "more bang for the buck," as Dulles so felicitously phrased it, but it hamstrung the ability of the government to use military force in a calibrated and credible fashion. Liberals of the John Kennedy ilk charged that massive retaliation was unpersuasive to ally and foe alike and that Communist aggression in all of its multiple forms, particularly including internal subversion and guerrilla warfare, went undeterred. According to Eisenhower's contemporary critics, it was simple nonsense to believe, as Dulles implied, that the United States would use nuclear weapons against China or the USSR in response to a Communist coup in the Middle East or central Africa. The melancholy fact was that the United States could not react convincingly when confronted with subtler forms of Communist assertiveness. Meanwhile, U.S. allies were frightened by the prospect of a thermonuclear war waged for reasons remote to West European or Japanese concerns.

Implementation of conservative fiscal policies also meant that by the time Eisenhower retired from office in 1961, the United States had fallen behind the Soviet Union in some areas, with potentially grave consequences for diplomacy. The launching of Sputnik in 1957 seemed to emphasize for critics the dangers of lagging behind in the space race; if the Russians could send a missile into outer space, they presumably could also strike the American mainland with their rockets. In the 1960 presidential contest, candidate Kennedy campaigned intensively against the alleged missile gap and implicated Richard Nixon in the shortsightedness of Eisenhower's inadequate and underfunded military-technology programs.

To various scholars of the 1950s, Dulles's major conceptual contribution was brinkmanship that on more than one occasion nearly precipitated World War III. His advocacy of the use of tactical nuclear weapons in order to rescue French troops at Dienbienphu in 1954 was certainly feckless. His brutal treatment two years later of the French and British during the Suez crisis strained the NATO alliance to the point of rupture. His clumsy, spiteful manner toward Nasser, exemplified by the secretary's refusal to lend assistance to the Aswan High Dam project, had earlier encouraged Egypt to shift toward the Soviet Union. Dulles had proved ineffective and even a little ludicrous on practically every front.

Dulles was also notorious for being ponderous and moralistic and for speaking in the most lurid terms of godless communism and the threat it posed. A staunch Presbyterian, and Calvinist to the core, Dulles and his stark black-white pronouncements on world problems seemed not only the worst sort of righteous self-indulgence, but also plainly simple-minded.[1] The inflated rhetoric of anticommunist crusade seemed to overwhelm or obscure any possibility of a thoughtful or refined understanding of U.S. foreign interests.

The view that Dulles was a pious dogmatist and that Eisenhower was a dullard has been increasingly challenged by a number of writers, however. While an early 1960s poll of historians ranked Eisenhower twenty-second among American presidents, nestled between Andrew Johnson and Chester Arthur, a similar poll conducted in 1984 placed him among the ten greatest presidents.[2] In fact, since the late 1960s, first journalists and then scholars have been busy rehabilitating Eisenhower, whom they have found to be far from an "unintelligent, inarticulate, bland, passive captive of corporate executives."[3]

This reevaluation of his reputation actually began nearly twenty years ago in an article by Murray Kempton, who saw in Eisenhower a cunning, almost Machiavellian, politician obsessed with subterfuge and disguise.[4] In 1969 Garry Wills glimpsed a political genius, who "had the true professional's instinct for making things look easy;"[5] in the following year Richard Rhodes wrote in *Harper's* that "no one seems to have understood that he was a brilliant man."[6] The historian Herbert Parmet began the first scholarly reappraisal in 1972 in his *Eisenhower and the American Crusades*.[7]

These and other kinder critics of Eisenhower and Dulles have been impressed that the United States emerged from the 1950s in an extremely strong position. The GNP had gone up without severe inflation, and the West European economies continued to expand and to prosper. NATO had not only survived Suez, but its power had also been much augmented by the inclusion of West Germany in 1955. Oil interests were intact in the Middle East. U.S. naval and air bases were secure throughout the Pacific. Even if the government was spending only two-thirds of the amount on military procurements that the Democrats recommended, the military prowess of the United States was by 1961 still far superior to the USSR.[8] As Kennedy discovered upon coming to office, a missile gap certainly existed, but it was one in which the United States enjoyed a vast advantage. Victory in the 1962 Cuban missile crisis was in some sense the result of Eisenhower's careful cultivation of superior strategic and naval forces in the 1950s; throughout his eight years in office, he knew, based on intelligence reports, just how paltry equivalent Soviet forces actually were.

Many liberals today praise Eisenhower for his perceptive warning about the military-industrial complex and the need to limit its expansion and political influence; his alarm about the effects on civil life and liberties of a militarized society was apparently deeply felt. As for Dulles, Eisenhower may have selected him to lead the State Department because of his knowledge and wide diplomatic experience, but there was never any question about who was in charge. The secretary took his every cue and decision from the president.[9] A veteran soldier with firsthand experience of the disasters of war, Eisenhower was moderate in his foreign policy, fully appreciated the complicated relationship between using military instruments and achieving sound diplomatic goals, and tried earnestly—and to a degree succeeded—in lowering the cold-war tensions that had so anguished the world during the final years of Truman's administration. Some recent historians of the Eisenhower period also claim that Dulles, too, was more complicated than indicated by the image of dour prig so cheerfully drawn by various pundits and liberal partisans of his era. Such scholars now argue that behind his sweeping public rhetoric, the secretary possessed a surprising gift for the give-and-take of foreign policy. His bombast seems to have been formulated to deflect aspersions by the right wing of the Republican party against his integrity—in 1946 he had recommended Alger Hiss to be president of the Carnegie Endowment for International Peace.

Despite political campaign rhetoric about the immorality of mere containment and the need to substitute for it a "positive" program of rollback and liberation, Eisenhower and Dulles never departed from Truman's course in Europe and certainly were not about to provoke a war by invading Russia's sphere of influence. When cracks appeared in the Soviet East European empire in 1953 (East Germany) and in 1956 (Hungary and Poland), the Americans prudently abstained from intervening and were content to register protests at the United Nations. Although the Republicans certainly talked tough, they were unwilling to take any forward movement on behalf of the "captive nations."

In the Third World, by contrast, a U.S. policy of interventionism was readily apparent during the 1950s: witness events in Iran (1953), Guatemala (1954), Quemoy and Matsu (1954, 1958), Lebanon (1958), support of the French in Indochina, and (after 1954) of the Vietnamese government in Saigon. Eisenhower's natural caution and good sense enabled the United States to maneuver through these crises without palpable damage to itself, and by 1961 American armies were nowhere engaged in combat—a considerable achievement, apologists argue, especially when compared with Truman and with Eisenhower's successors.

A full-scale reappraisal of Eisenhower is thus under way. Many commentators, of course, have continued to portray the old Eisenhower. Richard Rovere, Emmet J. Hughes, and Arthur Schlesinger, Jr., for example, have reiterated the earlier conventional wisdom;[10] but as new documentation has become available—most notably the remarkable Ann Whitman file at the Eisenhower Library—a more complex picture has begun to emerge. Among the first to take advantage of the Whitman file was Peter Lyon, whose 1974 *Eisenhower: Portrait of the Hero*[11] accepted the view of a politically astute leader, but rejected the claim that Eisenhower's foreign policy was essentially restrained. This latter interpretation had been offered in the early 1970s by more radical historians like Barton J. Bernstein and Blanche Wiesen Cook.[12]

While general treatments of Eisenhower have continued to appear— for example, Charles C. Alexander's *Holding the Line: The Eisenhower Era, 1952–1961*[13] and Elmo Richardson's *The Presidency of Dwight D. Eisenhower*[14]—the appearance of more specialized books and articles greatly accelerated during the late 1970s. Thus, scholars have offered new evaluations of Eisenhower's leadership style, dealings with Congress, relations with Dulles, management of the Defense Department, science policy, and handling of Joseph McCarthy.[15] In the 1980s, his nuclear strategy, disarmament proposals, foreign economic policy, organization of the National Security Council, role in defeating the Bricker Amendment, use of the CIA in Guatemala, and his philosophical convictions have been among the subjects studied intensively.[16]

In spite of this recent and valuable outpouring of Eisenhower scholarship, the editors hope that *Reevaluating Eisenhower: American Foreign Policy in the 1950s* can make a useful contribution for several reasons. First, although it is true that several general treatments and many monographic studies of Eisenhower have appeared during the last decade, no collection that demonstrates the current state of Eisenhower scholarship has appeared previously. Most of this volume's essays draw heavily on recently declassified materials to provide fresh insights into Eisenhower's foreign policy. In this sense, the anthology can be seen as an intellectual descendant of the two Richard S. Kirkendall books of 1967 and 1972 that assessed the Truman period as a research field with the help of then newly available documents.[17] Although these earlier works examined broad areas that included both Truman's foreign and domestic policies, while this one focuses on Eisenhower's diplomacy, all three are additionally characterized by a wide range of scholarly evaluations.

Indeed, the essays here represent something of the diversity of scholarly opinion about the foreign policy of Eisenhower and Dulles. Norman

Graebner, for example, is dismayed by Eisenhower's intransigent hostility toward Communist China. On the other hand, Kenneth Thompson and Anne-Marie Burley are cautiously sympathetic to Eisenhower and the solutions that he and his advisors sought for diverse foreign dilemmas. And David Mayers believes that Eisenhower and Dulles distinguished some national differences among the major Communist powers and fashioned diplomacy accordingly. In any case, most of the essays in this book do not ascribe either great praise or unalloyed blame to Eisenhower and Dulles. The general tone is dispassionate rather than partisan.

The two essays in Section 1 are broadly interpretative and provide conceptual frameworks for the other chapters, which deal with particular aspects of Eisenhower-Dulles foreign policy. Kenneth Thompson examines the faults and merits of Eisenhower's strategic thinking, and Richard Melanson assesses the domestic and philosophical sources that shaped and qualified Eisenhower's diplomacy.

The essays in Section 2 are more narrowly focused. Norman Graebner and David Mayers treat substantially the same issues—U.S. policy toward international communism and China—and yet come to startingly different conclusions. Readers will have to decide whether these interpretations are reconcilable. Richard Immerman, Thomas Zoumaras, and William Stivers examine discrete episodes, sometimes bizarre or tragic, of U.S. involvement in the Third World. Again, their evaluations of Eisenhower and Dulles are not entirely complementary. Finally, Anne-Marie Burley and Robert Strong consider issues central to Soviet-U.S. relations, the questions of German rearmament and of superpower arms control.

Reevaluating Eisenhower also takes advantage of documents that were fortuitously declassified before two executive orders made it more difficult for scholars to reconstruct the American diplomatic historical record of the 1950s. Although the general purpose of President Carter's 1978 Executive Order 12065 was to loosen government restrictions on classified records, it has had some undesirable consequences. "Foreign government information" is therein defined in an exceedingly narrow manner and is subject to a thirty-year review procedure; unfortunately, few documents of any significance to U.S. foreign relations are devoid of such information. Moreover, the State Department has used another provision of the order to tighten declassification guidelines that had been in place since 1972. State has also established the Classification/Declassification Center (CDC), which, instead of facilitating the declassification process, has actually become an obstacle to the orderly release of materials. But far more damaging to scholarly inquiry has been President Reagan's Executive Order 12356. Called an "exhortation to closure" by one leading academic critic, this order abolished previous provisions for mandatory agency review of classified records, further tightened the definition of "foreign government information," and allowed for the *re*classification of materials that had been released under the older guideline. As a result, some records have been withdrawn from public perusal;[18] the *Foreign Relations of the United States* series has also suffered. Some of the more recent volumes lack crucial material—for example, NSC minutes on Korea and CIA sources on Guatemala—and all are being released at an agonizingly slow pace.[19] It appears that slower and more selective declassification will continue for at least the remainder of the 1980s. This collection, then, appears at a time both when a critical initial mass of primary source material—chiefly the Whitman file[20] and several 1952–54 *FRUS* volumes[21]—has made significant scholarship possible, and when a similar documentary windfall does not seem likely soon again.

Although the essays in this volume cannot be fully definitive, they do demonstrate something of the spectrum of informed views now possible about Eisenhower's foreign policy and the complexity of international issues in the 1950s and, therefore, accurately reflect the current state of Eisenhower-Dulles scholarship. The essayists hope that their work will not only convey to students something about U.S. policy as it evolved between the Korean and Vietnam wars, but that it will also stimulate colleagues to further exertions of research in this vital field of inquiry. Even now, Eisenhower's first administration seems especially rich in possibilities for significant work in official attitudes and policies toward eastern Europe; U.S. perceptions of Khrushchev's de-Stalinization campaign; policy toward Southeast Asia and China; and U.S. relations with Japan, NATO countries, Israel and Egypt, and Latin America. Much has been sifted through and evaluated; much more remains unexamined.

Very likely the shibboleths of the past will not endure against the weight of new evidence, new arguments, and broader insights now being culled from the Eisenhower years. Indeed, as witnessed by most of the essays herein, much current scholarship is challenging the proposition that U.S. foreign policy during the 1950s was peculiarly lackadaisical, ideological, unperceptive, and intellectually flawed.

Notes

1. For examples of scholarship that portray the secretary as a combination of pious prig and pedantic moralist, see Townsend Hoopes, *The Devil and John*

8   *Reevaluating Eisenhower*

Foster Dulles (Boston: Little, Brown, 1973) and John Stoessinger, *Crusaders and Pragmatists* (New York: W. W. Norton, 1979).

2. Arthur M. Schlesinger, Jr., "Our Presidents: A Rating of 75 Historians," *New York Times Magazine,* 29 July 1962, 12, 40–41. Even in a 1970 poll of an Organization of American Historians panel, Eisenhower finished twentieth in achievements and twenty-second in strength of action.

3. Mary S. McAuliffe, "Eisenhower, the President," *Journal of American History* 68 (December 1981): 625. See also Vincent P. DeSantis, "Eisenhower Revisionism," *Review of Politics* 38 (April 1976): 190–207; Gary W. Reichard, "Eisenhower as President: The Challenging View," *South Atlantic Quarterly* 77 (Summer 1978): 205–81; and Karen J. Winkler, "Eisenhower Revised: From a 'Do-Nothing' to an Arch-Manipulator, a Low-Key Leader," *Chronicle of Higher Education,* 30 January 1985, 5, 8–9.

4. Murray Kempton, "The Underestimation of Dwight D. Eisenhower," *Esquire* 68 (September 1967): 108–9, 156.

5. Garry Wills, *Nixon Agonistes: The Crisis of the Self-Made Man* (Boston: Houghton Mifflin, 1969), 131.

6. Richard Rhodes, "Ike: An Artist in Iron," *Harper's* 241 (July 1970): 72.

7. Herbert S. Parmet, *Eisenhower and the American Crusades* (New York: Macmillan, 1972).

8. Stephen E. Ambrose, *Rise to Globalism: American Foreign Policy, 1938–1976* (New York: Penguin Books, 1976).

9. Interview of Arthur Flemming by David Mayers, 8 May 1984.

10. Richard Rovere, "Eisenhower Revisited: A Political Genius? A Brilliant Man?" *New York Times Magazine* 7 February 1971, 14, 59–61; Emmet J. Hughes, *The Living Presidency: The Resources and Dilemmas of the American Presidential Office* (New York: Coward, McCann, and Geohegan, 1972); and Arthur M. Schlesinger, Jr., *The Imperial Presidency* (Boston: Houghton Mifflin, 1973).

11. Peter Lyon, *Eisenhower: Portrait of the Hero* (Boston: Little, Brown, 1974).

12. Barton J. Bernstein, "Foreign Policy in the Eisenhower Administration," *Foreign Service Journal* 50 (May 1973): 17–20, 29–30, 38; Blanche Wiesen Cook, *Dwight David Eisenhower: Antimilitarist in the White House* (St. Charles, Mo.: Forums in History, 1974). But see also Cook, *The Declassified Eisenhower: A Divided Legacy* (New York: Macmillan, 1981) for a later view.

13. Charles C. Alexander, *Holding the Line: The Eisenhower Era, 1952–1961* (Bloomington: Indiana University Press, 1975).

14. Elmo Richardson, *The Presidency of Dwight D. Eisenhower* (Lawrence: University Press of Kansas, 1979).

15. See, for example, Fred I. Greenstein, "Eisenhower as an Activist President: A Look at New Evidence," *Political Science Quarterly* 94 (Winter 1979–80): 575–600; Gary W. Reichard, *The Reaffirmation of Republicanism: Eisenhower and the Eighty-Third Congress* (Knoxville: University of Tennessee Press, 1975); Richard H. Immerman, "Eisenhower and Dulles: Who Made the Decisions?" *Political Psychology* 1 (Autumn 1979): 21–38; Douglas Kinnard, *Presi-*

dent Eisenhower and Strategy Management: A Study in Defense Politics (Lexington: University Press of Kentucky, 1979); George B. Kistiakowsky, *A Scientist at the White House: The Private Diary of President Eisenhower's Special Assistant for Science and Technology* (Cambridge, Mass.: MIT Press, 1976); James R. Killian, Jr., *Sputnik, Scientists, and Eisenhower: A Memoir of the First Special Assistant to the President for Science and Technology* (Cambridge, Mass.: MIT Press, 1977); and Allen Yarnell, "Eisenhower and McCarthy: An Appraisal of Presidential Strategy," *Presidential Studies Quarterly* 10 (Winter 1980): 90–98. See also Robert A. Divine, *Blowing on the Wind: The Nuclear Test Ban Debate, 1954–1960* (New York: Oxford University Press, 1978) and Richard Aliano, *American Defense Policy from Eisenhower to Kennedy: The Politics of Changing Military Requirements, 1957–61* (Athens: Ohio University Press, 1975).

16. See, for example, David Alan Rosenberg, "The Origins of Overkill: Nuclear Weapons and American Strategy, 1945–1960," *International Security* 7 (Spring 1983): 3–71; Thomas F. Soapes, "A Cold Warrior Seeks Peace: Eisenhower's Strategy for Nuclear Disarmament," *Diplomatic History* 4 (Winter 1980): 57–72; Walt W. Rostow, *Open Skies: Eisenhower's Proposal of July 21, 1955* (Austin: University of Texas Press, 1983); Robert A. Divine, *Eisenhower and the Cold War* (New York: Oxford University Press, 1981); Burton I. Kaufman, *Trade and Aid: Eisenhower's Foreign Economic Policy, 1953–61* (Baltimore: Johns Hopkins University Press, 1982); Walt W. Rostow, *Eisenhower, Kennedy and Foreign Aid* (Austin: University of Texas Press, 1985); Anna K. Nelson, "The Security Council," *Diplomatic History* 7 (Fall 1983): 307–26; Duane A. Tananbaum, "The Bricker Amendment Controversy: Its Origins and Eisenhower's Role," *Diplomatic History* 9 (Winter 1985): 73–94; Richard H. Immerman, *The CIA in Guatemala: The Foreign Policy of Intervention* (Austin: University of Texas Press, 1982); and Robert Griffith, "Dwight D. Eisenhower and the Corporate Commonwealth," *American Historical Review* 87 (February 1982): 87–122. See also Stephen E. Ambrose, *Ike's Spies: Eisenhower and the Espionage Establishment* (New York: Macmillan, 1981); Fred I. Greenstein, *The Hidden-Hand Presidency: Eisenhower as Leader* (New York: Basic Books, 1982); and William B. Ewald, Jr., *Eisenhower the President: Crucial Days, 1951–60* (Englewood Cliffs, N. J.: Prentice-Hall, 1981).

17. Richard S. Kirkendall, ed., *The Truman Period as a Research Field* (Columbia: University of Missouri Press, 1967) and *The Truman Period as a Research Field: A Reappraisal, 1972* (Columbia: University of Missouri Press, 1973).

18. Thomas G. Paterson, "The Present Danger of Thought Control," *Society for Historians of American Foreign Relations Newsletter* 15 (September 1984): 38–39.

19. According to Anna K. Nelson, the documents obtained by Richard H. Immerman for *The CIA in Guatemala* would not be declassified under current conditions. "Classified History," *Organization of American Historians Newsletter* 12 (August 1984): 7.

20. The presidential papers of Dwight D. Eisenhower (Ann Whitman file)

constitute the richest collection in the Dwight D. Eisenhower Library. Among the most notable of its eighteen parts for foreign policy research are the Ann Whitman diary series, the Dulles-Herter series, the Legislative Meetings series, the International Meetings series, and the NSC series. Only small portions of the NSC series, however, have been declassified as of 1986.

21. As of March 1986, thirteen of the sixteen projected volumes in the 1952–54 series had been released. Furthermore, the 1951 series was still incomplete. According to Thomas G. Paterson, "documents for 1955–60 will not be opened to research for a long time . . . and apparently the Office of the Historian has suspended work on the volumes covering the early 1960s" ("The Present Danger of Thought Control," 38, 39).

Part One
Eisenhower's Public Philosophy

The Strengths and Weaknesses of Eisenhower's Leadership

Kenneth W. Thompson

In *Crusade in Europe,* General Dwight D. Eisenhower, discussing American differences with Winston S. Churchill, wrote: "The future division of Europe did not influence our military plans for the final conquest of the country."[1] Churchill had argued that it would have been wiser for the British forces to take Berlin and for the United States' troops to enter Prague, as he insisted they could have done. Eisenhower maintained that Berlin, although psychologically important, was not the logical or the most desirable objective for Allied forces. He pointed out that Churchill "held that because the campaign was now approaching its end, troop maneuvers had acquired a political significance that demanded the intervention of political leaders in the development of broad operational plans."[2] Yet neither he nor political leaders in the Roosevelt administration were persuaded by Churchill's thinking.

Churchill had favored a secondary invasion in the Balkans. The determining factor in his strategy was his conviction that the Germans, if hard-pressed enough in the Balkans and the Mediterranean, would have to divert forces from Western Europe. He also believed that a demarcation line which would extend the western sphere further east would diminish the temptation for the Soviet Union to expand to fill a vacuum in Central Europe. Reflecting on the debate over Balkan strategy, Churchill wrote: "It . . . constitutes . . . the most acute difference I ever had with General Eisenhower."[3] Their differences stemmed in part from their respective roles, for as Eisenhower explained: "I felt that the Prime Minister's real concern was possibly of a political rather than a military nature. He may have thought that a post war situation which would see the Western Allies posted in great strength in the Balkans would be far more effective in producing a stable post-hostilities world than if the Russian armies should be the ones to occupy that region. . . . I well understood that strategy can be affected by political considerations. . . . But I did insist that as long as he argued the matter on military grounds alone I could not concede validity to his arguments."[4]

Yet the two leaders' differences may also provide a clue to the contradictory evidence that pervades this volume on the strengths and weaknesses, successes and failures of President Eisenhower. Historians of social thought have put forward the concept of "professional deformation." We are each the products of our educational, social, and professional formation. In an informal discussion, former Secretary of State Henry Kissinger touched on this when he spoke of his deficiencies in the realm of economics. He recounted that his advisors carefully briefed him on issues concerning balance of payments, development, and the International Monetary Fund. He learned his lines, and, because of the prestige of his office and his considerable intellectual powers, he spoke with unquestioned authority. However, Kissinger acknowledged that he never grasped the stuff of economics as he did the truths of international politics. He went on to say that the American leader whom he respected most and whom he had once described as the single American he would trust most with the powers of the presidency, George Shultz, showed a similar limitation in the sphere of diplomacy and international politics. Kissinger could not remember a conversation with Shultz on diplomacy in which that respected economist had clearly demonstrated a full grasp of the realities of world politics. To these examples, we might add the long list of public figures who were at home in domestic politics, but who found international politics incomprehensible. For example, William Jennings Bryan as secretary of state under President Woodrow Wilson was so baffled and dismayed by the demands of the daily relations among states that he devoted himself almost entirely to the promotion of the arbitration movement, leaving the management of foreign policy to others.

Whether the glory and misery, the triumphs and tragedies of the Eisenhower presidency in foreign policy may not in part be attributable to the fact that the imperatives of world politics were merely one among many guideposts for his thought is a thesis worth exploring. Without such a thesis, one cannot escape puzzlement in following the account that runs through many of the chapters that follow. It remains a mystery, for instance, why Eisenhower should have expressed himself with such fervor on the need to bring the arms race under control and yet seemed oblivious to the consequences of actions that served the status quo yet conflicted with the search for accommodation. We must find some explanation for the priorities that guided his choices in practice that appear calculated to move away from, rather than toward, his objective of relaxation of tensions.

In 1982–83, the White Burkett Miller Center at the University of Virginia conducted a series of forums and interviews with intimates of President Eisenhower that resulted in the publication of *The Eisenhower Presidency*.[5] Contributors as diverse as the president's brother, Milton, Andrew J. Goodpaster, Bryce Harlow, Arthur Larson, Karl G. Harr, Bradley H. Patterson, Maurice Stans, Herbert Brownell, Arthur S. Flemming, Sherman Adams, and Eisenhower's biographer, William B. Ewald, joined in an effort to sketch the essence of Eisenhower's personality and leadership. Running through this oral history is a remarkably consistent presentation of the man and his works. The title of Harlow's interview summarized the picture that all of the participants sought to convey: "The Compleat President." Harr, who discussed "Eisenhower's Approach to National Security Decisionmaking," struck a note that echoes through the papers when he commented on "how much we all loved that man." Nobody who worked for Eisenhower went away and wrote a book that said bad things about him, in contrast with associates of many other presidents. This essay accordingly draws heavily on these Miller Center interviews and discussions.

Eisenhower's decision to run for president, according to his closest associates such as Herbert Brownell and his brother, stemmed from his commitment to internationalism. If he had been confident that Senator Robert Taft was a true internationalist, he would probably not have entered the race. However conservative he may have been on domestic issues (he warned Taft that some of his legislation verged on socialism), Eisenhower's experience in World War II and his relationships with leaders like Churchill and de Gaulle convinced him of the necessity of world leadership. He fought against the Bricker Amendment in part because it threatened usurpation of presidential power, but also because it would have crippled the United States in playing its essential role in the world (several of the conference contributors suggested that Eisenhower would have opposed the War Powers Resolution). Ewald, for example, revealed that "Eisenhower personally worked through that amendment word by word. He would write substitute amendments himself. He worked with the lawyers, he brought them in with great detail on certain things. That was a top drawer constitutional, presidential, national security issue and by golly he was going to know all about it. And he knew everything that anybody could tell him from State and from Justice on down, from Dulles and from Brownell, and from the people who worked for them."[6]

The most recent scholarship on Eisenhower, notably by Fred I. Greenstein of Princeton University, and the consensus of his closest associates make clear that Eisenhower had a political sense. Far from leaving all consideration of domestic political concerns to others, the president guided the ship of state through tempestuous domestic political waters as if by "a hidden hand." When his press secretary, James Hagerty, objected to an answer he was told to give to a particularly sensitive issue, Eisenhower responded: "Better you than me, my boy." When Eisenhower feared that he might say too much or too little on a particular issue, he reassured his colleagues by explaining: "I'll confuse them." On this point, his closest associates, and in particular his brother, broaden the discussion. Milton Eisenhower, in describing the criteria that the president used in press conferences, observed: "He would be doing two things. One, he would not reveal more than the security situation would permit. Second, he didn't want to make a dishonest answer. . . . So he would start and stop in the middle of a sentence and realize that he wasn't going to get it right so he would back up and start over again." While Eisenhower's double concern with security lapses and political deception led to muddled syntax, it protected him from the gaffes that during other administrations have harmed the nation's and its leaders' position and integrity.

Yet the Miller Center participants also emphasized that he was a man of principle. According to Larson, "Eisenhower could be said to be a man who made his decisions on the basis of principle rather than politics. He was politically shrewd but he was not a politician" insofar as "he wasn't motivated by political considerations."[7] Larson admitted that "principles may be a little bit too pretentious a word for what I have in mind. But I noticed very early . . . how often he said, 'I always' or 'I never' and then he would dredge down into some general principle of life or rule of life and come up with his decision." Eisenhower was a "principled pragmatist" whereas other postwar presidents have been "political pragmatists."[8] For example, Larson recalled that "if you wanted to get thrown out of the Oval Room, all you had to say is, 'Look, Mr. President, this is going to cost you votes in West Virginia.' Well, you wouldn't get past 'West'—you'd be out."[9] Goodpaster agreed that Eisenhower "worked from a set of principles. These were very high, often very broad principles. 'What's right for America?' was a question he would frequently ask. He would talk about a 'decent relationship' between countries, even countries that were in opposition to each other." And Goodpaster observed that "an interesting thing was his ability to use these principles instrumentally. He could call them into play in certain arguments around the Cabinet table."[10]

On the question of Eisenhower's approach to leadership, certain of his intimates expressed uneasiness with the term *hidden hand*. Thus, Goodpaster noted: "I think it may somewhat overstate and overdramatize the tendency he had always to work to multiple objectives. He would be looking, as he would put it, at how you kill two birds or many birds with one stone. Some of his objectives he would be reluctant to show. I think on occasion he deliberately kept some of them concealed. Especially some of the things of a longer term that he had in mind. Also, as to his methods, [he would] . . . take actions so that somebody else (maybe unknowingly) would be making a proposal that he really wanted to make."[11]

Milton Eisenhower gave another reason why his brother might have appeared always to be leading through indirect rather than direct measures, the "hidden hand." He remembered that "he was always building up the other fellow. He did this during the war and it was perfectly natural for him to do it in the presidency: He wanted people to be responsible and to grow and develop. He never said, 'I have told the secretary of agriculture to do so and so.' Never. He might say, 'I have approved the secretary's recommendation.' "[12] Eisenhower sought to delegate responsibility and to hold colleagues accountable for their acts. His assumption was that in so doing they would come forward and do their best.

Linked with his attitude toward individual responsibility was the fact that Eisenhower drew on his military experience to shape an organizational system to facilitate decision-making and follow-up. Eisenhower, of course, made heavy use of his cabinet as a forum for discussion ("If all I wanted was Foster Dulles' views on foreign policy, I would call him to the Oval Office to talk alone.") Again, according to Goodpaster, "He was a master executive. He knew what it was to be a superb executive and he knew that he knew it. He had great confidence in his powers of organizing, of delegating, of assuring that the people to whom these things were delegated did indeed work to carry out policies—policies that were set in broad guidelines, and were set after thorough deliberation and with his approval."[13]

Sometimes Eisenhower changed his mind during discussion, as an example that Flemming offered on legislation for aid to education demonstrates. Flemming and Eliot Richardson had developed a plan for a more significant involvement of the federal government in education. They had tried to sell the plan to the Bureau of the Budget and to several White House staffers but had not been notably successful. Then one day in the spring of 1959 Flemming went to the Oval Office to present the plan to Eisenhower. The president showed little enthusiasm, but

Flemming kept pressing for a decision. Finally, Eisenhower told General Persons to put the plan on the next day's Cabinet meeting agenda, a rather unusual thing to do. A long and lively Cabinet discussion took place, and Eisenhower finally said, "Well, I guess we better send something [an education bill] up [to Congress]." According to Flemming, "as a result of his listening to and participating in a very vigorous manner, he finally came around to the point where he decided that the best thing to do was to send it to the Hill."[14]

The president used Cabinet and staff secretaries to organize Cabinet agendas, to prepare papers and presentations, and to assign responsibilities for follow-up on the basis of a carefully kept record of action. He was an active participant in all Cabinet and National Security Council discussions, not waiting until everyone had been heard, but plunging into the discussion when direction or guidance was needed. Again, as Flemming remembered: "His work with the Cabinet as a collegial group did have an effect on the evolution of policy. Nothing was ever put to a vote and it was clear we were there talking about these matters as general advisers to him. He is the only person who voted. He is the only person who made a decision. He didn't have any difficulty making up his mind either usually. He gave us a decision and gave us a prompt decision."[15]

Perhaps this style reflected the confidence that Eisenhower had in his own powers of reasoning. In Goodpaster's words: "Oftentime he would question something, saying 'that's just not logical.' He would trace the line of logic through the problem, doing so, for example, where someone began to get off base (as he would term it) instead of following the central line of policy, or where someone would begin to pursue some parochial interest."[16] That Eisenhower had a quick mind and a vigorous personality was noted by all of his close advisors. Yet they also appreciated that he could make decisions without being overbearing. Goodpaster revealed that Eisenhower often referred to "desk pounders" as exhibiting false leadership.

Some would say that his strengths in certain instances became weaknesses. He deferred to professional politicians in his ill-fated decision to remove a reference to General Marshall condemning Senator McCarthy's attacks on him in a Wisconsin speech during the 1952 presidential campaign. The majority of the participants in the Miller Center oral history suggest that Eisenhower lived to regret his decision, although Adams defended him in the language of practical politics. According to Ewald, for example, "It was a mistake, it was a terrible mistake. Eisenhower regretted it. He was told it was a mistake; and people who were loyal to him around him knew it was a mistake. It went with him all through the rest of his life. He had to carry that weight with him, and it was one thing he was very defensive about, very uptight when we wrote about it in *Mandate for Change* and *Waging Peace*."[17]

But Adams recalled that Governor Kohler of Wisconsin thought that the remarks about McCarthy and Marshall were "gauche and awkward" and "a slap-in-the-face of a senator whose state was our host for the day." So Adams felt "duty bound" to take the objection up with Eisenhower.[18]

He made the following argument to the candidate: "You have spoken on this question before. Is the remark you make about General Marshall necessarily desirable or politically expedient, keeping in mind that this is the first time the subject has come up, probably, during the campaign? You have not been defending Marshall in your speeches in other states, but you wait until you get to . . . Milwaukee, before a great gathering, to put this record on."[19] Eisenhower "thought a minute and then said quickly, 'I guess you're right. Take it out.' " Adams "knew there was no love lost" between Eisenhower and McCarthy, but he "reasoned that they could have their differences if they wanted to, but they could do it without coming to blows on a platform in a state he needed to win the election."[20] And for Harlow, Eisenhower's handling of McCarthy was ultimately correct: "Truman attacked him personally, by name. Thereby he created a monster. Eisenhower killed him and he did it by ignoring him. The press almost went wild trying to force Eisenhower to attack him. There was White House friction over this, but Ike didn't bite. He wouldn't attack McCarthy by name. The result proved him right."[21]

Yet at what cost? John Eisenhower has argued that his father's tendency to subordinate his voice to others may have restricted his ability to galvanize public opinion in support of the policies that he sought to pursue.

Both Larson and Ewald stressed Eisenhower's sense of the nation's limits and his understanding of restraint and the need for international cooperation. When asked why he didn't intervene militarily in Indochina, the president replied: "Nobody asked us." For Larson, "if we had gone in [to Vietnam] unilaterally we would have contributed to the slaughter of thousands because we wanted to, not because somebody asked us. No Indochinese faction asked us, and that was what counted with Eisenhower." The president said, " 'The request has got to reflect the wishes of the population,' and, of course, the French couldn't have cared less about that."[22]

Eisenhower recognized the importance of damage limitation on occasions such as when he sought to reestablish a dialogue with the British and French after he had opposed their joint attack with Israel on Egypt. He had learned too well the importance of cooperation among the Allies in World War II to ignore its necessity in the cold war. Eisenhower was more prepared to restore relationships among friends than was Dulles, even when he found their actions unacceptable. According to Ewald, as soon as a truce had been established in Suez, Anthony Eden and Guy Mollet offered to fly immediately to Washington in order to resolve the dispute. Eisenhower agreed, but Dulles objected, saying "it's the wrong time." "So Eisenhower had to get back on the phone to Eden, and it was not an easy thing to do, to say 'Cancel your plane reservation. You are not coming.' "[23] Not until March 1957 did Eisenhower finally meet with Harold Macmillan in Bermuda "to put the whole alliance back together again. This is a key example of where Dulles overruled Eisenhower on timing."[24]

Above all, as his brother has eloquently explained, Eisenhower understood that possibilities of conflict in the nuclear age were too dangerous to allow a continuing deterioration in Soviet-American relations. He wanted to focus on the necessity for trade with the Soviets in his last speech in the 1952 campaign but was overruled by party strategists. "He said, 'Milton, I want you to write a paragraph in here someplace saying that I want to develop active two-way trade with the Soviet Union to our mutual benefit.' His brother replied, 'Well, I'll do it if you say so but let me say that as you know very well it's a complicated subject and here we are just the night before the election. Why do you want to introduce a new subject which you are not going to be able to spell out anyway?' Eisenhower said, 'Now you are trying to make a politician out of me.' But after visits from several Republican leaders he finally exclaimed, 'Oh, all right, I give up.' "[25]

Similarly, Eisenhower responded enthusiastically to suggestions by liberals like Emmett Hughes for a massive program of Soviet-American cultural exchange only to find that Secretary Dulles and State Department officials considered the plan utopian and unworkable. The president invited Khrushchev to visit the United States and demonstrated his willingness to meet the Soviet leader at the Paris summit. Historians continue to debate whether his approach might have changed the course of cold-war history if the summit had not been aborted by the shooting down and capture of Gary Powers in the untimely U-2 incident. (One intimate tells the story of Eisenhower making one last-ditch attempt to communicate with Khrushchev at Geneva only to discover that the Soviet leader had departed his conference headquarters minutes before the president walked down the hall to the Soviet delegation.)

Perhaps Senators George and Russell of Georgia influenced the president, or maybe some of Churchill's fervor for talks at the highest level had rubbed off on him. Whatever his motivation, and some of his thought processes may be mirrored in the account of his brother on the possibility of reaching an accommodation with the Soviet leader, Eisenhower was among a handful of Western chiefs of state who believed with Churchill that "jaw-jaw is better than war-war." From Milton Eisenhower's perspective, "Eisenhower did everything he reasonably could to develop better relations. He was sincere about it. He did succeed in reducing the intensity of the Cold War."[26] But according to General Goodpaster, "There was an interesting tension between Eisenhower's desire to project a positive sense of America to the world and the more cautious, more careful and reserved approach at the diplomatic level operated by Secretary Dulles. He supported that diplomacy very strongly. Nevertheless, at the same time, he felt that we should reduce the causes of tension with the Russians through an exchange of views and by making it clear that we harbored no offensive military designs against them. Once he had decided against rollback then he was prepared to see the Soviet Union continue without threat from us so long as they did not threaten us and our allies."[27]

One other of the president's strengths has not been mentioned, and for the future of the human race it may be his most important. As few Western leaders, Eisenhower understood the devastation of war. More than most, and certainly more than latter-day civilian leaders, he took hold of the realities of nuclear war and sought to educate the public on its differences from conventional warfare. He saw that thermonuclear destruction would be fundamentally unlike any larger-scale traditional war and undertook to check the unrealism of military and civilian leaders who spoke of "prevailing" in a nuclear war. Whatever the limitations of his own knowledge, Eisenhower drew on the greater scientific authority of world-class scientists such as James R. Killian and George Kistiakowsky. He could not simply look up to scientists who happened to espouse his own viewpoint. Thus, according to Ewald "He brought the scientists in. Eisenhower brought in the President's Scientific Advisory Committee, and believe you me he brought them into the Oval Office, and he had them talk to him, and he listened to them. He had all kinds of technical presentations from those guys. So, he understood the hazards of nuclear testing or where we are going with this weapon or with that weapon. He really went flat out to get the best kind of professional, academic, scientific, and technological advice that he could get and spent many, many hours on it."[28] The president could thus hold the Pentagon in check, because not only did he have as much or more military experience than they, but he also knew where to turn for authoritative scientific estimates.

In the words of one associate, Eisenhower knew where the bodies were buried in the Pentagon and the dynamics of the military procurement process. As Ewald put it, "He would go through the defense budget line by line: What do the marines need with an aircraft carrier? He could see these phony items. He wrote to friends and said, 'You know, someday there is going to be somebody sitting here in this office who can't look at that defense budget and separate the phony things from the valid things.' So he went over this with a fine tooth comb in great detail."[29] And in his much-quoted farewell, Eisenhower warned of the hazards of the military-industrial complex.

A less well known but equally significant strength was Eisenhower's grasp of politico-strategic arguments. Goodpaster, for example, in recalling Operation Solarium conducted in 1953, revealed that: "On hearing these final reports Eisenhower immediately jumped up himself and said, 'Now I would like to summarize and evaluate what we've heard.' He did this, speaking extemporaneously for forty-five minutes or so after the several-hour presentation that had been made, coming down finally on a policy that was essentially the containment policy. George Kennan in talking with me in later years about this used the phrase that 'in doing so Eisenhower showed his intellectual ascendancy over every man in the room.' "[30]

Perhaps this impressive understanding of national security options stemmed, in part at least, from Eisenhower's rather sophisticated, multidimensional conception of power. According to Larson, although Eisenhower's definition of power was simple—"the ability to produce a desired result"—it was comprised of many ingredients, only one of which was the raw military element. "He said never use force in international affairs. Never! But if you do, use it overwhelmingly."[31] "Eisenhower did not need any more playing with military toys, thank you, he had had enough of that. And as a result he placed a much greater value on the loss of human life because he had lived through that. It didn't come as easy for him as somebody else who might say, 'Well, we'll throw in so many thousand troops here or there,' knowing that many of them are going to get killed."[32]

But if force was to be employed, then it had to be used unanswerably, as it was, for example, in Beirut in 1958: "The marines came up to the beach in an overwhelming force and that was it. There was no more trouble. General Maxwell Taylor kept arguing that we ought to send our troops into Beirut and into the mountains and really drive these fellows out. Eisenhower said absolutely not. He said, 'They stay on the beach so they can get away just as fast as they can if anything goes wrong.' And he said, 'If with all that support, Camille Chamoun and Sami Sul don't survive, then maybe they don't deserve to.' "[33]

Eisenhower also believed in the conservation of power. When, for example, Nasser nationalized the Suez Canal and some of Eisenhower's advisors were urging a U.S. military response, the president gave Larson "a little sermon on what he called 'the tyranny of the weak.' He then really pulled me up in my seat by saying, 'I guess we'll just have to put up with it. Every conceivable kind of action should be considered: diplomatic, economic, UN, regional organizations, CIA, anything, but not open military action.'"[34]

In addition, Eisenhower was sensitive to world opinion as a source of power and believed that it could simultaneously constrain and provide opportunities. Closely related to this factor was his belief that a country's moral posture was a source of power: "I remember once I was sitting there by his side and Dulles called and Eisenhower hung up and said, 'Goddamn it, we've got to lose either Tunisia or France. Bourguiba is the best friend we've got. I've just given the French an ultimatum.' And a little later he said, 'I wish for once we would get on the right side of independence in advance.' "[35]

Finally, Eisenhower realized the crucial character of American public opinion as an ingredient of power. For Goodpaster; "He was quite aware of the rapport that he had with the American people and the support he had from them. We were pretty close to understanding the thinking of the American people."[36] As a result, Eisenhower worked hard to maintain that public consensus.

This complex understanding of power can perhaps be made clearer by examining in some detail a revealing, recently declassified memorandum written by Eisenhower to Dulles in April 1955.[37] There he confronted the issue of the defense of Matsu and Quemoy and its importance to the United States. Eisenhower began by acknowledging that the "intermixture of warfare, negotiations, public statements, and military understandings" since June 1950 had given Chiang Kai-shek "some right to expect U.S. help in the active defense of these islands." But he warned that such U.S. involvement would entail grave risks. First, "because the world generally regards the coastal islands as part of the mainland, our active participation would forfeit the good opinion of the Western world, with consequent damage to our interests in Europe and elsewhere." Second, "there is much opposition in our own country to becoming involved militarily in defense of the offshore islands, and in the event of such involvement our people would be seriously divided at the very time when increased global risk would underline the need for unity." Finally, "even a successful defensive campaign would not stabilize the situation; a new attack could be expected at any time . . ." and "a disproportionate amount of our disposable, mobile, reserves would be tied down indefinitely to this one spot."[38]

At the same time, Eisenhower acknowledged that a failure to help defend these islands might have had equally disadvantageous consequences, for "most observers assert that it would dismay the Chi Nats, *whose morale and military efficiency are essential to the defense of Formosa and essential to the best interests of the United States and the Western world.*"[39] Moreover, "further retreat in front of the Chinese Communists could result, it is alleged, in the disintegration of all Asian opposition to the spread of Communism in that continent."[40]

While "opinion in the free world appears to back the American determination to assist the Chi Nats in the defense of Formosa and the Pescadores," Eisenhower worried that Chiang was "gambling his whole position in Formosa and his future as a useful agent in helping to drive Communism from China against a local and possibly temporary success in a precarious defense of two island groups who are militarily weak."[41] In sum, "the principal military reason for holding these islands" was "the estimated effect of their loss upon morale in Formosa" and "to persuade Chiang to adopt any other plan" would result in "*the loss to the free world of that bastion of strength.*"[42] Furthermore, "the abandonment of Quemoy and Matsu would have a '*psychological* effect' on Asian nations like Thailand, the Philippines, Laos, and Cambodia."[43]

Yet Eisenhower also realized that both the United States and Chiang "would be much better off if our national prestige were not even remotely committed to the defense of the islands." Interestingly, he speculated that if Chiang could find a way to withdraw from the offshore islands so that the move would be seen in Formosa and Southeast Asia "as a shrewd move to *improve* his strategic position, his prestige should be increased rather than diminished."[44]

For Eisenhower, then, the problem was to help achieve a situation that would be consistent with U.S. treaty obligations to Formosa and the Pescadores, would solidify American and free-world opinion, would sustain the morale of Chiang and his forces on Formosa, and would win the support of our friends in Southeast Asia and the neighboring islands.

The president suggested that these somewhat contradictory goals could be achieved with the following policy:

1. In order to prevent a collapse of our position in the Far East, prohibit Chiang and the U.S. forces from making a "full-out" defense of Quemoy and Matsu.

2. Persuade Chiang to regard the offshore islands as outposts to be appropriately garrisoned.

3. Expedite the concentrating, equipping, and garrisoning of troops on Formosa in order to give Chiang the greatest possible strength to support his outpost troops and to take advantage of any opportunities on the Mainland.

4. Make adequate plans for a determined Nationalist defense of Quemoy and Matsu; evacuation should take place only after "defensive forces had inflicted upon the attackers heavy and bloody losses."

5. Protect Chiang's prestige and morale: "There must be no basis for public belief that the alterations came about through American intervention or coercion."

6. Send additional U.S. forces, including Marines, to Formosa in order to protect it against attack and to maintain internal morale.[45]

Eisenhower concluded by noting that even if Chiang ultimately lost the offshore islands, their fall "would occur only after the defending forces had exacted a fearful toll from the attackers, and Chiang's prestige and standing in Southeast Asia would be increased rather than decreased as a result of a gallant, prolonged, and bitter defense." And although "his own losses would be inconsequential, the losses of the Communists should be very great indeed."[46]

From this memorandum we see that Eisenhower understood power as a mix of military, political, and psychological factors. It is also evident that he emphasized the importance of public opinion and morale as essential to any policy. Finally, we should also mention—as a partial refinement of Larson's formulation—that although Eisenhower opposed the direct commitment of U.S. troops to a losing battle for political purposes, he favored the use of Nationalist forces for such ends.

On the other hand, despite the impressive analytic abilities obviously reflected in this memorandum—and in many others as well—Eisenhower was hugely, and perhaps inordinately, concerned with appearances, as his constant references to prestige, morale, public opinion, and psychological impacts make clear. Taken to extremes, an obsession with perceptions risked transforming the rhetoric of global, anticommunist containment into a foreign policy of great imprudence. Eisenhower's periodic threats to employ nuclear weapons against China in order to deter an invasion of the offshore islands—the April 1955 memorandum notwithstanding—may have been the logical consequence of a preoccupation with appearances.

How, indeed, can we account for Eisenhower's foreign policy failures? The most commonplace answer is to point to the intractability of the problems with which he had to grapple. No postwar leader has successfully resolved the stubborn problems of the cold war, and their amelioration may well exceed human competence. How could we expect Eisenhower to succeed where others have failed?

One explanation of the unsolved problems of the Eisenhower administration is the nature of foreign policymaking in a democracy. From Alexander Hamilton to Alexis de Tocqueville to Walter Lippmann, Hans J. Morgenthau, and George F. Kennan, informed observers have stressed the stubborn realities confronting those who seek to reconcile the demands of domestic politics with the imperatives of foreign policy. What early observers recognized as a troublesome obstacle to wise foreign policy has in the cold war become a nearly irreconcilable conflict. The two adversaries in the postwar world confront one another not only as superpowers but also as the carriers of political ideologies in competition for the allegiance of humankind throughout the world. In the Soviet Union, the government defends itself against internal opposition by depicting the external threat as requiring the perpetuating of a totalitarian regime. In the United States, the spector of crusading world communism introduces the spirit of countercrusades into domestic politics. For a relatively moderate and reasonable president like Eisenhower, the context of domestic politics can be less supportive than for more extreme spokesmen on the Right or the Left. For this reason, President Eisenhower discovered that moderate Democrats rallied to his side more often than right-wing Republicans. Secretary of State John Foster Dulles vowed that he would not fall victim to the critics on his political flanks who had destroyed the credibility of his predecessor. It seems difficult to explain some of President Eisenhower's rhetoric without reference to the play of domestic politics on policymakers. A China policy that took account of the possibility of a Sino-Soviet split in the wake of the Korean War ran counter to the forces of domestic politics in the 1950s. So, too, did a policy of rapprochement between East and West Germany in the face of the demand for a united Europe including West Germany as a means of upholding the status quo against Soviet expansionism.

A second explanation that some historians have advanced to explain the president's foreign policy failures is the thesis that whatever the strengths of the Eisenhower pattern of leadership domestically—as with his strategy to not lend credibility to Senator McCarthy by debating him publicly—his failure to formulate foreign policy in clear and unequivocal terms was a weakness. Political scientists have noted that presidents whose only preparation for the presidency is service in the

U.S. Senate suffer from this weakness. They tend to look for compromises and lowest common denominators in policy. They are prone to avoid taking positions until they sense where the public and the Senate is moving. They are always seeking deals and tradeoffs. In a curious way, President Eisenhower's practice of leading without staking out a clear public position resembles the pattern of leadership common to those who come to the presidency with only legislative experience. The seeming tactic of political evasion that is sometimes a virtue in domestic politics is a source of weakness for a president who would exercise world leadership. Those who would negotiate policy are more likely than not to sound an uncertain trumpet.

A third explanation of Eisenhower's difficulties rests on the proposition that he had an excessive faith in professionalism. The debate over whether Eisenhower or Dulles was the more dominant influence in determining foreign policy continues to this day. Where important military and strategic questions were involved, as in the debate over U.S. intervention in Indochina, Eisenhower's views would seem to have prevailed. But the president appears to have yielded to Dulles on other questions, for example, Soviet-American cultural exchanges and visits by British and French leaders to Washington following the debacle of the intervention over Suez. A more telling example may be Eisenhower's embracing of the political warfare campaign launched by C. D. Jackson and Radio Free Europe. The contrast between the cautious and prudent general and president and the flamboyant Time-Lifer could not be more striking. Who could imagine the former unleashing eleven thousand balloons and fourteen million leaflets over Poland and Czechoslovakia to "boost the morale of the entire non-Communist population and to fortify 'spiritual resistance' until 'the day of liberation' arrived. Yet Eisenhower thanked Henry Luce for the sanity that Jackson brought to his efforts.

Having reviewed the three possible explanations for Eisenhower's limitations in foreign policy, we return to our original suggestion. How was it that so experienced a leader could have imagined that policies such as his Atoms for Peace or Open Skies could bring about arms control given the reality of the impenetrability of sovereignty, especially in the Soviet Union? How could he have thought that simultaneously he could negotiate a political settlement with the Soviet Union based on the status quo and pursue a foreign policy of liberation? How did he reconcile his call for "massive retaliation" with his solemn warning about the military-industrial complex? What were the connections between his respect for the might of the Red Army and his scaling down of appropriations for the Army and for one-half of the Navy?

The answer may lie in Eisenhower's concept of the nature of international politics. Students of foreign policy today do not turn to Eisenhower for clear and coherent definitions of interest and power as they do to statesmen such as Churchill. The conceptual framework within which the president thought about world politics was rather that of a vague if inspiring internationalism. He believed that the United States should lead the world, but he was never quite clear how and where. He was stronger in formulating broad, if sometimes rigid and unchanging, ends than in relating the means to those ends. In any debate over diplomatic strategy with Dulles, he had difficulty standing his ground. In approving Dulles's foreign policy of liberation or Jackson's political and psychological warfare, Eisenhower appeared not to understand the consequences. He had dealt with national leaders throughout much of his career, yet he was strangely oblivious to the constraints imposed by national sovereignty. He understood the principle of doing what "was right for America," as General Goodpaster explained, but was somehow unprepared for the advantages that the Soviet Union gained when the United States turned against its allies in the Suez Crisis. He acted skillfully in sending fourteen thousand Marines into Lebanon in July of 1958 and withdrawing them in October, illustrating the dual principle that Larson ascribes to him: Seek never to use force, but when you must use it, employ overwhelming force. However, Eisenhower seemed less understanding of the cultural, ethnic, and sectarian divisions in Lebanon on which any national government must rest. He was able to contrive ways in World War II to bring quarreling leaders together, but he failed to bridge the deep chasm separating East and West.

To reflect on President Eisenhower's strengths and weaknesses is in no way to detract from the quality of his leadership. Indeed, a recital of his limitations leads to a broader question. If a president with the strengths of Dwight D. Eisenhower is found wanting in at least some sectors of cold-war leadership, what will be the fate of the United States and the world in the hands of far more mediocre leaders? If Eisenhower lacked the intellectual and political resources to cope with the manifold dimensions of world diplomacy, where are we to look for hope when lesser men are in the White House? No more sobering question can be posed as we think about human survival.

Notes

1. Dwight D. Eisenhower, *Crusade in Europe* (Garden City, N.Y.: Doubleday, 1948), 396.
2. Ibid., 399.

3. Winston S. Churchill, *The Second World War,* vol. 5, *Closing the Ring* (Boston: Houghton Mifflin, 1951), 218.

4. Eisenhower, *Crusade,* 283–84.

5. Kenneth W. Thompson, ed., *The Eisenhower Presidency: Eleven Intimate Perspectives of Dwight D. Eisenhower,* Portraits of American Presidents, vol. 3 (Lanham, Md.: University Press of America, 1984).

6. William B. Ewald, "A Biographer's Perspective," in Thompson, *The Eisenhower Presidency,* 26.

7. Arthur Larson, "Eisenhower's World View," in Thompson, *The Eisenhower Presidency,* 42.

8. Ibid.

9. Ibid., 44.

10. Andrew J. Goodpaster, "Organizing the White House," in Thompson, *The Eisenhower Presidency,* 74.

11. Ibid., 75–76.

12. Milton J. Eisenhower, "Portrait of a Brother," in Thompson, *The Eisenhower Presidency,* 9.

13. Ibid., 11.

14. Goodpaster, "Organizing the White House," 74.

15. Arthur S. Flemming, "Perspective on Eisenhower's Values," in Thompson, *The Eisenhower Presidency,* 236–37.

16. Ibid., 237.

17. Goodpaster, "Organizing the White House," 74.

18. Ewald, "A Biographer's Perspective," 29–30.

19. Sherman Adams, "The Eisenhower Presidency," in Thompson, *The Eisenhower Presidency,* 187.

20. Ibid.

21. Ibid., 187–88.

22. Bryce Harlow, "The 'Compleat' President," in Thompson, *The Eisenhower Presidency,* 161.

23. Larson, "Eisenhower's World View," 43, 44.

24. Ewald, "A Biographer's Perspective," 34–35.

25. Ibid., 35.

26. Eisenhower, "Portrait of a Brother," 10.

27. Goodpaster, "Organizing the White House," 71–72.

28. Ewald, "A Biographer's Perspective," 28.

29. Ibid., 26.

30. Goodpaster, "Organizing the White House," 65.

31. Larson, "Eisenhower's World View," 47.

32. Ibid.

33. Ibid., 48.

34. Ibid., 49, 50.

35. Ibid., 51.

36. Goodpaster, "Organizing the White House," 70, 71.

37. Eisenhower to John Foster Dulles, 5 April, 1955, White House Memoranda Series, Dwight D. Eisenhower Library.

38. Ibid., 1–2.

39. Ibid., 2 (emphasis in the original).
40. Ibid.
41. Ibid., 2, 4.
42. Ibid., 4 (emphasis in the original).
43. Ibid., 5.
44. Ibid.
45. Ibid., 6, 7, 8.
46. Ibid., 9.

The Foundations of Eisenhower's Foreign Policy
Continuity, Community, and Consensus

Richard A. Melanson

Most of this volume's essays focus on specific parts of Eisenhower's foreign policy—China, the Middle East, Germany, Indochina, arms control, foreign economic policy. Here, however, I will examine some of the broader concerns that lent coherence to and posed dilemmas for his world view. By illuminating Eisenhower's public philosophy, leadership style, and national security strategy, I hope to explore his deep commitment to foreign policy continuity, domestic consensus, and his vision of an international corporate commonwealth. Finally, I will probe some of the paradoxes that confronted Eisenhower as he tried to prevent the emergence of an American "garrison state" while simultaneously defending U.S. global interests against international communism. But first it is necessary to understand the policy of containment articulated by the Truman administration, whose overall goals Eisenhower believed had to be sustained by him.

Although he first ran for president, in part, as an "outsider" committed to ending "the mess in Washington," Eisenhower implicitly embraced the underlying values and policy preferences of the so-called foreign policy Establishment. Indeed, his outlook cannot be understood apart from its liberal internationalism.

The origins of this Establishment can be traced to a small group of advisors—dubbed "The Inquiry"—that Colonel House gathered around him at Versailles.[1] After the treaty was defeated in 1920, these businessmen and academics—joined by a handful of international bankers and their lawyers—continued to struggle against a resurgent isolationism, largely through the newly formed Council on Foreign Relations in New York. But it was clearly World War II (and thus the lessons of Munich) that crystallized the cold-war Establishment of New York lawyers, bankers, and corporation executives; high federal officials; and leading scholars. Specifically, the common experience of wartime (and often OSS) service imparted to these youngish men a sense of power, accomplishment, destiny, and international involvement that would survive the Axis surrender. And when Soviet communism replaced fascism as America's chief adversary, these men returned to Washington to construct the new policy soon known as containment.

What was the outlook of this nascent Establishment? Conceived as bipartisan counterweights to an anticipated revitalized isolationism (particularly in Congress), members of the Establishment called themselves "liberal internationalists." They were convinced that America's reluctance to exert its power during the interwar years had helped to bring on World War II; these men remembered the bitter fights over neutrality legislation in the 1930s and were determined to employ the presidency to build an internationalist consensus at home. Certain that the United States possessed the material resources to achieve world leadership, the Establishment believed that it had to supply the missing moral and spiritual ingredients necessary to transform crude power into international authority. Although they themselves rarely stood for election, these men had an instinct for the political center—an instinct that buttressed their aspiration to serve as educators to an America whose traditional tendency was to vacillate dangerously between self-righteous isolation and indiscriminate intervention. Finally, while members of this Establishment feared international communism as a mortal threat to Western values and institutions, they were unsympathetic to those who wished to ferret out domestic subversives.

Containment became the preferred policy of the Establishment, but it had not originally been the first choice. Its members had envisioned a postwar world resting on collective security, free trade, national self-determination, and the rule of law under American leadership and had sought to institutionalize these concepts in the United Nations Organization, the International Monetary Fund, the International Bank for Reconstruction and Development, and the International Trade Organization. Yet their early hopes were frustrated as Soviet vetoes hamstrung the UN, European economic weakness prevented the IMF and the World Bank from performing their assigned tasks, and Congress destroyed the ITO. Looked at in this way, containment was a strategic adaptation designed to salvage as much as possible from the wreckage of these universal organizations by roping off the noncommunist world, placing it firmly in the hands of American economic and military power, and improvising responses like the Marshall Plan, GATT, and NATO. Containment, then, was the symbol of a truncated crusade to reform international relations through the reflection of American values and interests. But although containment did constitute an implicit admission of the failure of liberal internationalists to realize their fondest dreams, it nevertheless came to form the foundation of the cold-war consensus. And it did so in large measure because the Establishment quickly recognized that containment rested on American values while serving American national interests and then conveyed these truths to the American public.

The free world—that is, that area lying within the protective wall of containment—was to reflect significant American values, although the Establishment realized that some parts of this world were "freer" than others. Nevertheless, while not all the countries within it "had liberal democratic forms of government, . . . they all had the freedom to take decisions on both internal and external policies without the fear of intervention by 'socialist internationalism' if they displayed too much independence."[2] In short, members of the free world, in theory at least, had the right to national self-determination. By means of its example and good works America's mission was to encourage such positive attributes of self-determination as religious toleration, free elections, an uncensored press, and a private economy. Even anticolonialism "could be squared with containment by persuading the West European imperial powers that satisfying the natural desire of colonial peoples for emancipation was the only way to prevent them from turning to the greater tyranny of Marxism-Leninism."[3]

But containment, of course, also served important American political and economic interests, and, as we know, on more than one occasion, liberal values were sacrificed in the name of the present danger of international communism. Above all, containment was designed to halt Soviet expansion, and thus "it attempted to shore up the position of allies and maintain an international distribution of power favorable to its alliance structure."[4] Collective security—now in a variety of regional guises but clearly under American auspices—became the institutional expression of this power system, and it was underwritten by an international currency regime dominated by the U.S. dollar. Or, as the Establishment probably would have preferred to put it: The mortal threat of international communism had thrust upon the United States primary responsibility to defend the security and enhance the well-being of the free world. Containment was intended to accomplish these tasks.

Yet however central to the cold-war consensus, containment should not be perceived as a single, all-encompassing strategy fully articulated in 1947 and simply inherited by Eisenhower. In fact, containment gradually evolved over several years, and at no time did it receive the unqualified endorsement of both American political parties. When Truman left office in January 1953, it had seemingly become the discredited legacy of the demoralized Democrats.

Actually the Truman administration had pursued a variety of Soviet policies. For example, until early 1947 it tried to negotiate with Moscow a formal end to World War II and to rely on the UNO to resolve differences; then until the outbreak of the Korean War it followed a limited form of containment in order to deny further successes to the Soviets in Europe and the Middle East; finally, from June 1950 onward the administration was guided in its national security strategy by the global guidelines offered in NSC 68.

In order to appreciate fully the scope of *anticommunist* containment embodied in NSC 68, it is first necessary to review the more restricted policy that it supplanted: that version of containment recommended by Kennan, not as "X," but as director of the Policy Planning Staff.[5] Kennan believed that the chief danger of the Soviet Union derived from the psychological malaise that afflicted the European and Near Eastern states bordering Russia—not the Soviet military threat or the appeal of international communism. Accordingly, Kennan's strategy of containment was primarily psychological in nature. As a first step toward creating a stable and hospitable international environment, he asserted that the self-confidence of those borderlands, particularly the European ones, had to be restored. It was essential that America lend economic and political support—but not military commitments—to help ensure the survival of these threatened states. The United States should function as an "arsenal of democracy" by offering economic assistance and the power of its example to these temporarily weakened but basically healthy societies. After self-confidence had been restored and after the Soviets had suffered a consequent loss of influence in these areas, the West could expect that Moscow would gradually modify its approach to international relations, so that negotiations might eventually become feasible. Made paranoiacally insecure by its history and its regime's ideology, this neurotic Bear might eventually mellow if constantly frustrated by a patient and steady American policy. Kennan further recommended that the United States attempt to fragment systematically the Soviet empire. Deeply impressed by the Yugoslav heresy, Kennan argued that Moscow's insecure rulers could not tolerate ideological diversity and predicted that Maoist China would follow its own nationalist path. While he believed that the Truman administration could hasten the fragmentation process by, for example, extending diplomatic recognition to the new Peking government, Kennan thought that the United States could best foster splits in the Communist camp by demonstrating its own commitment to domestic and international diversity. The ultimate goal of Kennan's containment was not a *Pax Americana* but the reemergence of independent power centers in Europe and Japan, the eventual domestication of Soviet power, and the growth to maturity of American diplomacy.

In short, Kennan's strategy was more or less traditional, but it had to deal with a world temporarily dislocated by World War II, and it was to be implemented by what he feared was a most untraditional nation: America. His approach evinced skepticism for permanent and global alliances, military commitments, and ideology, and favored instead the creation of an international order based on diplomacy, limit, and balance. John L. Gaddis has offered this summary of Kennan's outlook:

> Kennan's was, then, a concept of interests based on a pessimistic view of the international order, but on a degree of measured optimism as to the possibilities for restraining rivalries within it. This could be done . . . by making use of the organic equilibrium maintained by the very tensions inherent in the system. It was a view conscious of the fact that because capabilities are finite, interests must be also; distinctions had to be made between what was vital and what was not. It was also sensitive to the need to subordinate means to ends; to the danger that lack of discrimination in methods employed could corrupt objectives sought. Finally, it insisted on using this perception of interests as a standard against which to evaluate threats, not the other way around: threats had no meaning, Kennan insisted, except with reference to and in terms of one's concept of interests.[6]

This approach formed the essence of what can be termed *selective containment,* a policy at least partially implemented by the Truman administration between 1947 and 1950.

Yet events, ideas, and personalities intervened to challenge the sufficiency of selective containment. The Berlin blockade, the Czech coup, the successful Soviet testing of the atomic bomb, and Chiang's defeat in China provided powerful evidence for those in the Truman administration like Paul Nitze, who suspected that the Soviet Union was both a revolutionary state bent on world domination and the director of a unified, international Communist movement. Kennan's Neurotic Bear, while undeniably disturbed, remained a quasi-traditional power with whom negotiations might in the future be possible, but by 1949 a more extreme Soviet metaphor—the Great Beast of Revolution—grew increasingly persuasive. Diplomacy with such an adversary, except perhaps from a position of overwhelming military superiority, had no chance for success. Furthermore, a series of bureaucratic changes and maneuvers during 1949 and 1950 gradually encouraged the emergence of a more ambitious strategy of containment, one that would be fully articulated in NSC 68. It was this more extensive notion of containment that prevailed and that would do so until the late 1960s. And it was *this* containment, anticipated in the ringing words of the Truman Doctrine, that received ratification in the form of the cold-war anticommunist consensus.

These bureaucratic shifts included the "retirement" of Kennan, who felt increasingly ignored by Acheson, the transfer of State Department Counsellor Charles E. Bohlen to Paris, and the resignation of Secretary of Defense Louis Johnson. Yet despite the "shocks" of 1948, the Truman administration was extremely reluctant to respond militariiy to Soviet expansionism. Truman "had set an arbitrary $15 billion ceiling on defense spending, and a blue-ribbon panel declared in 1948 that even the proposed $14.2 billion budget for fiscal 1950 was 'unduly high,' given 'the ability of the economy to sustain' such high costs."[7]

This more cautious conception of containment was not unanimously shared by Truman's advisors, as can be sensed by reading "Measures Required to Achieve U.S. Objectives with Respect to the U.S.S.R.,"[8] a top secret NSC paper completed on March 30, 1949. Among its ten major recommendations were a sharp escalation of the defense budget, significant increases in Western force levels, a global propaganda campaign, and an economic policy that would encourage domestic dissent in the Soviet Union.

This document, which anticipated the major thrust of NSC 68, was attacked by Bohlen and Kennan as "hysterical"[9] and "dangerous."[10] But as the shocks of 1948 were replaced by those of 1949, Bohlen, Kennan, and Johnson increasingly found themselves part of a losing coalition. Their defeat was assured by the replacement of Edwin Nourse, a fiscal conservative, with a Keynesian, Leon Keyserling, as chairman of the Council of Economic Advisors.

Soon after Kennan stepped down as director of the Policy Planning Staff, the new secretary of state, Dean Acheson, recommended that the president create a special joint committee to study American objectives and strategic plans in light of the Soviet atomic test. This committee, officially known as the State-Defense Policy Review Group, took advantage of Kennan's absence to draft a report during February and March 1950 that eventually became NSC 68. During its deliberations this group called in only one outside witness, James B. Conant, who questioned the report's basic assumptions. Furthermore, Secretary of Defense Johnson was "deliberately kept out of the picture"[11] until the document was virtually complete. Paul Nitze quickly gained effective control of this special committee and was primarily responsible for the recommendations it produced.[12]

NSC 68 implicitly rejected Kennan's efforts to distinguish vital U.S. interests from peripheral ones. All interests were essentially identical and hence global in scope.[13] For Nitze and his colleagues, the world balance-of-power was dangerously fragile and could not tolerate any further Communist victories. Even the loss of a seemingly insignificant territory would have ominous psychological effects on more obviously central U.S. interests in Europe, Japan, and the Near East. In short, because the *appearance* of a shift in the global balance could prove to be as damaging as an actual, material change, the United States needed to oppose *all* Communist advances or risk a fatal loss of credibility. By stressing the importance of perceptions and images in world politics, NSC 68 vastly expanded the number of American interests.

Whereas Kennan had emphasized the finiteness of the resources available to secure U.S. interests, the framers of NSC 68 were more impressed with the dyr.amic potential of the American economy. By relying on the tools and concepts of Keynesian economic theory Nitze and friends argued that the United States could afford to possess global interests. Long-term economic growth could "pay for" short-run budget deficits and thus allow significant increases in defense spending. The expansive nature of the American economy would permit American foreign policy to treat all parts of the world as vital to our security. The U.S. need not be hampered by Kennan's "obsolete" distinctions: "Considerations of priority and economy might be appropriate in normal times, but in the face of a threat such as that posed by the Soviet Union, preoccupations of this sort had to go by the board."[14] Indeed, NSC 68 seemingly legitimated every conceivable sort of instrument: "The integrity of our system will not be jeopardized by any measures, covert or overt, violent or non-violent, which serve the purpose of frustrating the Kremlin design, nor does the necessity for conducting ourselves so as to affirm our values in actions as well as words forbid such measures, provided only that they are appropriately calculated to that end and are not so excessive or misdirected as to make us enemies of the people instead of the evil men who have enslaved them."[15] Kennan, of course, had suggested that the American example constituted our most effective foreign policy instrument and had worried that cold-war pressure could easily lead to its betrayal. NSC 68 justified his fears.

Nitze and Kennan also disagreed about the nature of the Soviet threat. Kennan had no illusions about the nature of the Soviet Union, but he had argued that American strategy needed to respond to Soviet intentions and that these intentions did not include aggressive war. Nitze, on the other hand, was more impressed with Soviet capabilities and claimed that unless the United States dramatically improved its military position, Moscow would be able to launch a preemptive attack by 1954. Nitze would discover another "window of opportunity" in the mid-1970s. In the meantime, the authors of NSC 68 predicted that the Soviet Union would wage proxy wars on the periphery (as they did in Korea two months later) and attempt to intimidate U.S. allies into submission. (This process was not yet called "Finlandization," although it is what these men had in mind.) Again, Gaddis has presented the best description of this contrast:

> At the heart of these differences . . . was a simple inversion of intellectual procedure: where Kennan tended to look at the Soviet threat in terms of an independently established concept of irreducible interests, NSC 68 derived its view of American interests primarily from its perception of the Soviet threat. Kennan's insistence on the need to deter hostile combinations of industrial-military power could have applied as well to the adversaries of World Wars I and II as to the Soviet Union. No comparably general statement of fundamental interests appeared in NSC 68. . . . Instead it found in the simple presence of a Soviet threat sufficient cause to deem the interest threatened vital.[16]

In short, NSC 68 defined the Soviet Union essentially as a *moral* problem so immense that traditional geopolitical calculations had lost all relevance. Fortunately the enormity of (potential) American power allegedly liberated the United States from these geopolitical constraints.

What policies did Nitze and his colleagues recommend to counter the Soviet threat? First, they urged the adoption of a strategy geared to defend all American interests through the application of appropriate military force. This approach, which Nitze was to term "flexible response" when he offered it to the Kennedy administration a decade later, presumed that every Communist threat needed to be contained by a calibrated U.S. conventional or nuclear response. Such a strategy obviously necessitated a much larger defense allocation than the $14 billion Truman had recommended by fiscal 1950, and although NSC 68 did not specify the magnitude of the increase, its framers concluded that it should be on the order of 250 percent. Second, Nitze and his colleagues believed that the United States could not afford to pursue a policy that sought to fragment the Soviet empire. Less impressed than Kennan with the immediate significance of nationalism which might erode Moscow's grip on other Communist regimes, NSC 68 claimed that the fragility of the balance-of-power prevented America from patiently waiting for nationalism to do its work. Furthermore, because the issues of credibility, appearance, and image were taken so seriously, NSC 68's authors evidently felt that the United States could not presume to lead the free world while conducting normal relations with national Communist states. Consequently, unlike Kennan, who wished to encourage the reemergence of several power centers, Nitze emphasized the bipolar (even Manichean) character of contemporary international relations and urged the United States to treat international communism as a monolith. Finally, NSC 68 stressed the near impossibility of meaningful negotiations with the Soviet Union. Until the Soviet regime underwent a fundamental domestic transformation no real diplomatic progress could be expected, because the Kremlin's ideological imperatives ruled out compromise with the West. Yet at the same time, the drafters of NSC 68 recognized that the United States was under strong and growing public pressure to negotiate with Moscow. Accordingly, they recommended that we *appear* to conduct negotiations in order to expose the insincerity of Soviet intentions, while recognizing that agreements would not be forthcoming until the United States had created "situations of strength." And, "If, contrary to our expectations, the Soviet Union should accept agreements promising effective control of atomic energy and conventional armaments, without any other changes in Soviet policies, we would have to consider very carefully whether we could accept such agreements."[17] In short, NSC 68 conceived of negotiations as a public relations ploy designed to placate public opinion, to embarrass Moscow, and to give the United States time to rearm.

This analysis and these recommendations were expressed rather feverishly in a melodramatic tone more appropriate to the *Congressional Record* than to a top-secret national security document. But, of course, NSC 68 was designed to do something more than serve as a Soviet strategy for the executive. Members of the foreign policy Establishment—Nitze included—shared an acute appreciation of the need for a broad domestic consensus to undergird containment. Deeply affected by the "lessons" of the 1930s, when serious public disharmony had allegedly crippled Roosevelt's ability to respond to the dictators until the last moment, these postwar policymakers were horrified by the probability that America would slip again into isolationist irresponsibility. Furthermore, their fears of an isolationist resurgence were heightened by their realization that American world leadership would entail substantial domestic sacrifices. In short, anticommunist containment had to be "sold" to Congress and the American people if an internationalist consensus was to be built, and the apocalyptic tone of NSC 68 reflected that recognition.

Yet NSC 68 should not be dismissed simply as a cynical attempt to manipulate public opinion. Nitze and his colleagues believed what they wrote. If they inflated their rhetoric to curry congressional support, these men did not distort their essential analysis of Soviet-American relations. The articulators of anticommunist containment were convinced that the United States neither could nor should conduct a European-style foreign policy grounded exclusively in geopolitical realities. These hard-headed Wilsonians appreciated power, but they also believed that power needed to be guided by moral purpose. The American people would only support a diplomacy that defended and exported liberal democratic values. They would retreat into isolationism rather than sacrifice in the name of *realpolitik*. An internationalist consensus had to be constructed on an ethical base. Furthermore, the nature of the Communist enemy apparently prevented the United States from pursuing a traditional balance-of-power policy, because the USSR represented much more than a geopolitical threat. The Soviet regime was fundamentally evil, driven by a totalitarian ideology that compelled unlimited expansion and absolute control. The character of international communism conspired with the character of the American people to produce the only policy capable of dealing with both: anticommunist containment.

The outbreak of the Korean War seemingly confirmed NSC 68's analysis of the Soviet threat, and the Truman administration's military response to the invasion was undertaken according to the precepts of anticommunist containment. At first Truman's actions received overwhelming public and congressional support. Even the "Asialationist" wing of the Republican party led by William F. Knowland, "the Senator from Formosa," applauded Truman's efforts, although it qualified the endorsement by accusing the Democrats of paving the way for the Communist attack through "secret deals" at Yalta, their abandonment of Chiang, and their preoccupation with Europe. This bipartisan enthusiasm increased in the wake of the Inchon landing, and Truman and his advisors, in their excitement, briefly forsook containment in favor of Korean reunification by force of arms. But when the Mainland Chinese massively intervened in late November 1950, public support for the war waned dramatically. Whereas in September 1950 81 percent of those identifying themselves as Republicans supported the "police actions," by December, as MacArthur fell back again below the 38th parallel, only 42 percent still did. Democratic support fell from 84 percent to 62 percent.[18] According to one student of public opinion, "the majority of Americans in 1951 and 1952 considered entering the war a mistake, wanted to pull American troops out of Korea as rapidly as possible, and supported numerous proposals to achieve a negotiated peace."[19] Despite the exhaustive efforts of the Truman administration and the foreign policy Establishment to construct a solid anticommunist consensus, "for two full years—from January 1951 until Eisenhower became President in January 1953—the nation had both an unpopular war and a highly unpopular President."[20] Truman's determination to wage a limited war in Korea (except for his brief flirtation with forcible reunification after Inchon), and the subsequent stalemate led MacArthur and his supporters to conclude that there was no substitute for victory. Yet these critics had enormous difficulty in suggesting exactly how victory was to be pursued, and their prescriptions included at various times the use of atomic weapons against North Korea and the PRC, conventional bombing of Manchuria, a ground assault across the Yalu, the acceptance of Chiang's offer to send troops to Korea, allowing the Nationalists to invade the Mainland, refusing to negotiate with the Communists on any terms short of Korean reunification, and the unilateral withdrawal of American forces from Korea.[21] So controversial had Truman's diplomacy become that of the three major issues emphasized by the Republicans in the 1952 presidential campaign—corruption, Korea, and containment—two of them involved foreign policy.

In short, foreign policy had become a divisive, increasingly partisan domestic political issue. Senator McCarthy and his supporters had placed the blame for America's diplomatic failures on the "communistic" proclivities of our highest public officials. The policy of containment had seemingly been discredited as "no-win appeasement." Yet at the same time, American voters in 1952 had rejected the inflation, taxes, and "New Dealism" of the Democratic party. It was this rather ambiguous history of containment and this unstable political situation that President Eisenhower inherited.

Through his public philosophy,[22] presidential style, and national security strategy, Eisenhower tried to reconstruct and strengthen the containment consensus that had been seriously weakened by 1952.

At the core of Eisenhower's public philosophy lay a conservative vision of community that Robert Griffith has called a "corporate commonwealth,"[23] and that will be termed here the "international corporate commonwealth" in order to emphasize the indissoluble link in Eisenhower's outlook between domestic and foreign affairs. I will, accordingly, first recapitulate Griffith's arguments and then extend them to

Eisenhower's understanding of international relations. For Griffith, Eisenhower "was a product of the organizational revolution that had transformed American life in the twentieth century, a member of the new managerial class that led the nation's great public and private bureaucracies,"[24] but "it was from the military . . . that Eisenhower absorbed the principal elements of his education: a respect for the efficiencies of organization, a contempt for politics and politicians, a distrust of popular democracy and of the masses whose 'class fears' and prejudices are easily aroused, and . . . a strong commitment to duty and to the ideal of disinterested public service."[25] Deeply upset by the industrial strife, serious inflation, and debilitating partisanship of the Truman years, Eisenhower searched for ways to moderate the fundamental conflicts created by "industrialization, mass production and distribution, and the growth of a complex, interdependent social system."[26] More specifically, he feared that the new forms of corporate organization—while in many ways a welcome element of order against chaos and irresponsibility—"posed grave dangers for traditional economic and political liberties" and worried that organized interests— many of which the Democrats had built through appeals to narrow self-interest—would impose their short-sighted ends "upon the state or that the state itself would become little more than a battleground for class conflict."[27] But Eisenhower did not believe that these clashing interests were necessarily irreconcilable, and like Herbert Hoover, Bernard Baruch, Herbert S. Dennison, "and other apostles of welfare capitalism," he "repeatedly called for voluntary cooperation among America's diverse economic interests."[28] Upon assuming the Columbia University presidency in 1948, Eisenhower warned that competition and self-interest must be "accompanied by a readiness to cooperate wholeheartedly for the performance of community and national functions,"[29] and at Columbia one of his proudest achievements was the creation of the American Assembly, in which he hoped the leaders of business, labor, government, and the professions would meet to study and plan cooperatively for the future.[30] To achieve his vision of a mutually cooperative, voluntarist society Eisenhower proposed "the middle way"—"a phrase that dominated almost all of his thinking after 1948."[31] The Middle Way was political centrism of course, poised between capital and labor, the New Deal and the Old Guard, but it also involved a distinctive approach to government and a particular leadership style. In short, "he believed that government should actively promote social harmony and encourage those mutually beneficial, voluntary and cooperative activities that lay at the center of his vision of the good society; the essence of citizenship entailed 'blend[ing], without coercion, the individual good, and the common good.' "[32] Furthermore, "Eisenhower's commitment to social harmony, self-discipline, limited government, and a depoliticized, administrative state all dictated, in turn, an approach to leadership that stressed restraint, patience, moderation, and flexibility"[33]—a style termed the *hidden hand* by Fred I. Greenstein.[34] Finally, "his belief in the mediatory role of government and his fear of popular politics was also reflected in his intense concern with public relations, which he saw . . . as a technique for defusing political conflict, limiting the role of the state, engineering support for administrative decisions, and forging consensus."[35]

Yet Eisenhower's public philosophy cannot be fully grasped without reference to his world outlook, for his vision of a consensual, domestic community required active American participation in international affairs. Indeed, this essential link between these two realms separated him from isolationist Republicans like Hoover and Robert Taft despite their wide agreement on domestic issues. The following entry from Eisenhower's personal diary emphasizes this crucial difference: "One of the men I've admired extravagantly is Herbert Hoover. I am forced to believe he's getting senile. God knows I'd personally like to get out of Europe and I'd like to see the United States able to sit at home and ignore the rest of the world. What a pleasing prospect until you look at ultimate consequences, destruction."[36]

Eisenhower, like the foreign policy Establishment that embraced him in 1952, believed that the United States possessed a moral obligation to employ its power in order to contain international communism, strengthen the economic, political, and ethical bonds within the free world, and protect American political and economic institutions from the chaos of international instability. But he also believed that a firm and steady internationalist foreign policy could not be sustained in the absence of a domestic consensus about the purposes of American power, and he—again, like his Establishment supporters—feared the outbreak of a divisive new national debate reminiscent of the bloodletting that had paralyzed American diplomacy in the 1930s. In fact, Eisenhower's decision to seek the presidency in 1952 as a Republican was primarily based on his conviction that he was the only man in America who could "internationalize" the Republican party and reconstruct the domestic foreign policy consensus that had been severely shaken by the Korean stalemate. According to Herbert W. Brownell, attorney general during Eisenhower's first term, "he was faced with the fact that Taft was the leader of the Republican Party and . . . he was in essence an isolationist. [Eisenhower] thought the issue of foreign policy was so critical that he withdrew his opposition to the idea of a military man being President, [and he ran as a Republican] because he thought it could do the most good in solidifying the country behind an internationalist policy."[37] Thus, despite his concern that the New Deal had unleashed a host of narrow economic interests that threatened domestic harmony, it alone was insufficient to impel Eisenhower to run for president. That motivation was provided by the imminent prospect of a Taft administration.

But for what international ends did Eisenhower propose to mobilize this domestic consensus? At bottom, of course, he accepted the outlines of Woodrow Wilson's world outlook: a pluralist international order respectful of national self-determination and democratic institutions, committed to collective security animated by free (as free as prudently possible) trade and investment, and underwritten by American moral, political, and economic leadership. Although he fretted over the socialism that crept behind the Fair Deal, Eisenhower wholeheartedly (although discreetly) supported the major elements of Truman's foreign policy: aid to Greece and Turkey, the Marshall Plan, NATO, and limited war in Korea. And fully as many Democrats as Republicans visited his NATO headquarters in Paris during 1951 and 1952 to implore him to be their party's standardbearer. Eisenhower, in short, combined domestic conservativism with international liberalism, mixing Hoover with Wilson to produce a vision of enormous appeal to cold-war America.

At the same time, his wartime and NATO experiences convinced him that consensus at another level—the Western Alliance—was a fundamental requisite for a stable international order. Here, too, Eisenhower worried about the weakness and conflicts that could be produced by narrow, shortsighted interests. As he wistfully noted in his personal diary in July 1953:

> Leadership must find a way to bring men to a point where they will give to the long-term promise the same value that they give to immediate and individual gains. If we could produce clear and dispassionate thinking in this regard, if we could get today the questions of world trade and world cooperation studied and settled on the basis of the long-term good of all, we could laugh at all the other so-called "contradictions" in our system, and we could be so secure against the communist menace that it would gradually dry up and wither away.
>
> As it is, the danger is very real and very great that even the so-called enlightened areas of Western Europe, Britain, United States, and the other English-speaking peoples will, by stubborn adherence to the purpose of achieving immediate gain, actually commit suicide.[38]

While NATO Commander Eisenhower had become so frustrated over the inability and unwillingness of the Western Allies to formulate long-range, comprehensive, unselfish defense plans that soon after his arrival in Paris he concluded that some sort of West European union was essential:

> I am coming to believe that Europe's security problem is never going to be solved satisfactorily unless there exists a United States of Europe, to include all countries now in NATO. . . .
>
> It seems scarcely necessary to enumerate the problems that arise out of or are exaggerated by the division of West Europe into so many sovereign nations. Norway is short of manpower, Italy way over. Italy has excess productive capacity in vehicles and plants. Many others have none at all. France and Germany (the key powers in the region) are on opposite sides in many problems because of French hatred of the Boche as well as the fear of a restored Western Germany. Each nation watches its neighbor to see that the neighbor's contribution to the common security is at least equal to the first nation's ratio, and none is ever so convinced.[39]

At the urging of Jean Monnet, Eisenhower even pressed the idea on the West European leaders meeting at Rome in November 1951 because: "America has spent billions in ECA and is spending more billions in MDAP [Military Defense Assistance Plan] and much of it will be sheer waste unless Europe coalesces. Denmark, Holland, Belgium, Luxembourg, France, Italy, and Western Germany should form one federated state. To help this America could afford to spend a lot, because we'd get something successful, strong, sturdy."

But the politicoes throw up their hands in fright and hopelessness.[40] In short, Eisenhower dreamed of a postnationalist West European consensus about defense and economics that would be immune to Communist intimidation. This vision—shared by many in the Establishment (perhaps most notably George W. Ball)—formed the international analogue to Eisenhower's domestic outlook. Whereas American leadership was essential to transform Europe into a harmonious whole, a president such as himself, he thought, could be instrumental in creating a cooperative community at home.

By itself Eisenhower's public philosophy would have possessed great appeal for an America frustrated by Korea and frightened by the extremist political atmosphere of the early 1950s. His Middle Way seemed to offer the country a respite, "a quieter time in which agreements overshadowed differences . . . [and] accepted standards held more appeal than change. . . ."[41] But Eisenhower's deep faith in the necessity for consensus extended well beyond his public philosophy to encompass both his style of presidential leadership and his actual policies.

Contemporary liberal critics delighted in dismissing Eisenhower as a lazy, passive, inarticulate, golf-playing, grinning mediocrity who presided over the presidency. Typical was Walt Rostow's critique in his very influential *The United States in the World Arena,* which appeared in 1960:[42] "He was unresponsive to the bipartisan internationalist coalition which, in a sense, he was chosen to lead and which certainly elected him. He was sluggish in response to new problems defined within the Executive Branch, and he virtually rejected the President's role of personal leadership and innovation in the political process until inescapable circumstances and strong pressures within his staff persuaded him to act."[43]

Furthermore, "Eisenhower did not appear to understand the extent to which the Congress must count on a degree of Presidential assertion and even conflict to find a basis for supporting an effective military and foreign policy."[44] This exaggerated deference also spilled over to his relations with the Republican party, so that Eisenhower allegedly lost the chance to reshape it in the image of his values and purposes and settled instead for an unimaginative consensus produced by negotiation.[45] For Rostow, Eisenhower similarly forfeited opportunities to lead the people: "In his relations with the public Eisenhower concentrated on one important function of the President which was wholly congenial to his style: namely, the articulation and projection of the unifying principles and moods of the nation. As head of state for all the people, he executed with conviction the roles of ceremony; and in this dimension he was aided by the personal reticences and inhibition of his conception of leadership."[46] By instituting an elaborate staff system, by avoiding personal involvement in divisive issues like McCarthyism and civil rights, and by portraying himself as "above politics," Eisenhower struck Rostow (and other heirs of the Roosevelt revolution) as little more than a constitutional monarch.

The liberal orthodox interpretation of Eisenhower's leadership has, of course, recently come under heavy attack by several scholars, most notably Greenstein, although parts of this revisionism were anticipated by Murray Kempton more than fifteen years ago.[47] Greenstein argues that Eisenhower pursued subtle, sophisticated, and generally effective political and organizational strategies that "enabled him to exercise power without seeming to flex his muscles."[48] This repertoire included hidden-hand leadership, instrumental use of language, refusing to "engage in personalities" publicly, privately basing actions on personality analyses, the selective delegation of authority, and building a public support that transcended many of the nation's social and political divisions.[49] Although the individual techniques were not uniquely Eisenhower's, "he fit them together in a way that made his presidential leadership distinctive."[50] But by practicing "a politics of unobtrusive guidance . . ." Eisenhower

> did not subscribe to the idea that problems automatically go away. He believed that they should be attacked, but not necessarily with publicity. Undoubtedly, his long experience with the bureaucracies of the interwar army helped shape his belief, as did perhaps his parental tradition of religiously based pacifism. In its mature manifestations, this predilection is reflected in Eisenhower's remark to Paul Helms that making enemies is inconsistent with leadership. Thus he preferred compromise to a public fight. An ex-boxer and competitive sportsman, his conciliatory impulse does not seem to have stemmed from fear of conflict. Rather, he thought in terms of feasibility and concluded that fights often cost more than they yield.[51]

What Greenstein might have added is that this instinct for consensual techniques stemmed from more than family values and early military experience. It stemmed also, as we have seen, from Eisenhower's conservative vision of a free-world community of harmony and cooperation.

Yet Greenstein's revisionism embraces some of Rostow's preferences. Indeed, the burden of *The Hidden-Hand Presidency* is to refute orthodox charges that Eisenhower failed to exert presidential leadership, but Greenstein and Rostow agree that such leadership is the *sine qua non* of effective national policy. While Greenstein, with the help of the recently opened Whitman file, finds a decisive, personally involved, politically astute president, Rostow, although he clearly admired these attributes, thought they were lacking in Eisenhower. Similarly, both share the conviction that presidential leadership depends on broad public support, but whereas Rostow claimed that Eisenhower failed to mobilize it to win approval for new programs, Greenstein concludes that he actively (although quietly) curried such support.

But in other areas revisionists and contemporary liberal critics see the same Eisenhower, however they assume contrasting attitudes toward him. For example, both Greenstein and Rostow agree that Eisenhower self-consciously sought to build public support for domestic and foreign policies. Rostow, however, echoing those who characterized this technique as "the bland leading the bland," argued that Eisenhower's constant search for consensus resulted in timidity, inaction, and policy drift. Instead of using the power of the presidency to initiate domestic reforms and to invigorate American foreign policy (especially in the Third World), Eisenhower's fears of controversy led him to counsel patience and inordinate caution: "Eisenhower's style as President, taken as a whole, was admirably geared to situations in which the nation could solve its problems and protect its interests by slow, gradual change in the classic American manner."[52] In short, President Eisenhower failed to appreciate that the revolutionary nature of the times demanded bold, assertive, risk-taking leadership. Greenstein agrees that the president did not seek "sharp departures from existing policies,"[53] and he acknowledges that hidden-hand techniques may not always be appropriate, but he suggests that "a number of the enactments in Roosevelt's historic '100 Days' . . . had extensive bipartisan support and were *not* accompanied by publicized presidential wheeling and dealing."[54] FDR's approach worked because "for the moment, leaders of both parties were willing to treat normally divisive presidential proposals as if they were the appropriate initiatives of a nonpartisan head of state."[55] Greenstein concludes that "Eisenhower's style could have been equally successful in producing major innovations at such a time. But except in such a period of crisis, Eisenhower's leadership style is not suited to effecting major political change, though . . . other approaches normally do not succeed either."[56]

Thus, while Rostow condemned Eisenhower for conducting a "business-as-usual" administration despite the winds of revolutionary change that were supposedly sweeping the globe, Greenstein claims that Ike fostered "a *sense* of calm by quietly dealing with likely sources of controversy and by adopting a crisis-minimizing demeanor in volatile situations."[57] In other words, orthodox critic and revisionist alike look at essentially the same Eisenhower, but do so with sharply different values. For one, a somnolent president lulled America into a false sense of security in the face of world revolution; for the other, a crafty chief executive "successfully implemented his hold-the-line domestic policies, . . . kept intact a bipartisan internationalist foreign policy coalition and avoided allowing the cold war to retreat into military encounters and confrontations."[58]

Put differently, both orthodox interpreters of the 1950s and revisionist rehabilitators of the 1980s agree that Eisenhower's commitment to consensus lay at the root of his presidential style. But whereas the pre-Vietnam critic mourned this commitment as the symbol of myopia and lost opportunity, the present-day revisionist applauds its modesty and common sense. Neither view, as will be later suggested, is wholly satisfactory, but both are correct in suggesting the centrality of consensus in Eisenhower's presidential behavior.

Eisenhower's desire to encourage the growth of a consensual and harmonious free-world community also helps to explain the main outlines of his foreign policy. At bottom he believed that his background, experience, and personality uniquely qualified him to lead the Western Alliance against international communism. On one level, and unlike many of his presidential successors who would cling to public opinion polls in order to ward off self-doubt, Eisenhower felt confident that his values and policies accurately reflected those of the vast majority of Americans. Because he allegedly embodied the national interest, he hoped that his leadership could contain those selfish and shortsighted groups that threatened to fragment the society. According to General Andrew Goodpaster, who served as Eisenhower's staff secretary from 1954 to 1961, "He was aware of the support that he had with the American people, and we talked about that. The fact that he and I grew up about three hundred miles apart, although twenty-five years difference in time was something that we talked about and . . . we thought coming from the midwest [meant] . . . that we were pretty close to understanding the thinking of the American people."[59]

On another level, and again unlike many of his successors whose experiences were rooted in congressional or statehouse politics, Eisenhower's military service had enabled him to meet and frequently befriend most of the West's leaders before assuming the presidency. He was convinced that such first-hand knowledge allowed him to understand the perspectives and interests of the Allies as no other American could.

Thus Eisenhower formulated his foreign policy with the confidence that it best represented the preferences of the American and European publics if they could be wisely educated. In his Middle Way, Ike thought, lay the most realistic chance to bring about the kind of international community that he so deeply valued. Yet he also worried that the unprecedented dangers posed by the Soviet threat to the United States, the natural proclivity of most Americans to isolationism, and the precarious base on which the "American way of life" rested combined to make the task of building such a community extraordinarily difficult.

Eisenhower constantly confronted these dilemmas as his administration attempted to formulate a national security strategy that would constitute a middle way between the Fortress America isolationism of Taft and the Keynesian internationalism of Truman. A Fortress America approach suffered from several liabilities. First, as mentioned earlier, Eisenhower feared that any attempt to return to such a policy would inevitably be sponsored by the isolationist wing of the Republican party and would thus reopen the partisan and divisive debates of the 1930s. Moreover, he was convinced that the "lessons" of World War II and continuing rapid changes in military technology made it extremely unlikely that isolationism could ever again serve as the basis for a domestic foreign policy consensus. Second, Eisenhower concluded that the determination of the Soviet Union to develop long-range nuclear striking power made it imperative for the United States to possess reliable allies in order to intercept Soviet air assaults from forward bases. Thus, by the early 1950s a Fortress America was allegedly becoming a geostrategic impossibility. Third, Eisenhower agreed with those internationalists who argued that the United States could not afford to lose Western Europe; a fully communized Europe would deprive America of essential markets and investment opportunities, would shift the global military balance decisively toward the Soviet Union, and would endanger our domestic institutions by making the American example a moral irrelevancy. Finally, and perhaps most important, Eisenhower believed that the social requirements of a true Fortress America would likely lead to a garrison-state type of regimentation inimical to individual freedom and representative government. For all of these reasons, Taft had to be prevented from obtaining the 1952 Republican nomination.

But if Eisenhower was a committed internationalist, he was no less a fiscal conservative, and he was certain that a continuation of Truman's national security strategy would bankrupt the United States and destroy its social fabric just as surely as would a Fortress America. The new president had been acutely distressed by the Truman administration's final strategic statement—NSC 141—which was approved by the outgoing president the day before Eisenhower took office. Essentially this document reconfirmed NSC 68, but warned that the Soviet threat had grown even more ominous since 1949. Moscow's increased striking power not only exposed East Asia and the Middle East to danger, but even the continental United States was becoming increasingly vulnerable to air attack. NSC 141 accordingly recommended the accelerated development of "flexible, multi-purpose forces to meet the varied threats that confront us,"[60] including a vastly expanded continental air defense system and a large-scale civil defense program. Eisenhower accepted NSC 141's portrayal of a global, multi-layered integrated Soviet threat, but he worried about America's ability to pay for the response envisioned by it. Thus at the February 11, 1953, meeting of the NSC he "explained to the Council the value of NSC 141 as a legacy from . . . the previous administration," but "the President went on to state that the great problem before his Administration was to discover a reasonable and respectable posture of defense. If we can find such a level it may be possible to secure the money and resources necessary to enable the world to reach a decent economic position. In short, it may be possible to figure out a preparedness program that will give us a respectable position without bankrupting the nation."[61] This early formulation—a respectable defense without economic bankruptcy—formed the fundamental premise for subsequent NSC discussions as Eisenhower sought to retain the Truman administration's global definitions of American interests and the Soviet threat while exploring new ways to cut defense costs.

On May 8, 1953, the president met in the White House sun room, or solarium, with Robert Cutler, special assistant for National Security Affairs; Allen Dulles, director of the CIA; C. D. Jackson, chairman of the Psychological Strategy Board; and Undersecretary of State W. Bedell Smith[62] to begin to take a "new look" at national security strategy. They decided to appoint three study groups at the National War College to consider and make the strongest possible case for three separate options "in the same spirit as an advocate works up a case for court presentation."[63] Each team was to be issued guidelines for its particular alternative. Task Force A—chaired by George F. Kennan apparently at Eisenhower's insistence—was instructed to argue in favor of "the general policy towards the USSR and its block, which has been in effect since 1948; as modified by the determination expressed in NSC 149/2 (April 29/53) to bring the Federal budget into balance as rapidly as is consistent with continuing our leadership in the free world and barring basic change in the world situation."[64] Interestingly, this charge implied that U.S. policy had been unaltered since 1948 despite the fact that NSC 68 had not been signed by Truman until mid-1950. And indeed, when Kennan's team made its presentation to the NSC on July 16, its report reflected NSC 68/141 much more than Kennan's original version of containment. It was not without irony that Kennan made the case for global containment with Dulles seated approvingly in the front row, because presumably neither favored it. Furthermore, all three teams were enjoined from considering policies in "conflict with the realities of the world situation" or, in other words, isolationism, global unilateralism, world government, and preventive war.[65] It was as if a policy of selective containment had never been pursued and could not now be imagined (even if only to be rejected). Major General James Mc-Cormack, Jr.'s Task Force B was told to articulate a policy that would: (1) "complete the line now drawn in the NATO area and the Western Pacific so as to form a continuous line around the Soviet bloc beyond which the U.S. will not permit Soviet or satellite military forces to advance without general war"; (2) "make clear to the Soviet rulers . . . that the U.S. has established and is determined to carry out this policy"; and (3) "reserve freedom of action in the event of indigenous Communist seizure of power in countries on our side of the line to take all measures necessary to re-establish a situation compatible with the security interests of the U.S. and its allies."[66] Finally, Task Force C, headed by Admiral Richard L. Conolly, was to frame a policy "against the background of Alternative A or Alternative B, which would seek to restore the prestige of the West by winning in one or more areas a success or successes" in order "to produce a climate of victory, disturbing to the Soviets and their satellites and encouraging to the free world."[67]

After hearing the three presentations Eisenhower characteristically remarked that he discerned more similarities than differences among the alternatives and hence wanted the task forces to agree on the best features of each into a "unified policy."[68] The president then emphasized several themes that would be constantly reiterated during the course of discussions about the "New Look." First, he predicted that individual freedom would perish everywhere after the next global war regardless of who was victorious. Second, he suggested that "if you demand of a free people over a long period of time more than they want to give," "more and more controls" will be necessary until finally America becomes "a garrison state." Third, Eisenhower pondered what the United States would do with a defeated Russia inasmuch as "the American people" had "demonstrated their reluctance after a war is ended to take the necessary action properly to occupy the territory conquered. . . ." And fourth, Eisenhower warned that any tax increase to pay for defense would require "a vigorous campaign" to educate the American people and the people of our allies.[69]

The NSC referred the Solarium Task Force reports to the Planning Board to assist its consideration of a basic national security policy, and by October a draft of NSC 162 was ready. In the meantime, Eisenhower continued to wrestle with the problem of providing a respectable defense at a reasonable cost. For example, in a September memorandum to Dulles he complained that "our own people want tax relief; but they are not well informed as to what drastic tax reduction would mean to the security of the country," for they unrealistically expected better relations with Moscow after the Korean armistice: "The individual feels helpless to do anything about the foreign threat that hangs over his head and so he turns his attention to matters of immediate interest— farm supports, Taft-Hartley Act, taxes, drought relief, and partisan politics."[70]

Eisenhower admitted that a new national security policy, even if unanimously urged by "the President, the Cabinet, and the bipartisan leaders of the Congress would not in themselves be sufficient. . . . *We must have the enlightened support of the Americans* and the informed understanding of our friends in the world."[71] And when the NSC met later that month to consider NSC 159 regarding continental defense he explicitly raised his central dilemma:

> The United States was confronted with a very terrible threat and the truth of the matter was that we have devised no way of meeting this threat without imposing ever-greater controls on our economy and on the freedom of our people. We had been trying, in other words, to have our cake and eat it at the same time. We were engaged, continued the President, not only in saving our money or in defending our persons from attack; we were engaged in the defense of a way of life, and the greater danger was that in defending this way of life we would find ourselves resorting to methods that endangered this way of life. The real problem . . . was to devise methods of meeting the Soviet threat and of adopting controls, if necessary, that would not result in our transformation into a garrison state. The whole thing, said the President, was a paradox.[72]

And when the NSC convened on October 7 to discuss the draft of NSC 162, Eisenhower observed that "the issue before the Council . . . was the long-term capacity of the United States to survive. All of us . . . admit that we can endure anything for a year or two. . . . Nevertheless, in the long run this country must have a sound dollar. Moreover, this sound dollar lies at the very basis of a sound capability for defense."[73] Later he underlined the point by remarking that "NSC 141 which had been left on our doorstep by the outgoing Administration had called for additional expenditures in the neighborhood of $20 billions. . . . I think . . . that the American people ought to know when and how the law of diminishing returns sets in so heavy as to prove fatal."[74] A year later, when the NSC was deciding whether to amend the previously adopted NSC 162, Eisenhower cast the problem in the following way:

> The President commented that [one of the dilemmas he] was living with all the time [was] what do you do with the world after you have won victory in such a catastrophic nuclear war? . . . On the other hand, . . . the United States could not afford to fight all kinds of wars and still preserve its free economy and its basic institutions.

Then

> The President stated that our only chance of victory in a third world war . . . would be to paralyze the enemy at the outset. . . . Since we cannot keep the United States an armed camp or a garrison state, we must make plans to use the atom bomb if we become involved in a war. . . . We have got to be in a position to use that weapon if we are to preserve our institutions in peace and win the victory in war.[75]

In sum, President Eisenhower fretted that his vision of a cooperative commonwealth could be destroyed by the emergence of an American garrison state, and that nightmare, he concluded, could occur in several ways. First, a Taft-like Fortress America, deprived of access to external markets and raw materials and ideologically isolated in a totalitarian sea, would be required to adopt draconian measures in order to survive physically. Second, a deficit-ridden, high-tax America, although rightly committed to defending the free world from international communism, would witness the destruction of its individual liberties as its citizens were eventually demoralized by the long-term demands of the cold war. Finally, even Eisenhower's middle way New Look could not guarantee success, because even if defense costs could be controlled through an increased reliance on nuclear weapons, the president acknowledged that a third global war, regardless of its outcome, would transform the United States into a dictatorship.

In order to reconstruct the internationalist consensus that had been shaken by Korea, Eisenhower altered the means of Truman's foreign policy while preserving its main goals. Eisenhower embraced with conviction NSC 68's global definitions of the Communist threat and American interests, but he feared that the policy instruments sanctioned by it would ultimately undermine the domestic consensus and destroy the Western alliance. That is, while endorsing the broad outlines of a containment strategy, Eisenhower believed that the American economy could no longer tolerate the defense expenditures evidently required by NSC 68, and a faltering U.S. economy would in turn inevitably plunge our allies into depression.[76] In place of a strategy that demanded conventional, proportional military responses wherever communism threatened to expand, Eisenhower offered a dual-tracked alternative: the New Look and the increased use of the CIA. The New Look promised to reduce the military budget by taking advantage of America's atomic and air superiority. Convinced that his barely concealed threat to use atomic weapons against the Chinese during the spring of 1953 in the absence of progress at Panmunjon had led directly to the Korean armistice, Eisenhower concluded that the threat of "massive retaliation" might be effectively employed against a variety of Communist provocations in areas where the United States suffered conventional inferiority.[77] The construction of such an umbrella around the Soviet and Communist periphery was combined with a series of regional military pacts that placed the primary responsibility for conventional defense in indigenous hands. Such a course had been recommended by Solarium's Task Force B. This approach—derisively called "brinkmanship'' and "pactomania"—was designed essentially to protect America's global interests without risking new Koreas. But the second track of the strategy—the systematic use of the CIA for covert operations—was equally essential and appealed to Eisenhower for similar reasons. As Stephen E. Ambrose has recently pointed out in *Ike's Spies*,[78] during World War II Eisenhower had been an enthusiastic advocate of clandestine activities, and a heavy reliance as president on the CIA both supported his national security strategy and perfectly fit his leadership style. In those cases where the threat of massive retaliation might not be practical or where regional allies lacked reliability, the capability to quickly, cheaply, quietly, and relatively bloodlessly depose hostile or unstable regimes could be a significant cold-war asset, and Eisenhower clearly recognized the CIA's potential. Confronted with a public that had wearied of Korea, that was extremely wary of further direct U.S. military interventions,[79] but that adamantly opposed the loss of additional territory to the Communists, Eisenhower saw in the CIA an instrument that, if employed effectively, could help preserve the domestic consensus while not burdening allies or citizens with heavier expenditures.

In symbol as well as substance Eisenhower refused to dissociate himself from the Democratic diplomatic record. By opposing the Yalta Resolution and the Bricker Amendment, by nominating Charles E. Bohlen as ambassador to the Soviet Union, and by refusing to endorse explicitly the "liberation" plank in the 1952 Republican platform, Eisenhower signaled his endorsement of containment. Fearful of the partisan rancor that all but paralyzed the Truman administration during its last two years, he wanted to rebuild the bipartisan internationalist coalition of the late 40s and realized that acquiescence in any of these "unilateralist" schemes would be disastrous.

At the same time, however, Eisenhower felt that certain of Truman's actions had needlessly harmed the international image of the United States. His persistent refusal to negotiate with the Soviet Union except in "situations of strength" had occasionally allowed Moscow to wrap itself in the mantle of the peacelover. Furthermore, and related to his fascination with public relations,[80] Eisenhower believed that the Truman administration had been insufficiently sensitive to the psychological impact of its foreign policies. He took several steps to correct these alleged shortcomings. First, partly in response to West European pressure and partly because of his own conviction that Soviet-American tensions had to be reduced, Eisenhower initiated a number of limited diplomatic and cultural exchanges with Moscow and Peking, highlighted by the Big Four Geneva Summit in 1955. Second, with great fanfare he presented himself as the "military man of peace" through his Open Skies and Atoms for Peace initiatives. Although little of substance came from these proposals, as Robert A. Strong shows in his essay, they signified a symbolic break with the widely perceived rigidity of the second Truman administration. Third, with the help of C. D. Jackson, a *Time* magazine executive hired as Eisenhower's psychological warfare assistant, the National Security Council was restructured. According to Karl Harr, who was a Defense Department-NSC liaison during these years, "the Communists were doing such a good job of orchestrating all their resources and assets. Orchestrating meant so organizing our assets that we were in a position to give a positive and sensitive psychological twist to our activities."[81] Thus in the fall of 1953 the Operations Coordinating Board was created at the undersecretary level to ensure that actions "were consonant with the policies decided upon by the President, that they were coordinated with each other and . . . that they were conducted with a view to the impact on world opinion in a way most favorable to the United States."[82] Finally, a range of "psychological warfare" weapons, "anything from the singing of a beautiful hymn up to the most extraordinary kind of physical sabotage. . . ."[83] was sanctioned to seize the initiative in the cold war. Essentially, however, psychological warfare "meant simply a robust faith in the efficacy of public posture: the belief that by merely making pronouncements and striking poses" (especially by Dulles) "the United States could increase the difficulties under which its adversaries operated."[84] These black arts, moreover, were consistent with a containment strategy that sought to utilize America's strengths—in this case, the talents of the advertising industry!

A presentism lurks in many of us that wants to make Eisenhower into something that he was not. After Vietnam, the Great Society, Watergate, chronic inflation, and the institutionalization of the cosmetic presidency, we ache for another Eisenhower and wistfully remember his refusal to intervene in Indochina in 1954, his responsible fiscal conservatism that supervised the shrinkage of the defense budget, and a fierce personal integrity that tolerated neither scandal nor cheap politiking. Moreover, a new revisionism has suggested that Eisenhower possessed a previously unnoticed asset—the demonstrated capacity for sophisticated, quiet, effective leadership.

This presentism takes a variety of forms and has ranged from Vietnam to the Imperial Presidency, but a recent example is particularly suggestive. Commenting on a letter written by Eisenhower to Richard L. Simon of Simon & Schuster in 1956 and uncovered by David S. Broder of the *Washington Post,* Anthony Lewis claimed to know "what Dwight Eisenhower would have said to the MX: No. He had no hesitation in turning down grandiose military ideas. He knew the system from within."[85] In contrast to Ronald Reagan, who had allegedly used the Korean airliner incident in September 1983 as an excuse "to drum up support for a larger defense budget and new nuclear weapons," Lewis found "a serenity" in Eisenhower's letter, "the inner confidence of a man who knows he does not have to posture" and sadly concluded that "that air of confident restraint is what has been so lacking in American rhetoric about the Soviet Union in recent years."[86] Can this be the same Eisenhower who, for instance, suggested to Press Secretary Hagerty in February 1955, in response to Chou En-lai's demand for Taiwan's expulsion from the UN, that perhaps the United States should "go after" the Chinese Communists "right now without letting them pick their time and place of their own choosing?"[87] Would Eisenhower, if he had been constitutionally able to stand for reelection in 1960, have sent combat forces to South Vietnam? Would Eisenhower have tolerated double-digit inflation? Would he have allowed Reagan's budget deficits? Would he have built the MX? The B-1? Midgetman? Would he have made the Sandinistas cry uncle? The questions quickly become absurd.

As I have tried to show, Eisenhower's foreign policy cannot be grasped without reference to his public philosophy and to the domestic consensus that he sought to sustain. The "what if" historical questions of 1980s' hypothesizers frequently reflect justifiable disappointment with the last quarter-century of American foreign policy, but they risk deifying Eisenhower by transforming him into a paragon of wisdom and moderation. Rather than further such speculation, I will conclude by highlighting the dilemmas produced (in part, at least) by Eisenhower's public philosophy, by his commitment to anticommunist containment, and by his reluctance to build a domestic consensus on other than cold-war premises.

Eisenhower sensed that exigencies of the cold war threatened his vision of a cooperative, voluntary international corporate commonwealth. The perceived necessity for a global, coordinated, militant response to the international Communist conspiracy created opportunities, he feared, for narrow private interests and for domestic enemies of liberty to undermine the sort of community he valued. He noted the problems while still NATO commander: "It is interesting to speculate where we would now find ourselves had it not been for the communistic invasion of South Korea and the consequent awakening of the whole free world to the warning that people like Jim Forrestal had been expressing time and again in previous years. Now I am afraid that we are risking damage from the other horn of the dilemma—that is, the danger of internal deterioration through the annual expenditure of unconscionable sums on a program of indefinite duration. . . . If the Republicans place a political mantle on me, I would not attempt to evade it.''[88] Eisenhower's reference to "internal deterioration" meant more than economic insolvency. It included the danger that cold-war-induced political centralization, rapid technological change, and unchecked military spending posed to a free society.

As president, Eisenhower attempted to deal with the dilemma in several ways. First, he served, in effect, as his own secretary of defense. Confident that his own vast knowledge of military affairs would enable him to deal wisely with the Joint Chiefs' predictable pleas for expenditures, Eisenhower signaled his own commitment to fiscal responsibility through the largely symbolic appointment of Charles E. Wilson as defense secretary. But whatever public relations advantages "Engine Charlie" may have initially possessed were quickly dissipated by several unfortunate congressional appearances and excessive deference to military opinion. Eisenhower was apparently satisfied only with the performance of his final secretary, Thomas Gates, an insider who had gained a thorough knowledge of DOD during a slow rise through the ranks.[89] Second, in a further effort to evaluate the arguments of the Chiefs, Eisenhower sought the counsel of respected scientists and came increasingly to rely on what he perceived as their reputation for candor and prudence.[90] Third, President Eisenhower largely succeeded in stabilizing the defense budget. Between fiscal 1954 and fiscal 1961 absolute spending rose only $800 million, from $46.6 billion to $47.4 billion, and during the intervening years expenditures were at or below the 1954 figure. Moreover, military spending as a percentage of the overall federal budget fell from 65.7 to 48.5 during his presidential term. Many of these savings occurred, of course, because of a growing reliance on nuclear weapons and long-range delivery systems, both of which were relatively less expensive than the conventional instruments favored by NSC 68 and NSC 141.

Here, then, was the rub. Even as Eisenhower labored to control the military establishment that he feared could eventually impose intolerable burdens on American society, he authorized the development of increasingly sophisticated technologies designed to maintain U.S. nuclear superiority and to protect our land-based forces from Soviet attack. And while these new weapons may have been necessary to keep pace with Russian improvements, there was a heavy underlying cost—a cost that Eisenhower dramatically acknowledged in his Farewell

Address as the military-industrial (and scientific) complex and that his private utterances at NSC discussions had anticipated.

In that speech, which his brother Milton termed "about as one hundred percent Eisenhower as you can get,"[91] he summarized the major themes of his presidency—continuity, community, and consensus. Suggesting that presidential-congressional consensus on "issues of great moment" constitutes an essential prerequisite for effective government, Eisenhower claimed that "the Congress and the Administration have, on most vital issues, cooperated well to serve the national good rather than mere partisanship. . . ."[92] The president cautioned, however, that America's "noble goals" of "world peace and human betterment" were "persistently threatened by the conflict now engulfing the world" that "commands our attention, absorbs our very beings."[93] Implicitly embracing the images of NSC 68 and the language of "X," Eisenhower warned: "We face a hostile ideology—global in scope, atheistic in character, ruthless in purpose, and insidious in method. Unhappily the danger it poses promises to be of indefinite duration. To meet it successfully there is called for, not so much the emotional and transitory sacrifices of crisis, but rather those which enable us to carry forward steadily, surely, and without complaint the burdens of a prolonged and complex struggle—with liberty at stake."[94]

Moreover, this policy of global containment must be patiently pursued with the help of a military establishment, "mighty, ready for instant action, so that no potential aggressor may be tempted to risk his own destruction."[95] Yet the recognized "imperative" for "an immense military establishment and a large arms industry"—unprecedented in the American experience—had to exert enormous "economic, political, even spiritual" influence with "grave implications" for "the very structure of our society."[96] To meet this internal threat to liberty Eisenhower called upon "an alert and knowledgeable citizenry" to "compel the proper meshing of the huge industrial and military machinery of defense with our peaceful methods and goals."[97] But the consequences of the technological revolution that made the military-industrial complex possible must also be addressed. Research had become so "formalized, complex, and costly" that the survival of the "free university, historically the fountainhead of free ideas and scientific discovery," was now confronted with "the prospect of domination of the nation's scholars by Federal employment, project allocations, and the power of money."[98] While President Eisenhower evinced respect for scientific research and discovery, he noted that without viligance "public policy could itself become the captive of a scientific technological elite."[99]

Eisenhower concluded, appropriately enough, with his vision of community—"a proud confederation of mutual trust and respect" based on equality and dedicated to "disarmament with mutual honor and confidence."[100] And although admitting disappointment with his inability to build a "lasting peace," he contented himself with the knowledge that war had been avoided during his presidency and that "steady progress toward our ultimate goal" had been made.[101]

In short, Eisenhower publicly expressed his long-held fear that his goal of building a cooperative, decentralized domestic community was simultaneously being undermined by the regimentation and bureaucratization necessitated by America's defense requirements. He never resolved this dilemma; indeed, it was probably unresolvable. Eisenhower hoped that an enlightened Middle Way national leadership characterized by executive-congressional bipartisanship and supported by an alert citizenry could preserve the traditional liberties of American life. But he could only hope that a post-Eisenhower America would remain skeptical of higher taxes, deficit spending, social panaceas, and exhortations to intensify the cold war.

At the same time, Eisenhower's deep commitment to anticommunist containment and his consequent embrace of the Truman administration's grandiose definition of American interests guaranteed the future that he abhorred. Massive retaliation could only remain a credible threat so long as Soviet strategic forces were clearly inferior to our own, or if Eisenhower limited that threat to regions of primary interest to the United States. Eisenhower repeatedly acknowledged he could do little to stop Soviet strategic advances—except to continue to modernize American nuclear forces as he did—but his refusal to take Kennan's original advice and structure American interests in a hierarchy meant that brinkmanship on the periphery became increasingly vulnerable to attacks from critics like Nitze and Maxwell Taylor, who argued that the New Look placed exaggerated reliance on a noncredible nuclear threat.

Then why didn't Eisenhower redefine the *ends* of American foreign policy? Why did he accept the open-ended goals of NSC 68 and NSC 141 while he rejected the unlimited means? Why did he "nation build" in South Vietnam, create SEATO, and sponsor CENTO? Why, in the name of fiscal responsibility, could he not have shrunk the ends of foreign policy as he had shrunk its means? Confident of his immense political popularity and his leadership capacities, why didn't President Eisenhower push the foreign policy Establishment and the cold-war consensus to accept more modest foreign policy objectives? His unwillingness to take these steps represents the central dilemma of Eisenhower's foreign policy. While he was acutely aware that the national security instruments mandated during the Truman years threatened his conservative vision of American community, Eisenhower nevertheless believed that a failure to oppose communism everywhere posed an even more deadly challenge to that vision. Thus critics who chastize Eisenhower for not using his enormous popularity to redirect the cold-war consensus really miss the point. It was not Eisenhower's timidity but his deeply held anticommunist convictions that explain his refusal to transform the consensus. In the end, Eisenhower risked the destruction of his cooperative, decentralized domestic community in order to preserve a diverse, prosperous free world. By returning to the expandable means of NSC 68 his Democratic successors not only ultimately destroyed the domestic consensus via Vietnam but also gravely endangered the economic stability of the West as well. Compared to Kennedy and Johnson, Eisenhower's accomplishments were impressive, but all three men were imprisoned in an anticommunist outlook that required America to live beyond its means. Eisenhower's balancing act proved transitory and fatally vulnerable to New Frontiersmen eager to "get America moving again."

Notes

1. Godfrey Hodgson, "The Establishment," *Foreign Policy* 10 (Spring 1973): 8. For more recent accounts, see Robert D. Schulzinger, *The Wise Men of Foreign Affairs: The History of the Council on Foreign Relations* (New York: Columbia University Press, 1984), and I. M. Destler, Leslie H. Gelb, and Anthony Lake, *Our Own Worst Enemy: The Unmaking of American Foreign Policy* (New York: Simon & Schuster, 1984).

2. David Clinton, "Interests, Values, and the American Consensus on Foreign Policy," in Kenneth W. Thompson, ed., *Political Traditions and Contemporary Problems* (Lanham, Md.: University Press of America, 1982), 9–4.

3. Ibid.

4. Ibid.

5. Much of the following discussion of containment under Truman originally appeared in somewhat different form in my essay, "A *Neo-Con*sensus? American Foreign Policy in the 1980s," in Richard A. Melanson, ed., *Neither Cold War nor Detente? Soviet-American Relations in the 1980s* (Charlottesville: University Press of Virginia, 1982).

6. John Lewis Gaddis, *Strategies of Containment* (New York: Oxford University Press, 1981), 32–33.

7. Fred M. Kaplan, "Our Cold-War Policy, circa '50," *New York Times Magazine*, 18 May 1980, 88.

8. Ibid.

9. U.S. Department of State, *Foreign Relations of the United States, 1949*,

Diplomatic Papers, vol. 1, *National Security Affairs; Foreign Economic Policy* (Washington, D.C.: Government Printing Office, 1976), 271–77.

10. Bohlen Memorandum, 14 April 1949, ibid., 277–78.

11. Kennan to Acheson, 14 April 1949, ibid., 282.

12. Kaplan, "Our Cold-War Policy," 91.

13. Gaddis, *Strategies of Containment,* 90–98.

14. Ibid., 95.

15. Ibid.

16. Ibid.

17. Ibid., 98.

18. Ralph B. Levering, *The Public and American Foreign Policy, 1918–1978* (New York: William Morrow, 1978), 102.

19. Ibid.

20. Ibid.

21. Ronald J. Caridi, *The Korean War and American Politics: The Republican Party as a Case Study* (Philadelphia: University of Pennsylvania Press, 1968), 141.

22. See Kenneth W. Thompson, *The President and the Public Philosophy* (Baton Rouge: Louisiana State University Press, 1981), 1–2. Thompson suggests that a public philosophy consists of "a formulation that gives some minimum coherence of purpose to public endeavors" in order that broader social interests are not "overridden by a surge of special interests."

23. Robert Griffith, "Dwight D. Eisenhower and the Corporate Commonwealth," *American Historical Review* 87 (February 1982): 87–122.

24. Ibid., 88.

25. Ibid.

26. Ibid., 89.

27. Ibid., 90.

28. Ibid., 96, 91.

29. Inaugural Address, October 12, 1948 in ibid., 91.

30. Ibid. Corroborated by Milton S. Eisenhower in interview, 14 June 1983, Baltimore.

31. Ibid., 92.

32. Ibid.

33. Ibid., 93.

34. Fred I. Greenstein, *The Hidden-Hand Presidency: Eisenhower as Leader* (New York: Basic Books, 1982).

35. Griffith, "Dwight D. Eisenhower," 93.

36. Entry from 5 March 1951 in Robert H. Ferrell, ed., *The Eisenhower Diaries* (New York: W. W. Norton, 1980), 189.

37. Interview, Charlottesville, Virginia, 8 July 1983.

38. Entry from 2 July 1953 in *The Eisenhower Diaries,* 245.

39. Entry from 11 June 1951 in ibid., 194–95.

40. Entry from 24 November 1951 in ibid., 206.

41. Robert Dallek, *The American Style of Foreign Policy: Cultural Politics and Foreign Affairs* (New York: Alfred A. Knopf, 1983), 187.

42. Walt W. Rostow, *The United States in the World Arena: An Essay in Recent History* (New York: Harper & Brothers, 1960).

43. Rostow, *The United States in the World Arena*, 395.

44. Ibid., 392.

45. Ibid., 393.

46. Ibid., 393–94.

47. Murray Kempton, "The Underestimation of Dwight D. Eisenhower," *Esquire* 68 (September 1967), 103–9, 156.

48. Greenstein, *The Hidden-Hand Presidency*, 57.

49. Ibid., 57–58.

50. Ibid., 58.

51. Ibid., 247.

52. Rostow, *The United States in the World Arena*, 395.

53. Greenstein, *The Hidden-Hand Presidency*, 229.

54. Ibid.

55. Ibid., 230.

56. Ibid.

57. Ibid., 232.

58. Ibid.

59. Interview, Washington, D.C., 7 July 1983.

60. Quoted in Gaddis, *Strategies of Containment*, 125.

61. U.S. Department of State, *Foreign Relations of the United States, 1952–1954*, Diplomatic Papers, vol. 2, pt. 1, *National Security Affairs* (Washington, D.C.: Government Printing Office, 1984), 236.

62. Glenn H. Snyder, "The 'New Look' of 1953," in Warner R. Schilling et al., *Strategy, Politics, and Defense Budgets* (New York: Columbia University Press, 1962), 407.

63. *Foreign Relations of the United States, 1952–54*, vol 2, pt. 1, 324.

64. Ibid., 325.

65. Ibid., 361–62.

66. Ibid., 365.

67. Ibid., 326.

68. Ibid., 397.

69. Ibid.

70. Ibid., 461.

71. Ibid., 462 (emphasis in the original).

72. Ibid., 469.

73. Ibid., 519.

74. Ibid., 520–21.

75. Ibid., 804, 805–6.

76. Interestingly, however, contemporary opinion polls indicated that the American public was willing to support higher defense budgets than those offered by Eisenhower. See, for example, Samuel P. Huntington, *The Common Defense* (New York: Columbia University Press, 1961).

77. See Gaddis, *Strategies of Containment*, 168–69.

78. Stephen E. Ambrose, with Richard H. Immerman, *Ike's Spies: Eisenhower and the Espionage Establishment* (New York: MacMillan, 1981).

79. See Levering, *The Public and American Foreign Policy,* 116–17.

80. See Griffith, "Dwight D. Eisenhower and the Corporate Commonwealth," 93–94.

81. Miller Center of Public Affairs Forum, University of Virginia, Charlottesville, 10 February 1983.

82. Ibid.

83. Quoted in Gaddis, *Strategies of Containment,* n. 61, 155.

84. Ibid.

85. Anthony Lewis, "If It Were Eisenhower," *New York Times,* 8 September 1983, 21.

86. Ibid.

87. Robert H. Ferrell, ed., *The Diary of James C. Hagerty: Eisenhower in Mid-Course, 1954–1955* (Bloomington: Indiana University Press, 1983), entry from 3 February 1955.

88. Entry from 22 January 1952, *The Eisenhower Diaries,* 212.

89. Interview with Arthur S. Flemming, Charlottesville, Virginia, 9 June 1983.

90. Goodpaster interview.

91. Milton S. Eisenhower interview.

92. *Public Papers of the Presidents of the United States, Dwight D. Eisenhower, 1961* (Washington D.C.: Government Printing Office), 1036.

93. Ibid., 1037, 1036, 1037.

94. Ibid., 1037.

95. Ibid.

96. Ibid., 1038.

97. Ibid.

98. Ibid., 1038, 1039.

99. Ibid., 1039.

100. Ibid.

101. Ibid., 1040.

Part Two
Foreign Policy Issues

Eisenhower and Communism
The Public Record of the 1950s

Norman A. Graebner

Dwight D. Eisenhower inherited from his Democratic predecessor a body of attitudes and purposes regarding China, but no policy for achieving them. Having failed to share with its potential critics its diminishing choices during the months of Nationalist China's collapse, the Truman administration permitted the Republican party to extract uncontestable political and emotional advantage from Chiang Kai-shek's final retreat to the island of Formosa in late 1949. The China White Paper, published in August when the Nationalist cause was already doomed, attributed the Communist triumph of Mao Tse-tung to revolutionary forces in China beyond American control. Republican senators Kenneth Wherry of Nebraska, William Knowland of California, and William Jenner of Indiana denounced the White Paper as "a 1,054-page whitewash of a wishful, do-nothing policy which has succeeded only in placing Asia in danger of Soviet conquest."[1] Wisconsin Senator Joseph McCarthy added the cry of treason to explain such apparent failure. Recognizing the potential of his accusations, Republicans fell into line behind the Wisconsin senator. Under intense Republican pressure the Truman administration promised to recognize only the Republic of China on Formosa and sustain its presence in the United Nations. Nonrecognition of the Peking regime, Republican leaders argued, would prevent it from consolidating its power and assure Chiang's triumphant return to the Mainland. As president after January 1953, Eisenhower faced the challenge of satisfying such partisan expectations with neither a promising course of action nor the prospects of creating one.

Chiang's supporters in the United States declared emphatically that Eisenhower's election was a mandate that the administration abrograte Truman's limited commitment to the Nationalist cause and give all possible assistance to the Republic of China. A *Life* magazine editorial asserted that the first requirement of a sound China policy was the need of binding "free China's fate and policy to ours with hoops of steel. Only on that basis will there be anything to defend." Henry R. Luce, its editor, declared after a visit to Formosa that the Nationalists were living completely for the purpose of liberating China from the Communist regime. The time had come, he believed, to join hands with the Kuomintang in its struggle to free the Mainland. Geraldine Fitch, in her *Formosa Beachhead,* added genuine expectations of success to the proposed venture by asserting that the overwhelming majority of the Mainland Chinese were "working, watching and praying" for Chiang's return.[2] Any integrated invasion by six to eight hundred thousand Nationalist troops, she predicted, would make "the liberation crusade snowball from South China to Manchuria." William C. Bullitt observed in *Look* magazine that the United States could turn the balance of power against the Communist world in Asia "by a concerted attack on the Chinese Communists, employing no American soldiers except from Korea, but using the American Navy to blockade the China coast and the American air force to bomb appropriate targets, while assigning the great burden of the ground fighting to the Koreans and the Free Chinese. . . ."

Members of the China bloc in Congress were equally determined to force the China issue to its necessary conclusion. For them, coexistence with the Mainland regime was tantamount to surrender. "There can be no American policy for the Pacific," Jenner warned the Senate, "if the Communists are allowed to retain the heartland of Asia. . . . All American policy must start from a firm decision to reestablish the legitimate anti-Communist government on the China mainland."[3] Knowland could no longer visualize any long-run alternative to military action against the mainland of China. "We must not fool ourselves into thinking we can avoid taking up arms with the Chinese Reds," he wrote. "If we don't fight them in China and Formosa, we will be fighting them in San Francisco, in Seattle, in Kansas City." Knowland emerged as Chiang's leading spokesman in the Senate. Congressman Walter Judd of Minnesota assumed direction of the House's broad commitment to the Nationalist cause. The Republican stalwarts moved quickly to commit the Eisenhower administration to the indefinite nonrecognition of the Peking regime. They closed in as early as June 1953, when they attached a rider to an appropriation bill that declared that the United States would cut off all financial support to the UN if it should seat a Red Chinese delegation. Senator Knowland soon captured the headlines when he announced that he would resign his position as majority leader in the Senate and devote his full efforts to seek the withdrawal of the United States from the UN should that body admit the Peking regime. Only when Eisenhower and Dulles assured Chiang's congressional supporters that they would vigorously oppose any effort to bring Peking into the world organization did the China bloc relax its pressure.[4]

Conscious of the abuse that former Secretary of State Dean Acheson and other Truman officials had suffered at the hands of Chiang's supporters in Congress, the new administration was not inclined to challenge them. Eisenhower established his liaison with the China bloc by appointing Walter S. Robertson, a staunch friend of Chiang, to the position of assistant secretary of state for Far Eastern affairs. "If we had paid attention to the reports [from China] of Walter Robertson," Knowland observed bitterly, "we wouldn't be in the mess we are today." In naming Admiral Arthur W. Radford as chairman of the Joint Chiefs of Staff, the president placed in a high advisory post a powerful member of the Nationalist China bloc. Radford made no secret of his belief that the Peking regime must be eliminated even if it required a fifty-year war. For Dulles, the necessary opposition to Peking came naturally enough. He shared the fears of Robertson and Radford that a China-based Communist expansionism threatened the whole of Asia. These men possessed the power to bind the United States inflexibly to the Nationalist cause, nothing more. They had no plan to return Chiang Kai-shek to the Mainland peacefully; nor could they assume that the American people would support a war to achieve their purposes in China.

Nothing revealed the emptiness of the Eisenhower posture toward China as did the "unleashing" of Chiang Kai-shek in February 1953, when the president, in a dramatic gesture of reversing Truman's Korean War order to the Seventh Fleet to defend Formosa, announced that the fleet would no longer protect, not Formosa, but the Mainland.[5] The president added emphatically that the United States had "no obligation to protect a nation fighting us in Korea." To add reality to the notion that the unleashed Nationalists would shortly seize the offensive against the Mainland, the administration pressed Chiang to place regular troops on the Tachens off the China coast some two hundred miles from Formosa. Chiang resisted, believing that the Tachens were too distant from his home base. Eventually he conceded and placed a division under one of his ablest generals on the distant outposts.

This new posture of firmness conveyed the impression that Eisenhower and Dulles had successfully forged something more promising than Truman's island defense perimeter. Congressional acclaim was most pronounced among those who had condemned Truman's neutralization of the Formosa Straits. Senator Robert A. Taft of Ohio thought the new posture "a step in the right direction." Admiral William Leahy termed it a "bright idea" to let the Chinese Nationalists settle the "problems along the China coast." General Douglas MacArthur asserted that it would "correct one of the strangest anomalies known to military history." It would strengthen the American position in the Far East by releasing the Nationalists for raids on the Chinese coast and would give notice to the reds that their unprecedented sanctuary would now come to an end. "The modification of the Seventh Fleet's orders," he concluded, "should be supported by all loyal Americans irrespective of party."[6] Predictably Eisenhower's "unleashing" had no effect on the Far East whatever. Thereafter the United States posture toward China settled down to the perennial recognition of the Republic of China on Formosa as the legitimate government of China, alone deserving representation in the United Nations. This relationship demanded nothing of the nation beyond limited military and economic aid for the Nationalist regime. Meanwhile, nonrecognition of the Peking regime, backed by a rhetoric of open defiance, sustained the promise of Chiang's return and enabled the administration to avoid the hard necessity of formulating a policy for China. What permitted such behavior was simply the absence of any Chinese threat to the United States, perhaps not even to Asia itself.

Administration officials devoted themselves to the necessary task of rationalizing nonrecognition as a promising response to the Chinese challenge. State Department officer Alfred Jenkins offered the standard formula. After recounting the many misdeeds of the Peking regime, he warned that recognition of the Communist government, granting it the moral approval of the United States, would shatter the confidence of those resisting communism elsewhere in Asia. Nonrecognition thus became a powerful, even essential, deterrent to Chinese expansionism. Beyond containment Jenkins offered the promise of liberation by delineating the superior qualities of the government on Formosa which, he added, "is far more representative of the will of the Chinese people than is the Peiping regime."[7] If the Peking regime was illegitimate, as Jenkins charged, it was also ephemeral. "We recognize with concern an increase in the incidence of cancer in recent years," he wrote, "but we refuse to recognize cancer as the inevitable wave of the future." Perhaps it was true that if the cancer were properly ignored it would eventually disappear, and even without a quarantine. Perhaps it was equally true, as Eric Hoffer wrote in *Harper's,* that "an uncompromising attitude is more an indication of inner uncertainty than of deep conviction. The implacable stand is directed more against doubt within than the assailant without."[8] This rationale, whatever its intrinsic merits, managed to build an overwhelming national consensus of unrelenting opposition to Peking. Dulles responded to that consensus when, at the Geneva Conference of April 1954, he avoided the outstretched hand of Chinese leader Chou En-lai and instructed the American delegation to ignore the presence of the Chinese delegation.[9]

Whether the United States could extract itself from its burgeoning commitments in East Asia without coming to terms with Peking was doubtful. Joseph C. Harsch, Washington correspondent for the *Christian Science Monitor,* posed the question in September 1953: "If Secretary Dulles is firmly set on a policy of 'disengagement' from the Far East and if [UN Ambassador Henry Cabot] Lodge really expects to get American troops out of Korea, then both of them must contemplate the possibility of some sort of progression from the Korean peace conference which would lead to a seat for Communist China in the UN."

Indeed, in meetings with his staff early in his adminstration Eisenhower expressed uneasiness over the United States' commitment to the Nationalist regime. Robert J. Donovan, who attended such meetings in preparation of his semiofficial history of the administration, *Eisenhower: The Inside Story,* recorded the president's views in the following passage: "The President was not convinced that the vital interests of the United States were best served by prolonged nonrecognition of China. He had serious doubts as to whether Russia and China were natural allies. . . . Therefore, he asked, would it not be the best policy in the long run for the United States to try to pull China away from Russia rather than drive the Chinese even deeper into an unnatural alliance unfriendly to the United States?" On occasion the president admitted to newsmen that the country could not eliminate the red government and therefore had no choice but to live with it peacefully. But never in his public statements did the president admit his doubts or counter the continuing anti-Chinese rhetoric of administration spokesmen. Officially he remained committed to Chiang Kai-shek as the legitimate leader of all China.

Having cast its lot with Chiang Kai-shek, the United States could not escape its ultimate entrapment in the ongoing Chinese civil war. In September 1954, after months of threats and counterthreats between Taipei and Peking, shore batteries near Amoy opened fire on Nationalist-held Quemoy. The Pentagon immediately authorized Chiang's air force to strike coastal installations and shipping in the vicinity of the offshore islands. Admiral Radford admitted that the offshore islands were not essential for the defense of Formosa, but he insisted that the

loss of the islands would destroy Nationalist morale, an essential element in the defense of free Asia.[10] Amid the growing crisis Dulles, on
December 1, 1954, announced a new security pact with the Republic of
China which promised that the United States would defend Formosa,
the Pescadores, and other Nationalist-held islands. Chiang agreed not
to attack the Mainland without previous consultation with the United
States. What made the ongoing shelling of the offshore islands especially
disconcerting was the assertion of Chinese leaders that it was merely a
prelude to the conquest of Formosa. After a lull, Chou En-lai announced
in January 1955: "The government of the People's Republic of China
has repeatedly and in solemn terms declared to the world that the
Chinese people are determined to liberate their own territory of Taiwan
[Formosa]. . . . Taiwan is an inalienable part of China's territory."
Dulles responded by assuring Chiang that the Nationalists on Formosa
would not stand alone against any invasion from the continent. With
Formosa protected from the Mainland by the Seventh Fleet and one
hundred miles of water, the United States' commitment to its defense
did not appear to Americans or Europeans as particularly dangerous.

What quickly subjected the Eisenhower adminstration to open criticism throughout the noncommunist world was the doubtful posture that
it assumed on the question of the offshore islands. The president ordered
a retreat from the Tachens but added the tacit promise to Nationalist
Foreign Minister George Yeh that the United States would defend
Quemoy and Matsu, the offshore islands along the coast facing Formosa. Dulles informed newsmen that the Mainland Chinese were mass-
ing enormous forces along the coast, that an attack could come at any
moment. Yet the assault on the offshore islands that he predicted would
have left the United States only two impossible alternatives. If, on one
hand, American forces rushed to the aid of Chiang's exposed position,
the United States would be involved in another open conflict with China
on Asian soil; the resort to atomic bombs, as Dulles warned, might
shortly involve the United States in a general war. If, on the other hand,
the United States backed down and deserted Chiang, as it did in the
Tachens, it would suffer a tremendous loss of prestige. Successful
diplomacy always seeks to avoid the hard decision between war and
diplomatic defeat. Yet any all-out Chinese attack on Quemoy or Matsu
would have placed the United States in precisely that dilemma.

Actually there was little strategic connection between the offshore
islands and Formosa. The offshore islands were not even remotely
required for the defense of Formosa. C. L. Sulzberger of *The New York
Times* reported from Tokyo following a trip to Formosa: "Chiang Kai-
shek would like to see a battle for the strategically unimportant offshore

islands develop into a world war so he could gamble on returning to the mainland. But as far as we are concerned they have no military value.'' By maintaining a posture of doubt, the administration hoped to deter the mainland Chinese and to save itself the embarrassment of turning on Chiang's friends in order to avoid a war over two tiny islands hugging the China coast ten thousand miles away.

In the Formosa Resolution of late January 1955, Congress authorized the president to resist any effort to capture the offshore islands if it appeared that the assault was an initial move against Formosa itself. "Clearly, this existing and developing situation," warned the president, "poses a serious danger to the security of our country and the entire Pacific area and indeed to the peace of the world."[11] The president agreed to use United States' force only in situations that he could recognize as part of a general assault on Formosa itself. His purpose, he said, was to demonstrate American determination to maintain its commitment to the defense of Formosa. Eisenhower's decision to remain in the thick of the Chinese civil war troubled Europeans and Asians alike. Europeans seldom objected to the American defense of Formosa, but they questioned the wisdom of any commitment to the offshore islands. *The Times of London* observed characteristically: "Mr. Dulles is chiefly concerned with the defense of Formosa, and many are with him there. But even on the score of defense, it is surely better to put 100 miles of sea between the two sides than leave provocative and exposed outposts on [red] China's doorstep." For Nehru and other free Asian leaders, the final outcome of the Chinese civil war had been determined years earlier; they blamed the United States, not China, for the tension in the Formosa Straits.[12] Except for the assumption that Chiang would return to the Mainland, they noted, the American involvement in the Straits had no purpose whatever.

Only if it foreswore its vision of a prewar China could the United States give up its commitment to the offshore islands. To Chiang, the offshore islands, as stepping stones to the Mainland, were symbols that the Nationalists would one day return to power over all China. With a fourth of his best troops on Quemoy and Matsu, Chiang asserted his right to hold the islands as essential for his ultimate victory in the Chinese civil war. Without the anticipation of success, his regime was in danger of disintegration. Tingfu F. Tsiang, Chinese representative at the UN, defended the Nationalist position in June 1955: "We cannot do that [give up the offshore islands] because withdrawal from Matsu and Quemoy weakens our material strength and undermines our moral position." Any effort to force compromise on the Nationalists, he warned, would "liquidate the Republic of China."[13] The diminution of

Nationalist morale, the administration concluded, would produce a wholesale desertion of Kuomintang forces and their return to the Mainland. Walter Lippmann saw danger in this assumption. "If, as a matter of fact," he wrote, "the internal strength of Nationalist China rests on the fantasy that Chiang Kai-shek will some day return to China, we are headed for trouble." Clearly the United States could not defend the offshore islands at any cost commensurate with their value. At the same time, it could not declare them outside the American defense perimeter without endangering the Nationalist regime and undermining the official purpose of unseating the Peking government. The United States could maintain the myth of Chiang's popularity on the Mainland, but it could not eliminate his enemies there except through a general war.

Eisenhower's Formosa Resolution confronted the United States with some of the most profound questions that had plagued the nation's foreign relations in a decade. Yet the entire affair was over in less than a week. Congress again demonstrated its reluctance to oppose Eisenhower's leadership in matters of foreign policy. So completely did Senator Walter George, chairman of the Foreign Relations Committee, surrender the right of debate that the result could scarcely be termed bipartisan. George accepted the president's assurance that he alone would make the decision to employ American forces in defending the Formosan commitment. "I believe that President Eisenhower," he said, "is a prudent man. I believe he is dedicated to a peaceful world. I believe what he says, and I am willing to act upon it." There were two days of testimony from Dulles and the Joint Chiefs in the Senate Foreign Relations and Armed Forces committees, meeting jointly. The House Foreign Affairs Committee listened to five hours of testimony and discussion. The debate on the Senate floor lasted somewhat more than two days; on the House floor less than three hours.[14] No one inquired why Congress would permit the administration to hold it jointly responsible for an unpredictable, perhaps unwanted, presidential decision. No one knew whether the resolution would result in an ultimatum to the mainland Chinese or a Nationalist withdrawal from the offshore islands. One senator summed up the congressional action: "We gave the President authority that we don't have for the purpose of doing something that we are by no means agreed we want to do. And we did it in the name of national unity."

Several days later the Senate approved the Mutual Defense Treaty with Nationalist China with less than six hours of debate. Democrats complained that Senator George refused to consider any amendments and gave little quarter on the floor to those who opposed him. Supported by Chiang's Republican friends, he effectively silenced the younger

Democrats on the Foreign Relations Committee—Hubert Humphrey, J. William Fulbright, John Sparkman, and Mike Mansfield. Those who questioned the juridical distinction between Formosa and the offshore islands George accused of "legalistic quibbling." There was no retort when H. Alexander Smith, New Jersey Republican, asserted that the mere accumulation of a Chinese army could be accounted as an act of war, or when Knowland added that a Mainland attack on an American ship during the evacuation of the Tachens would call for preventative action on the part of the United States. Throughout the entire discussion of the defense pact congressmen asked no questions about the conditions under which the administration would seek to avoid involvement in the Formosa Straits. The refusal of Democratic leaders, who controlled both houses of Congress in 1955, to question the administration's foreign policy positions left the area of debate too restricted to permit the introduction of either new analyses or more limited objectives. Eisenhower escaped the crisis by resisting the appeals of Radford, Knowland, and Dulles for strong responses to the Chinese shelling while he avoided the charges of appeasement.[15] The president anchored his moderation, not to the defense of the offshore islands, but to the supposition that the Mainland Chinese would not attack them. They did not. This enabled the president to stand firm, yet preserve his reputation as a man of peace.

From Bandung, Indonesia, in April 1955, came the first major challenge to the Eisenhower administration's rejection of the Peking regime as the government of China. At this fateful meeting Asian leaders asked that Washington reevaluate its policies in the Far East, especially toward China. The notion that the United States might go to war over Quemoy and Matsu terrified even its friends in Asia.[16] Nor could Chou En-lai resist the pressure for peace in the Formosan Straits. Before the conference adjourned, Asian leaders forced him to assure the world that the Chinese government did not want war with the United States and was ready to enter negotiations to seek a relaxation of tensions in the Far East, especially in the Formosa Straits.[17]

Mainland China's offer at Bandung produced such an immediate and favorable response around the world that a reluctant Eisenhower administration could not ignore it. Chou's announcement led one Indian official to remark, "As a result of the Bandung conference, there is a lessening of fear among Communist China's neighbors if not actually a lessening of tension in that area." Premier Ali of Pakistan believed Chou's offer "a great move for relaxing tension, particularly in the critical Far East." Burmese Premier U Nu and Indonesia's Ali Sastroamidjojo agreed. A British Foreign Office spokesman declared that Britain was "interested in any idea which might provide a basis for a settlement." V. K. Krishna Menon, India's traveling envoy, after a hurried trip to Peking, warned officials in Washington that the offshore islands would be attacked unless the United States either induced the Kuomintang to release them or started negotiations with the implication that they would be given up. In its response, the State Department reminded Chou that the United States had an ally in the Republic of China and would insist on that government's participation as an equal in any negotiations. In his press conference of April 26, Dulles wondered about the sincerity of the Chinese proposal, but assured newsmen that the adminstration intended to find out. "In doing so," he added, "we shall not, of course, depart from the path of fidelity and honor to our ally, the Republic of China."[18]

Senator George objected. Speaking before the American Society of Newspaper Editors in Washington, he urged the administration to seek a Far Eastern conference with Peking without insisting that Nationalist China be represented. If Chou indicated at Bandung that he was willing to talk, said George, "this nation should be big enough and great enough, through its highest officials, to talk to him." The senator reminded Dulles that he could not please everyone at home and still maintain a position of leadership in the noncommunist world. Thereupon Dulles modified the administration's position. Direct talks were feasible, he said, as long as they did not infringe on the interests of Nationalist China. Such administration Republicans as Alexander Smith of New Jersey, Leverett Saltonstall of Massachusetts, Clifford Case of New Jersey, James Duff of Pennsylvania, and Irving Ives of New York took the lead in supporting the administration's more flexible position. "The president of the United States," ran their joint statement, "has a right and obligation to wage peace as well as to wage war. Waging peace is what he's trying to do." Humphrey called for negotiations with Red China, even over Quemoy and Matsu. He warned the nation that the administration was too concerned with the offshore islands, not enough with India, Burma, and Indonesia. "Our relations with Quemoy and Matsu are good," he said, "but for nine solid months we had no ambassador to Burma. . . ."[19] For almost a year, Humphrey complained, the prime minister of Burma saw no important officials from the United States, but every other weekend someone ran from Washington to visit Chiang.

With equal determination the Nationalist China bloc closed in on the administration to prevent any negotiation with the Peking regime, whatever world and domestic pressures might be. Knowland demanded simply that Chiang be represented. "The policy of this government," he said, "is not to barter away the territory of any country without its presence at the negotiations." Judd joined Knowland in warning against any talks with the Chinese Communists. He could see no value "in law-abiding citizens sitting down with outlawed gangsters to discuss how order should be maintained." What these friends of Chiang suspected was a growing American willingness to barter away the offshore islands. Senator Jenner warned that "the air is full of foreboding that a carefully laid plan is under way for the United States to give up bit by bit its commitments in the Formosan Straits." McCarthy rushed to the defense of the Nationalists with his resolution that they be included in any United States-Mainland China talks. In urging this resolution on the Foreign Relations Committee, McCarthy declared: "It involves a very important question as to whether or not we are going to sell out our Allies." Chairman George refused to change the order of committee business; the resolution never came up for a vote. When Eisenhower and Dulles finally agreed to ambassadoral talks with the Mainland Chinese in August 1955, they admitted that they could no longer avoid negotiations with Peking. Dulles assured the China bloc, however, that the administration would pursue the interests of Nationalist China and maintain its commitments to the offshore islands. With its diplomatic postures fixed, the administration assigned the talks in advance to the realm of lost causes.

Throughout 1956 and 1957 the situation in the Formosa Straits remained calm. Nothing had occurred, however, to encourage the administration either to modify or to alter its commitment to the offshore islands, or to adopt measures that might prevent a recurrence of the previous crisis. In large measure the immobilism in the American posture reflected Dulles's unchanging conviction that the entire United States position in the Far East rested on Chiang's success in holding the offshore islands. As he observed in 1957:

> I realize full well that to many people, including some of the leaders of our Allies, it seems ridiculous to think of defending the off-shore islands . . . with the possibility of bringing on a major war with Communist China, perhaps also with the Soviet Union. But I strongly believe that to give them over to the Chinese Communists would not prevent war but promote it, because this would stimulate their desire and demands for more, namely Formosa, and then the other free countries in the area. . . . Therefore, to me the defense of Quemoy is essential to the defense of Formosa.[20]

Dulles had raised the issue, first suggested by Eisenhower, that Chiang reduce his garrisons on the offshore islands to token forces, but on that point, he recorded, "Chiang would bow only to pressure so tremendous that it would in fact break him." Such a reaction in Taipei would defeat the objectives of the United States.[21]

Committed as it was to the defense of the offshore islands, the administration could avoid embarrassment only as long as the Chinese made no effort to take them. For that reason the situation became tense when in 1957 the Chinese began to mass guns and planes in the vicinity of Amoy and to build new rail lines to the air fields. "Has not the time come," asked the *London Observer* in July, "for the Administration to see the picture as a whole and to move boldly to bring policy in line with realities?" That summer, Admiral Felix Stump, commander of all U.S. forces in the Pacific, warned that the situation along the Chinese coast was more ominous than at any time since the Korean War.

Finally, in August 1958, the Chinese began their heavy shelling of Quemoy to create another major crisis and reveal again the potential price that the country was paying for binding itself to the cause of Chinese liberation. The administration had lost the power of decision; it could neither choose war nor desert Chiang's objectives. Dulles looked on in disbelief. Certainly, he reported, the Chinese would not attempt to take the islands. He responded formally to the attack on Quemoy by making public a letter he had written to the chairman of the House Foreign Affairs Committee: "It would be highly hazardous for anyone to assume that if the Chinese Communists were to attempt to change this situation by attacking and seeking to conquer those [off-shore] islands that this act could be considered or held to a 'limited operation.' It would, I fear, constitute a threat to the peace of the area."[22] Chiang, terrified over the possible loss of Quemoy, requested an immediate, unambiguous United States commitment to the defense of the island. Eisenhower refused to respond.

But on September 4, Dulles traveled to Newport, Rhode Island, where Eisenhower was vacationing, with a well-prepared statement that represented the views of the Pentagon, the CIA, and his advisors in the State Department. The document assumed that the United States faced a major threat to its security in the Pacific. The loss of Quemoy, it concluded, would expose the Nationalist government on Formosa to subversion, if not military attack, causing its overthrow and the emergence of a government prepared to join the Mainland. Second, Dulles's statement predicted that the fall of Formosa to the Communists would lead to the destruction of the entire anticommunist barrier in the western Pacific—Japan, Korea, the Philippines, Thailand, the states of Indo-china, Indonesia, Malaya, Burma, and even Okinawa. The resulting decline of Western security would exceed that which followed the initial fall of the Nationalist government in China. Clearly the United States had no choice but to defend Quemoy. To that end Dulles recommended that the United States, if it could not persuade the Mainland Chinese to abandon their goals, prepare for the use of nuclear weapons. The world might object, but a swift, total victory would soon cause it to forget. At any rate, said Dulles, any other response would be inconsistent with "the safety of the free world and our influence on it." After suggesting a few minor changes in the text, Eisenhower accepted the Dulles proposal and authorized the secretary to release it to the press. Dulles could now confront the Quemoy issue with threats of massive retaliation, leaving the Chinese the choice of living peacefully or facing nuclear destruction.[23]

Eisenhower soon entered the fray publicly. If the United States permitted the Chinese to take Quemoy, he warned on September 11, it would "encourage the aggressors. It would dismay our friends and allies there. If history teaches anything, appeasement would make it more likely that we would have to fight a major war."[24] The president presented to the country as ambivalent a position as the Chinese dilemma required. His assurance was complete: "There is not going to be any appeasement. I believe there is not going to be any war." No American boy would die over Quemoy, but there would be no Munichs. He defended his administration's commitment to Quemoy by declaring that the Chinese designs on the offshore islands were part of a general plan to liquidate the entire Western position in the Far East. He reminded the American people that Quemoy was symbolic of containment's success throughout Asia. "Powerful and aggressive forces are constantly probing," declared the president, "now here, now there, to see whether the free world is weakening. . . . There must be a sober realization by the American people that our legitimate purposes are again being tested by those who threaten peace and freedom everywhere."[25] The president's message divided the American populace into two tidy groups: those who favored holding Quemoy advocated peace, freedom, and justice; those who favored ceding the islands were appeasers. Eisenhower would not retreat. At the same time, he would not make "absolute advance commitments, but . . . use [his] judgment according to the circumstances of the time."

When on September 29 Senator Theodore F. Green, now chairman of the Foreign Relations Committee, questioned the importance of Quemoy to the defense of Formosa and the United States, the president responded that a successful Chinese attack on Formosa would drive the United States from the western Pacific. To prevent that the country had no choice but to protect the status of Quemoy and Matsu. "We must not forget," Eisenhower concluded, "that the whole Formosa Straits situation is intimately connected with the security of the United States and the free world."[26]

Americans who accepted the view that the issue of Formosa and the offshore islands were one upheld the president's address. *Life* lauded the president for the firmness and clarity of his stand. Whatever the vulnerability of Quemoy to attack from the Mainland, the United States had an uncompromisable obligation to Chiang Kai-shek. Knowland termed the speech "a forceful reminder to Communist aggressors that America will not abandon her allies or defenses in the Far East." For Europeans and Americans who could detect no strategic relationship between Formosa and the offshore islands, it seemed strange that the president would risk war over an island situated inside the harbor of Amoy. John S. Knight, editor of the *Chicago Daily News*, commented: "Let's protect Formosa, as we have pledged. But defense of Quemoy and Matsu by United States forces would be an act of monumental madness." *The New Republic*, on October 6, accused the administration of involving the United States in the internal affairs of China. It declared editorially: "We consider the administration's Quemoy policy indefensible morally, militarily, and politically." Dean Acheson accused the administration of pursuing a policy designed to keep everybody guessing because it had "unwisely maneuvered itself, with the help of Chiang Kai-shek, into a situation of which it [had] lost control." Europe was visibly shaken by the crisis. Its leading spokesmen and editors denied the relationship between Munich and the alleged dangers posed by Quemoy; they wondered why the United States would expose itself to war for the fiction that Chiang would return to the Mainland. *Le Monde* declared that "it would be unbelievable for a world conflict to arise from the contest." Europeans favored concessions; to them China was no threat to the western Pacific. American correspondents seemed to agree that American attitudes toward China, and the dangers of nuclear war, were undermining the nation's influence in Europe.

Throughout the crisis it was fully evident that Chiang was the controlling factor in American action. Privately Eisenhower preferred that Chiang reduce the tension in the Straits by reducing his garrisons on Quemoy and Matsu. There was, however, no formula available that would satisfy Chiang and still diminish the confrontation over the offshore islands. Dulles announced in advance that the United States would agree to no settlement that injured the Nationalist regime. That ruled out any concessions to the Mainland Chinese. When in October the administration did suggest partial demobilization of the offshore islands as a basis of negotiation, Chiang declared that he would ignore any agreement negotiated with Peking that weakened the prospects of his return to the Mainland. Chiang's belligerence prompted Dulles to fly to Taipei on October 19 to reach a *modus vivendi* with the Nationalist leader. Dulles reminded Chiang that his position in the world community had become precarious and that the time had come for easing tensions in the Formosa Straits. The agreement that they reached did not injure Chiang's position on the offshore islands, but it changed the symbolism.[27] Restoration of freedom on the Mainland remained the sacred mission of the Kuomintang, but the power that would achieve that goal would now reside within China itself. Walter S. Robertson assured the world that Quemoy and Matsu would never "be selected as bases from which to attack the mainland." The Taipei communique itself restated the American position: "The United States recognizes that the Republic of China is the authentic spokesman for Free China and the hopes and aspirations entertained by the great mass of the Chinese people. . . . The foundation of [the Nationalist] mission resides in the minds and hearts of the Chinese people." This explained why the mission would ultimately triumph without force. But the critical issue of what the United States would do if the Mainland Chinese assaulted the outposts remained the unanswered challenge.

Fortunately China's leaders ordered no assault on the offshore islands. Perhaps for them also the struggle over the islands was not worth the price. The Peking regime, moreover, shared with Formosa the dream of a united China, one that bound Formosa to the Mainland. Mao no less than Chiang rejected the principle of two Chinas. Thus, the Mainland Chinese had as much reason as the Nationalists to keep the Chinese struggle alive, exerting pressure on Formosa by threatening, not capturing, the offshore islands. At the end the Mainland Chinese announced that they would shell the offshore islands on alternate days. It was a strange commitment that would tolerate the shelling of islands on schedule whose defense only recently had been important enough to warrant the threat of nuclear war. Whatever the motive in Peking's behavior, its decision permitted the Eisenhower administration to weather the crisis without altering its commitment or facing its possible consequences. Privately the administration had buried the fiction that Chiang would liberate the Mainland. But the constant repetition of the myth of Chiang's power and popularity had created a pervading sentiment, no less than a body of bureaucratic commitment, that had itself become an obstacle to change.

Throughout the late 1950s the Eisenhower administration's approach to China remained unpromising, if not potentially dangerous. Still the official resistance to change was as determined as ever. Even as the president entered his final years, the rejection of China as a major, permanent element in world politics with interests to be understood, encompassed, or resisted as conditions might demand, was as complete as ever. The perennial identification of the Chinese revolution with Soviet imperialism underwrote the continuing fears of global Communist expansionism. In June 1957, Robertson could tell the nation: "Starting from zero in our generation, the international Communists now hold in a grip of ruthless power 16 nations, 900 million people—a circumstance recently described by the Secretary of State as 'the most frightening fact history records.' "[28]

Eisenhower's Washington in time dropped the earlier notion of complete Chinese subservience for that of a Sino-Soviet partnership. Dulles expressed his view of the changing relationship in an interview of July 1957: "As far as we can judge, the nations which are within the Sino-Soviet bloc are all dominated by what can fairly be called international communism, a single group which provides a guiding force." The State Department sustained that judgment in its August 1958 memorandum to all United States' missions abroad. Attacking the notion that the recognition of Peking might weaken that regime's ties with Moscow, the memorandum declared: "The alliance between Moscow and Peiping is one of long standing; it traces its origin to the very founding of the Chinese Communist Party in 1921. . . . It is based on a common ideology and on mutually held objectives with respect to the non-Communist world."[29] Even as the Eisenhower administration entered its final months, Under Secretary of State Robert Murphy assured a New York audience: "Some day this might become a most uneasy partnership. However, this day seems far in the future, and in the present in which we must operate there is little doubt but that both Moscow and Peiping regard the continuation of their close alliance as being of overriding importance."[30]

Gradually the official antagonism toward China became so pervading that China often replaced Russia in official speeches as the dominant threat to Asian stability. In Asia at least, China had become the senior partner in the Communist monolith. In his noted San Francisco address of June 1957, Dulles reminded his audience that China "fought the United Nations in Korea; it supported the Communist war in Indochina; it took Tibet by force. It fomented the Communist Huk rebellion in the Philippines and the Communists' insurrection in Malaya. It does not disguise its expansionist ambitions. It is bitterly hateful of the United States, which it considers a principal obstacle in the way of its path of conquest."[31] Later that year William J. Sebald, ambassador to Australia, condemned China in what had become standard phraseology. The core of the problem in the Pacific, he said, "is the deadly hostility of the Chinese Communist regime with its unwavering espousal of the principles of Marxism-Leninism. These principles, as we know, envisage the conquest of the non-Communist world and the destruction of free institutions."[32]

However grave the Chinese threat to Southeast Asia, nonrecognition still carried the chief burden for both the containment and ultimate liberation of the Mainland. Whatever the changing perception of Chinese power and subservience during the Eisenhower years, nonrecognition demanded a perennial denial that the Peking regime represented the Chinese people. Official rhetoric continued to accuse the Mainland leadership of imposing an alien minority rule on an intimidated Chinese populace and of flouting every Chinese treaty obligation and every principle of the United Nations. As late as March 1959, Robertson reminded a Canadian audience: "Let no one say that representation is being denied to 600 million mainland Chinese. The fanatical Marxists of Peiping come no closer to representing the will and aspirations of the Chinese people than the puppet regime of Budapest comes to representing the will and aspirations of the Hungarian people or William Z. Foster comes to representing the will and aspirations of the American people."[33]

This denial of Peking's legitimacy enabled Washington to maintain its allegiance to Nationalist China as an essential element in the containment of Communist expansion. Indeed, United States' officials defended nonrecognition as the key to Asia's resistance. "Many an Asian has told me," reported Walter P. McConaughy, director of the Office of Chinese Affairs, in January 1954, "that American nonrecognition of the Communist regime in Peiping has had much to do with checking the impetus of the Communist advance in Asia."[34] Conversely, recognition of the Peking dictatorship, declared McConaughy, would comprise "the hardest psychological blow against the will to resist the further spread of communism that could be devised." Recognition, Dulles warned an Australian audience in March 1957, would "strengthen and encourage influences hostile to us and our allies and further imperil lands whose independence is related to our own peace and security."[35] Shortly thereafter Sebald observed, "a change in the status of Free China would, I believe, have a chain-reaction effect which would seriously weaken the free world." Robertson declared in even more dramatic language in March 1959: "If the United States were to abandon its commitments to the Republic of China in order to appease the threatening Red Chinese, no country in Asia could feel that it could any longer rely upon the protection of the United States against the Communist threat. These comparatively weak nations would have no alternative but to come to terms—the best they could get—with the Peiping colossus."[36]

Beyond containment, nonrecognition sustained the hope of China's eventual liberation. The Republic of China on Formosa remained the symbol of hope for all who opposed the Mainland regime. Unlike other countries suffering under Communist tyranny, observed Karl Lott Rankin, the United States' ambassador in Taipei, China had its Formosa as "a bastion and rallying point where hope is being kept alive and preparations made for a better future."[37] One day, predicted Rankin, Formosa might prove to be the Achilles heel of communism in Asia. Rankin shared Washington's faith in nonrecognition as the one means of keeping the hope of Chinese liberation alive. But he complained increasingly after 1953 that nonrecognition did not comprise a policy. He rejoiced in Eisenhower's order of February 1953, which allegedly unleashed Chiang Kai-shek to attack the Mainland. Unfortunately, noted Rankin, it changed nothing on Formosa. Taking the promise of liberation seriously, Rankin continued to press Washington for the creation of a policy that would liberate the Mainland. In January 1957, Chiang reminded Rankin that despite the intent of nonrecognition, he still languished on Formosa. The ambassador observed that the United States did not want a war in the Far East. "At the same time," Rankin informed Washington, "I said that I hoped and believed that there was today in the United States a growing understanding that China could not remain permanently divided, and that since we certainly did not want it united under communism, it must be united in freedom."[38]

During March 1957, Rankin acknowledged that the United States had done much for the Republic of China. But, he again complained, the government on Taiwan remained "as far as ever from its great objective of bringing about the liberation of mainland China from Red tyranny. In fact," he added, "the disparity between the two protagonists in total military and economic strength is increasing at an accelerated pace, to Free China's disadvantage."[39] Continued drift would end in disaster, for there would be one China. On April 25, Rankin sent his final warning: "A great people like the Chinese will never accept the permanent mutilation of their country. . . . There can be no genuine lasting peace in Asia while half a billion Chinese remain under communist rule. Peace will remain in jeopardy and freedom a word of mockery until a reunited China joins the free world. . . . China is half of Asia and Asia is half the world. The fate of China may well determine the fate of all."[40] For Dulles, nonrecognition still carried the assurance of liberation. As he declared in June 1957: "We can confidently assume that international communism's rule of strict conformity is, in China as elsewhere, a passing and not a perpetual phase. We owe it to ourselves, our allies, and the Chinese people to do all we can to contribute to that passing."[41] What troubled Chiang and his supporters everywhere was the realization that, beyond nonrecognition, the United States had no policy of liberation.

Nonrecognition and the extravagant language that underwrote it sustained an overwhelming anti-Chinese consensus within the United States. As an official position it was untouchable and thus contributed immeasurably to the public approbation that the Eisenhower administration enjoyed. But nonrecognition did not prepare the American people to rid the world of a regime declared a danger to Western interests in East Asia; nor did it prepare them to come to terms with its existence. In no way did nonrecognition alter China's progress or influence that nation's internal or external policies. It rendered American power irrelevant to China's evolution into a major force in Asian affairs. Eisenhower never permitted the extremist attitudes of his administration to degenerate into war. But his refusal to challenge those who, for reasons of politics or conviction, sustained the nation's anti-Chinese sentiments and the fears that they sustained aggravated the notion of an expanding communism in Asia and compelled the nation to strengthen its commitment to all pro-Western regimes in Asia, including those of Taipei and Saigon. The Eisenhower posture toward China turned out to be meaningless rather than dangerous, but the conviction that China underwrote the Communist expansionism of Southeast Asia ultimately demanded its heavy price of the American people.

Notes

1. Norman A. Graebner, *The New Isolationism: A Study in Politics and Foreign Policy since 1950* (New York: Ronald Press, 1956), 45.

2. Geraldine Fitch, *Formosa Beachhead* (Chicago: Henry Regnery, 1953), 289–59, 262.

3. William Jenner in the *Congressional Record*, 83 Cong., 1st sess., vol. 99, pt. 8, 11000–1.

4. The newly opened transcripts of Dulles's telephone conversations reveal that Knowland and Judd reported every rumor or newspaper report that suggested a softening of administration policy toward China. Dulles always reassured them that there had not been and never would be a change in the official United States' posture toward the government on the Chinese Mainland.

5. Graebner, *The New Isolationism*, 129.

6. William Henry Chamberlain, *Beyond Containment* (Chicago: Henry Reg-

nery, 1953), 372; MacArthur quoted in *San Francisco Chronicle*, 1 February, 1953.

7. Quoted in Lawrence Lafore, "The Problem of Diplomatic Recognition," *Current History*, March 1956, 154.

8. Eric Hoffer, "The Passionate State of Mind," *Harper's*, January 1955, 25.

9. Townsend Hoopes, *The Devil and John Foster Dulles* (Boston: Little Brown, 1973), 222.

10. At the outbreak of the shelling the Joint Chiefs agreed that the offshore islands were not essential for the defense of Formosa and that the Chinese Nationalists could not hold them without American assistance. Eisenhower said in his reply to Radford: "We're not talking now about a limited, brush-fire war. We're talking about going to the threshold of World War III. If we attack China, we're not going to impose limits on our military actions, as in Korea. Moreover . . . if we get into a general war, the logical enemy will be Russia, not China, and we'll have to strike there." See Dwight D. Eisenhower, *Mandate for Change, 1953–1956: The White House Years* (Garden City, N. Y.: Doubleday, 1963), 463–64.

11. President Eisenhower to Congress on Defense of Formosa, 24 January 1955, Russell D. Buhite, ed., *The Dynamics of World Power: A Documentary History of United States Foreign Policy, 1945–1973*, vol. 4: *The Far East* (New York: Chelsea House Publishers, 1973), 211.

12. A. M. Rosenthal in the *New York Times*, 13 February 1955.

13. Quoted in *The Commonwealth*, 27 June 1955, 156; Eisenhower, *Mandate for Change*, 470–71.

14. Douglas Cater, "Foreign Policy: Default of the Democrats," *The Reporter*, 10 March 1955, 21–23.

15. Eisenhower, *Mandate for Change*, 483. Eisenhower admitted that his choices were between peace with honor and war or dishonor.

16. See, for example, Carlos P. Romulo, "Watching Bandung," *This Week Magazine*, 17 April 1955, 29.

17. Statement by John Foster Dulles, 26 July 1955, Buhite, *The Far East*, 214.

18. Ibid.

19. Hubert Humphrey in *The Commonwealth*, 7 March 1955, 58.

20. Andrew H. Berding, *Dulles on Diplomacy* (Princeton, N.J.: Princeton University Press, 1965), 59–60.

21. Ibid., 60–61.

22. Quoted in Dwight D. Eisenhower, *Waging Peace, 1956–1961: The White House Years* (Garden City, N. Y.: Doubleday, 1966), 296.

23. Hoopes, *The Devil and John Foster Dulles*, 446–49; Eisenhower, *Waging Peace*, 299–300. For the September 4 memorandum in full, see ibid., 691–93.

24. Address by President Eisenhower, 11 September 1958, Buhite, *The Far East*, 248.

25. Ibid., 250.

26. Eisenhower to Senator Green, 2 October 1958, ibid., 253.

27. Hoopes, *The Devil and John Foster Dulles*, 453–57.

28. Walter S. Robertson, "America's Responsibilities in the Far East," 3 June 1957, *Department of State Bulletin* 36 (24 June 1957): 997.

29. For August 1958 memorandum, see ibid. 34 (8 September 1959): 388–89.

30. Address before the Institute of World Affairs, New York, 20 October 1959, ibid. 41 (9 November 1959): 661.

31. Dulles's speech before the convention of Lions International, San Francisco, 28 June 1957, ibid. 37 (15 July 1957): 91.

32. Address before the New South Wales chapter of the Australian-American Association, Sydney, 26 July 1957, ibid. 37 (2 September 1957): 389.

33. Speech before the Canadian Club, Ottawa, 13, March 1959, ibid. 40 (6 April 1959): 475.

34. Walter P. McConaughy, "China in the Shadow of Communism," ibid. 30 (11 January 1954): 41.

35. Dulles's statement on United States China policy, Canberra, 12 March 1957, ibid. 36 (1 April 1957): 531.

36. Ibid., 37 (2 September 1957): 390; 40 (6 April 1959): 474.

37. Karl Lott Rankin, *China Assignment* (Seattle: University of Washington Press, 1964), 114–15.

38. Ibid., 311.

39. Ibid., 315.

40. Ibid., 323.

41. Dulles's speech in San Francisco, 28 June 1957, *Department of State Bulletin* 37 (15 July 1957): 95.

Eisenhower and Communism
Later Findings

David Mayers

Standard interpretations of U.S. foreign policy during the Eisenhower-Dulles period invariably make the point that the American government was unaware of actual and potential Sino-Soviet problems in the 1950s; policy against these two states was based on the assumption of an international Communist monolithic movement directed by Moscow. According to this view, U.S. policy amounted merely to a series of ad hoc responses to Chinese and Soviet initiatives. Containment never included a serious appraisal of the security and national differences among Marxist states, and precluded anything so imaginative as trying to spoil Communist systems of alliance. Norman Graebner's preceding essay is an especially graceful and thoughtful representative of this school of interpretation.

A strong case can be made that official U.S. understanding of the Sino-Soviet alliance and policy toward it were not nearly so primitive as Graebner and others believe. I contend that Dulles and Eisenhower hoped and expected that China would one day play an independent role in international politics and contribute to a stable balance of power in the Far East. Consequently, they sought to weaken the Communist alliance by pressing China economically, diplomatically, and militarily very hard, forcing it to make demands of the Soviet Union that were imprudent or otherwise impossible for Moscow to meet. Unrelenting pressure on the alliance was designed essentially to disrupt it; this overall method was reasonably effective and tailored not to offend conservative opinion in the United States.

U.S. Perceptions of the Sino-Soviet Alliance, 1953

Stalin died less than two months after the new Republican administration assumed office. The CIA believed that the initial impact of his death on Sino-Soviet cooperation was slight. Yet the CIA also doubted that any successor to Stalin would have prestige in Asia comparable to his. "The stature of Mao as leader and theoretician of Asian Communism will inevitably increase with the disappearance of the former supreme leader. Mao will almost certainly have more influence in the determination of Bloc policy affecting Asia." Although the CIA believed that Mao would not seek leadership of the international Communist movement, Moscow would probably deal very cautiously with him. Otherwise, "serious strains in Sino-Soviet relations will almost certainly develop."[1]

The new administration had some evidence of Sino-Soviet tensions that, if not promising severe discord between the two powers, at least offered reason to hope. A case in point was the autumn 1952 Sino-Soviet meetings, which revealed ample evidence of difficulties: Soviet promises to relinquish privileges in Manchuria and Port Arthur were unredeemed, and Russian military and economic aid to China was not increased substantially. According to General Walter Bedell Smith, director of Central Intelligence, the inadequate Soviet help was not a coincidence but was perfectly predictable. Shortly before the Sino-Soviet conference, he commented, "the Chinese are obviously coming to Moscow to ask for more help because they are losing a great deal of material and energy in Korea. The Russians will drive a hard price. At all costs they do not intend to see built up on their eastern frontier a Chinese military Frankenstein monster."[2]

Early 1953 Voice of America broadcasts to China, aimed at stirring popular unrest with the regime and exciting Peking's impatience with Moscow, stressed the disastrous effects for China of dependence on the Soviet Union. Moscow's return of the Changchun Railway to Peking, for example, was ridiculed by the Voice of America for granting China only "paper control of its transportation."[3] VOA celebrated the third anniversary of formal Russian-Chinese alliance with an imaginary Chinese citizen on the street, who reported that the Peking-Moscow observance day festival was "nice. It ought to be. It was very expensive. We paid with Port Arthur, the Changchun Railway, Sinkiang and—let's see—the war in Korea."[4] Also, according to VOA, China's economic rehabilitation was lagging thanks to underwhelming Soviet aid. Even so, Chinese soldiers were useful cannon fodder in Moscow's imperialist adventures.[5]

Stalin's death also inspired themes for American propagandists. VOA reporters wondered whether Mao would continue to obey Moscow, now under a revolutionary novice, Malenkov, and whether China would still mindlessly fetch and serve as a Soviet lackey in foreign policy. One broadcast ended with these words: "Will Mao allow himself to be again humiliated? Is the Communist regime's grip on the Chinese people strong enough to survive another era of Soviet contempt for and exploitation of China?"[6]

In addition, Stalin's death provided an unusual opportunity for the "imaginative" handling of covert operations. Harold Stassen, director of the Mutual Security Administration and Psychological Strategy Board, arranged to send an American newspaper publisher to Peking in order to interview Mao. Stassen believed the journalist's "attempts to get to see Mao will cause uneasiness in both the USSR and China, and if he does see him, it will increase suspicions in every respect."[7] Rumors and speculations were also planted among Western commentators and writers that Malenkov had a hit-list, and that Mao was the first to be liquidated. In this context VOA broadcast a report, *Whose Funeral Is Next?*

Meanwhile, Sino-Soviet problems entirely unrelated to American machinations were evident to CIA analysts. In a September 1953 report covering the period 1949–52, the agency examined Mao's theoretical corpus in relation to its relevance (and China's) to colonial struggles and predicted that a deterioration in relations between Peking and Moscow would first be signaled by divergent assertions regarding theoretical matters. The CIA also observed that Soviet critiques of Mao's written works, while praising him, were careful to avoid the attributions of originality reserved only for Lenin and Stalin. To have made such claims, argued intelligence analysts, would have meant Mao's promotion to an unacceptably high position of esteem. Its ideological supremacy indirectly challenged, Moscow's socialist leadership would be jeopardized. Soviet reviewers therefore insisted on referring to Marx, Engels, Lenin, and Stalin as the important contributors to Communist theory; Mao's work, albeit worthy, was essentially derivative and depended on Lenin and especially Stalin's pioneering. Similar appraisals were made of Mao as a military tactician who had skillfully and faithfully applied Lenin's and Stalin's ideas during the Chinese civil war.

Not fully appreciated abroad, the master was revered at home, however. Shen Chih-yuan remarked that "Chairman Mao is indubitably the world's most outstanding teacher of creative Marxism-Leninism since Lenin and Stalin"; Chou En-lai expressed similar sentiments. According to the CIA's September report, Chinese critics originally implied, and later explicitly proclaimed, that China's revolution—not Russia's— was pertinent to other Asian revolutionary struggles. One Chinese apologist was quoted as predicting, "China's revolution today . . . is the tomorrow of Vietnam, Burma, Ceylon, India and the other various Asian colonial and semi-colonial nations."

Earnest Soviet ideologues were neither convinced nor amused. The agency noted that in late 1951 all Chinese discussions of "Mao's road" and China as revolutionary exemplar ceased, presumably the victim of Soviet censorship; Mao, in effect, was forced to retract exalted claims that he was an outstanding, creative Marxist-Leninist theorist. That November at a conference of the Soviet Oriental Institute, the principal speaker, Ye Zhukov, explained, "it would be risky to regard the Chinese revolution as some kind of 'stereotype' for people's democratic revolutions in other countries of Asia"; rather, Lenin, Stalin, and the Soviet experience were the progenitors of true doctrine applicable in the East. The CIA analysts wrote that the Chinese accepted these pronouncements only after a delay and even then unwillingly. "It would be surprising if the Chinese Communist elite had not been disturbed by these conclusions. The consequent decline in prestige for China's revolution and for its theoretician, Mao Tes-tung, was unmistakable."

The agency concluded cautiously that ideological and political problems between China and the Soviets were latent, although full of possibility. The Chinese might eventually rebel. But for the time being, China's industrialization program depended on Soviet aid, and thus Moscow's influence in Peking was considerable; Mao was having "a sufficiently difficult task in the consolidation and stabilization of China's economy and can look to few other countries for assistance."[8]

If the CIA authors of the quotation above meant to imply that America might still use its economic might to lure China away from the Soviet Union, they were not alone among observers urging such a line. Retired Admiral Ellis Zacharias had earlier in the year advised Sherman Adams, "today, China is offered no realistic alternative to her present orientation. An operational plan to provide such an alternative, *without appeasement*, but with a realistic and positive approach, is both feasible and vital. Such a plan should *not be discussed openly*, but it has been formulated in detail."[9] Only a couple of weeks after Zacharias sent his letter, Charlton Ogburn, an advisor for State's Bureau of Far Eastern Affairs, complained to his superiors that the only rational policy toward China was to detach it from the Soviet camp, but so far American actions were merely encouraging Chinese reliance on Moscow. He urged emphatically that the entire China policy of the United States ought to be overhauled.[10]

Yet the administration in 1953 was hardly in a position to take advantage of these recommendations; to pursue a policy even remotely smacking of conciliation with Mao would have been tantamount to challenging the McCarthy wing of the Republican party, something that neither the administration nor most members of Congress were willing to do. In addition, an inflexible anticommunist pose helped reassure Taiwan. As Ambassador Rankin explained in July 1953, many Chinese on Taiwan feared that Mao actually did enjoy a high degree of independence from Moscow. And they worried even more that if the United States should accept this as true, it would then follow the lead of Britain and India and adopt a more generous policy toward the People's Republic. "Only so long as they are persuaded that Americans continue to regard Mao simply as a Soviet tool will they [the Nationalists] feel reasonably assured as to our policy."[11] In fact, as early as 1949, Chiang had tried to disabuse Western observers of "insidious," "false" speculation that Mao would imitate Tito's defiance.[12]

Still, the administration and John Foster Dulles managed to perpetuate a clearheaded, pragmatic policy, but from political and diplomatic necessity one that was sheltered from public scrutiny. As a member of the Democratic administration in 1950 and later as secretary of state, Dulles believed that the Soviets had in China a somewhat doubtful ally, and he favored harassing the Communist alliance.[13] Certainly, splitting the Communist powers was entirely consistent with his view of international politics. His rigid, moralistic rhetoric did not rule out the possibility that virtue and the Lord's work could be advanced by duping Lucifer's agents into confounding each other.

During a February 1952 interview on "Meet the Press," Dulles stated as a general proposition, "if your major objective is to get a break [between a given Marxist state and] Moscow, the way to get that is to make the going tough, not easy." He asserted that Tito broke from Moscow because Western resistance to Yugoslavia in Greece and the economic blockade caused severe problems for Belgrade, problems that the Soviets could not alleviate. Therefore, in order to check the spread of economic and social deterioration at home, the Yugoslavs sought an accommodation with the West at the expense of their connection with Moscow. Regarding Moscow and Peking, Dulles claimed that the alliance between them posed a "great danger" for the United States. "If we could break that, that would certainly be a great advantage." He then said, "I would have a policy which is designed to make the going so tough for the present regime in China that it's going to change in some way." It might be changed from within; it might be changed by a radical shift away from Moscow. "The essential thing is to have action which will bring about a change."[14] In mid-November 1952 Dulles, by then secretary-designate, explained that Sino-Soviet bonds could be severed by "keeping [Communist China] under pressures which would, in turn, keep the Communists pressuring Russia for more than Russia would give."[15]

Dulles's proposed handling of the Sino-Soviet alliance fitted logically into his general foreign policy. In effect, it emphasized the bludgeon—consider the administration's doctrine of massive retaliation—over the rapier. Applied to the Communist alliance, Dulles hoped it would menace or at least fatigue the allies apart. Diplomatic pressures against Peking should be combined with implied threats of instantaneous nuclear destruction of China and Russia if the former misbehaved. And in peacetime, Russia would risk overextending its limited financial and material resources; as much as possible, Moscow should bear alone the full weight of aiding impoverished China.

The newly constituted Republican National Security Council admitted in November 1953, "the primary problem of U.S. foreign policy in the Far East is to cope with the altered structure of power which arises from the existence of a strong and hostile Communist China, and from the alliance of Communist China with the U.S.S.R."[16] Furthermore, reckoned the NSC, even if Far Eastern problems—over Taiwan, Korea, and Indochina—should be resolved to Peking's satisfaction, its hostility toward the West, especially the United States, would fester on. Respecting the Sino-Soviet alliance, the NSC believed—despite intelligence analyses such as the one just considered—that "powerful ties of common ideology" secured the partnership. Coinciding national interests also bound the alliance, and its value to each state had recently been proven. China had obtained Soviet material and technical assistance to develop the armed forces, build extracting industries, establish power plants, and improve transportation facilities. The Russians also supported Chinese attempts to gain international acceptance and proclaimed Peking as a great power. Finally, the Soviet connection provided China with immunity from direct American attack during the Korean War. In turn, Moscow profited from China's defense of Korea, which prevented installation of a hostile government along part of the Soviet frontier. Chinese propaganda also helped spread Soviet influence in the Far East. In short, the alliance effectively promoted the interests of each party, and "the conflicts of interest of both partners with the non-communist world are for the present much more intense than conflicts of interest between the partners."

Immediate and long-term hazards, however, could rot Sino-Soviet friendship. These "potential dangers to the alliance will stem primarily from the inner workings of the partnership and only secondarily from the nature of external pressures or inducements." The primary dangers were rooted in Chinese nationalism, whose ambitions, embodied by the Chinese Communist party included international Communist leadership and national goals incompatible with Soviet aims. Over the short term, Chinese desires to reclaim sovereignty over Port Arthur might cause Russian irritation. Other specific, unresolved problems—such as Soviet intervention in Manchuria, Sinkiang, and Mongolia; Mao's undetermined status in world communism; CCP influence in South Asian and Japanese Communist parties; and Chinese repayment of Soviet military and economic aid—jeopardized the alliance. In addition, Chinese self-development was thought to anguish the Russians. The Kremlin could "hardly view with equanimity the development of an independent China on its frontiers which was powerful, well armed, industrially competent, and politically united. Chinese Communist successes in achieving reduction of Western power and influence in the Far East might confront the Russians with a partner whose ambitions could be achieved at cost not to the West but to the Russians themselves." Peking's military and industrial prowess might eventually threaten Moscow's hold on Siberia.

Although persuaded that external pressure alone could not break the alliance, the NSC declared, "The West . . . can strive to create those pressures or inducements which might be most apt to provide the context for increase of tension in the partnership." To this object several policy options were considered. First, either alone or in conjunction with Taiwanese forces, the United States could on an appropriate occasion overthrow and replace the Peking regime. The problems, however, with such a policy were numerous. In the first place, America's European allies would probably balk and oppose such a venture. And should general war result, China could at least expect considerable Soviet military aid, while for the United States, war would exact large costs in mobilization, inflict high casualties, and divert forces from Europe. Global war would be risked, atomic weapons might be used. The dangers of such a policy were obviously too great.

Another possibility was to offer China concessions designed to overcome its hostility and distrust. Perhaps agreements favorable to Peking could be reached on Taiwan's disposition, UN forces in Korea, and France's struggle to recover Indochina. This policy too was rejected on the grounds that America's security position would seriously weaken if Taiwan reverted to Mainland control and Western forces withdrew from areas contiguous to China. It was thought that Peking's influence would fill the void, and "free Asia" would soon capitulate. Besides, concessions could not ease Chinese ideological antagonism toward the West nor necessarily provide incentive to loosen ties with Moscow.

Despite limited capabilities for increasing pressures inside China, the

NSC decided to seek through continued economic restrictions to delay and make more difficult "Chinese Communist efforts to achieve industrialization and oblige the USSR to continue to carry the burden of assisting Communist China." Simultaneously, through various political measures, the United States should seek to impede universal acceptance of Peking and to reduce its propaganda value for the Soviets. The United States would meanwhile continue to buttress the political, economic, and military strength of noncommunist Asian countries. The NSC planned to refortify offshore island security, check any Chinese expansion—with American forces if necessary—assist in antisubversion programs of friendly states, establish a regional collective security system, and aid Taiwan and Japan in all important matters.[16]

By December 1953, it had become acutely evident to British and U.S. leaders that their approaches to China were very much at odds—London urged a moderate policy toward China designed to woo it from the Soviet Union—and that in the interest of allied cooperation these differences should be reconciled. Consequently, when French, British, and American heads of state met in Bermuda in early December, they discussed among other issues Western policy toward China. Dulles's assessment—for the assembled leaders—of Sino-Soviet relations was reasonable enough. However, it did not meet with general approval; both Churchill and Eden withheld their assent.

The secretary explained to his British colleagues that although he could not be entirely confident about the real nature of Sino-Soviet relations, he suspected that the Communist alliance was becoming more tenuous. After all, Mao was an outstanding Communist leader in his own right, whose prestige, although less than Stalin's, far outstripped Malenkov's.[17] Dulles reasoned that it was likely that Mao would no longer be content to play a role subordinate to the Soviets. Probably Soviet eulogizing of Mao was prompted by the need to treat him as an equal partner and an important world leader. Dulles punctuated his remarks with optimism when he said that ever-competitive Sino-Soviet relations held the promise of a future Russian-Chinese break.

Like a well-prepared lawyer outlining his brief, Dulles next contrasted British and American approaches to China. He doubted that British attempts at "being nice to the Communist Chinese" could succeed in weaning them from the Soviets.[18] On the other hand, American tactics relying on maximum pressure toward China could produce tangible strains on the alliance. Russia would simply not be able to meet Chinese demands, and the alliance's inevitable deterioration would speed along. Dulles argued that, short of war, the United States should concentrate its economic, political, and military strength against China; if America's allies joined this policy, it was probable that intracommunist problems would develop all the sooner. To Dulles, Britain's current policy would only lead to a dead end, and if the U.K.'s approach should be adopted by others, China before long would enjoy the best of all worlds as Russia and the West competed for Peking's favor. Dulles warned, moreover, that contradictory Western policies toward China impaired progress and enabled the Communist states to exploit Western differences. Naturally, he did not expect Great Britain to withdraw its recognition of China; British leaders, he regretfully allowed, believed "One must recognize even one's enemies." Even so, political, economic, and moral aid did not follow automatically from recognition. Dulles hoped very much that Britain would join America in thwarting China's UN admission and would in other ways coordinate policy with Washington against China.

Foreign Minister Eden, diffident but unimpressed by the secretary's analysis, agreed that allied actions could help undermine Sino-Soviet cooperation. He further stated his belief that the Communist leaders were intent on spoiling Anglo-French-American unity. And yet, that in itself was not a reason to break all contacts with Peking, no matter how unsatisfactory London's "relationship with the Chinese communists might be at present."[19]

Following Eden's slim rebuttal, the meeting adjourned without Anglo-American agreement. As the following episodes demonstrate, the United States persisted in its policy of pressure toward China, yet was alert to any Sino-Soviet problems accessible to a milder American diplomacy.

Geneva 1954

In February 1954, several months after the Korean armistice was signed, the foreign ministers of England, France, Russia, and the United States met in Berlin. Among other things, they scheduled a conference of all concerned parties, Peking included, to meet in the spring in order to resolve Korean-related issues and negotiate a settlement to the Indochina War. The Korean agenda at Geneva produced nothing. Far-reaching, disastrous repercussions sprang from the sessions devoted to Indochina, however.

Congressional pressures directed at Dulles before the Geneva Conference were aimed at discouraging any intentions he may have entertained about meeting with Chou En-lai or improving Sino-American relations. As recently as November 1953, Dulles had caused a stir in

Taiwan and among Chiang's congressional supporters because of some apparently loose remarks. He seemed to imply that the American line toward China was softening and that if Peking should renounce aggression and quit taking orders from the Soviet Union, then perhaps China would be eligible for American recognition and UN admission. Prompt "clarification" by Vice-President Nixon of the secretary's comments helped put the matter to rest.

American conservatives, still not mollified, were vociferous in early 1954 for fear that contacts between the Chinese and U.S. delegations might lead to Washington's recognition of Peking. To have done so would, in the words of Senator Welker of Idaho, subvert that policy for which "American soldiers have paid in blood on the icy hills of Korea."[20] Even the Berlin Communique specifying the conditions of invitation to the Geneva Conference did not placate Senator Knowland. He found little comfort in assurances that "neither the invitation to nor the holding of the . . . conference shall be deemed to imply recognition in any case where it has not already been acceded." Rather, the Senator from Formosa—as he was dubbed by the press—warned that the administration would be held accountable for any "slip" that led to recognition of the People's Republic or Communist expansion in Indochina. Facile parallels between Munich and Geneva were also drawn by various members of the Republican and Democratic parties.

Dulles's brief performance at the conference must have allayed all fears among China bloc congressmen. The secretary displayed singular diplomatic rudeness by refusing even to acknowledge the presence of Peking's delegation and wisecracked that he would not under any circumstances meet Chou En-lai, "unless our automobiles collide."[21] Formal contact was never established between Chinese and American representatives during the conference's entire eight weeks (April 26– July 21). As Dulles declared with characteristic earnestness, "It is one thing to recognize evil as a fact. It is another thing to take evil to one's breast and call it good."[22] Meanwhile, of course, the Americans did directly engage their Soviet counterparts and informally met with Peking's delegates.[23]

Thus Dulles's anticommunist policy at the minimum distinguished gradations of Marxist acceptability. Indeed, Dulles and the administration might have gone very much further had it not been for the inhibiting scorn of congressional critics. Eisenhower, toward the end of the Korean War, actually floated the idea that following a truce, China might rightfully enter the United Nations; and although the president never pushed the idea, it did at one point cause considerable domestic and international speculation. In June 1954 he suggested to Churchill that, under the right circumstances, the prime minister might use his good offices to help establish full, formal Sino-American relations.[24] However, sensibly impressed by the failure of Acheson to retain public confidence, Eisenhower and Dulles acted cautiously and indirectly when they tested the limits of right-wing tolerance. The experience of Arthur Dean, special ambassador to Korea and chief American delegate at Panmunjom, also revealed plenty to the president and his secretary.

Dean publicly suggested in early 1954 that Washington review its policy toward China. He resurrected the old idea that the United States could drive a wedge between China and Russia by improving relations with Mao's government.[25] Such an idea, though, was ludicrous, at least by the lights of Knowland, Welker, Judd, and others of their ilk. Welker, for example, countered that "the leaders of Communist China have, by their statements and their military actions, proved themselves to be complete tools of the international Communist conspiracy and its plan for world conquest." The senator ridiculed Dean's call for greater realism and asked rhetorically what was so unrealistic about America's China policy. "To me the refusal of a policy to offer the slightest concessions to the Red Chinese is the absolute height of realism. It is a real policy because it refuses to offer a bribe to the slave rulers of China . . . it refuses even to discuss the possibility of United Nations membership for a bloody aggressor whose policies have brought murderous ruin and destruction to millions."[26] Welker concluded by connecting Dean to a number of so-called Communist organizations, like the Institute of Pacific Relations, and supposedly unsavory characters such as Owen Lattimore. The charges were silly, of course, but they reached a wide audience and clung like a straitjacket around the diplomacy of Eisenhower's government. Dulles went to Geneva unencumbered by any illusions about the political price to be paid for even a brief conference with Chou En-lai.

Western diplomats during the Geneva meeting were absorbed with divisions among French, British, and American approaches to the Indochina fighting. The United States had previously sought British commitments to join an interventionist scheme if the French position crumbled further. To this Foreign Minister Eden objected and maintained that to widen the war would be folly. France's difficult position— exemplified by the debacle at Dien Bien Phu, discrediting the Navarre Plan—led London to assume that the war in the north was already lost. Besides, the Commonwealth would oppose a seemingly procolonial British policy. As for the French government, it wanted to extricate itself rapidly and gracefully from defeat and, if possible, salvage something of France's Southeast Asian possessions. As it was, French Prime Minister Joseph Laniel's government toppled before popular dissatisfaction with the slowness and inconclusiveness of negotiations; Pierre Mendes-France's premiership barely escaped the same fate before accomplishing what Dulles termed its "disguised surrender." France gave up, not so much for military reasons, but because two of its governments could not meet the cost and lacked internal support.

Despite preoccupations with Western difficulties, tensions among the Communist delegations were apparent to British and American observers. The most obvious intracommunist problem was the divergence between the Viet Minh's ambitious aspirations—a united Vietnam under Ho's party—and those of Russia and China. By themselves the Viet Minh probably could not conquer the whole country. And yet the Communist camp was not, unfortunately for Ho, forthcoming with needed diplomatic aid. The Americans largely attributed Chinese caution to fears instilled by Dulles, who had repeatedly warned that Peking's intervention in the war would invite American retaliation anywhere and at any time of Washington's choosing.[27] In view of China's first five-year plan aimed at economic reconstruction, Mao would surely be unwilling to risk another expensive, bloody war. American intelligence also recognized that to Peking, a united Vietnam under Viet Minh auspices might eventually threaten China's paramountcy in Southeast Asia.[28] As for the Soviets, Washington understood that Kremlin interests in Indochina were not so important as to require pressing France severely. Why, after all, should the Soviets antagonize Paris, thus encouraging French interest in the European Defense Community?

Although their goals were understood to be essentially compatible, some tactical divergence between the Mainland powers was perceived by Western analysts. Dulles thought that the Soviets had assumed a stand more moderate than China's, and at one point he thought this might lead to a serious rift over support of the Viet Minh. He certainly suspected that seemingly minor disagreements between Chou and Molotov concealed deeper cleavages within the Communist alliance. And both Laniel and Foreign Affairs Minister Georges Bidault felt that Moscow was becoming increasingly anxious about potential independent Chinese activity in Southeast Asia. The Soviets, so the French thought, "were deeply afraid that their Chinese friends might drag them into an adventure which they themselves did not at all desire."[29] Moreover, the French government believed that neither the Soviets nor the Communist Vietnamese would welcome an extension of Chinese influence anywhere in Southeast Asia. In any case, at the minimum the Soviets were generally thought to have been displeased by the unexpected, considerable prestige that accrued to China as a result of Chou's skillful Geneva performance.

According to Anthony Eden, Molotov attempted to impress upon the foreign minister that both of them had important roles to play at the conference as intermediaries between two hostile groups. Of the well-publicized Anglo-American differences, Eden recalls that Molotov remarked that he had read in the local newspapers that Britain and the United States were engaged in serious disputes, but he disbelieved such stories. "I said he was right not to [believe the news accounts], because allies often have to argue their respective points of view. Molotov said, 'That is right, we have to do that amongst ourselves, too.' And he emphasized to me once again that China was very much her own master in these matters."[30] Indeed, Peking was so much her own master that, in the view of the American Broadcasting Information Service, Moscow was eager to avoid responsibility for any Chinese actions in the Far East that might arouse American wrath.[31]

Dulles specifically was encouraged by intelligence gathered during the meetings from sources in Peking. Apparently, when American intrusion in Indochina seemed likely, Chou sought assurances from Molotov that the Soviet Union would intervene if America launched a war against China. The Soviet answer was ambiguous, noncommittal. Molotov replied that the Geneva negotiations "should be conducted in a way that military intervention, if it should take place, would not expand into a war on the mainland of China."[32] Dissatisfied, Chou pushed for a definite reply and stressed to Molotov that the war clique in the United States might take steps impervious to Soviet or Chinese influence. After receiving new instructions from Moscow, Molotov stated that only if the United States attacked China with atomic weapons would Russia retaliate against America. In the event of a conventional Sino-American war, the Soviet Union would provide weapons, industrial products, and technical skills, but no men. The Soviets argued, "It is to the advantage of China that Soviet Russia should temporarily stand aside. She may force a quick end of the war by threatening to participate, may rally the support of Asiatic countries for China against aggression and may mobilize world opinion in favor of China."[33]

The Russians clearly hoped to maintain their alliance with China at minimal costs. To Dulles, China's reaction was one of resentment; he believed, "they think the Russian comrades are somewhat selfish. If the United States does not make use of the atomic or hydrogen bomb, Soviet Russia will not be in danger and wants to stand aloof."[34] Heartened, Dulles's hope was reinforced that the Communist alliance could be divided through pressure. Yet, throughout the conference, he insisted that the American delegation not make public allegations of independent Chinese policy or Peking's displeasure with modest Soviet support. To do so, feared the secretary, would encourage Asian "wishful thinking" that China was more Asian than Communist and that reasonable accommodation could be reached with Peking.[35]

Despite China's problems with Russia, Geneva was an unqualified diplomatic success for Peking. The end of hostilities precluded any possibility that American bases would be established adjacent to, and hostile troops stationed along, China's southeastern border. An ideologically acceptable regime also occupied the zone between the People's Republic and the Franco-American-backed government in Saigon. In addition, Chinese participation in the conference dignified Peking's claims to international prestige; settlement of Asian issues would hereafter require Chinese inclusion. Peking's self-esteem and satisfaction in having been treated as a great power was apparent in the *People's Daily* editorial of July 22: "For the first time as one of the Big Powers, the People's Republic of China joined the other major powers in negotiating on vital international problems and made a contribution of its own that won acclaim of wide sections of public opinion. The international status of the People's Republic of China as one of the big world powers has gained universal recognition." Peking thereafter never lost an opportunity to portray itself as *the* Asian power championing all Asia against the West. During one of the conference's recesses, Chou exploited recently won good will by traveling to India for meetings with Nehru. Together on June 28, 1954, they proclaimed for the first time the five principles of coexistence, adopted a year later by Asian and African leaders at Bandung. Meantime, China's relationship with the Soviets seemed to grow steadily more ambiguous.

In early June, American intelligence reported that Chinese domestic programs aimed at expanding and modernizing the military continued to benefit directly from Soviet assistance. Peking's dependence on Moscow was predicted to last for a fair period, and maintenance of the alliance would probably continue as "a dominant aspect of China's foreign policy."[36] Taking nothing for granted, though, Soviet leaders allegedly treated their Chinese ally with extreme deference and refrained from issuing straight orders. Yet, the intelligence analysts pointed out, Moscow's predatory policies in Northeast Asia continued unabated to compromise Chinese sovereignty. At the same time, the Americans had good reason to suspect that popular Chinese resentment against Russia was mounting. According to Humphrey Trevelyan, Britain's ambassador to China, most Chinese disliked the Russians and grumbled about unfair rates for goods exchanged. He told C. L. Sulzberger of the *New York Times* that ordinary people in Peking were friendlier to the ambassador on learning that he was British, not Russian.[37] Nevertheless, as far as the Chinese government was concerned, the important question was whether or not the Soviets would support Peking in completing the social revolution and eliminating Mao's foe on Taiwan. In this—as with other issues with Moscow—the Chinese leaders were in for some sharp disappointments.

To the American government, neither the Korean truce nor the Geneva Conference represented victories for the West. In fact, the Geneva Accords, in the words of the *Pentagon Papers,* "completed a major forward stride of communism which may lead to the loss of Southeast Asia." Eisenhower's government, over the advice of the National Intelligence Board, consequently undertook measures to bolster the sagging Saigon regime. Aid to Bao Dai was increased, and clandestine operations in the North to disrupt and embarrass the Communist regime were undertaken. By these policies the United States began to relieve France of its colonial obligations and hoped to smooth the way for French integration into the European Defense Community. Ironically, in August 1954 France refused to accept membership in the organization.

Because of the disquieting Geneva decisions, the Manila Treaty negotiations were hurried along. On September 8, 1954, a treaty was signed that pledged the United States, Australia, New Zealand, Thailand, the Philippines, France, and Great Britain to Southeast Asian collective security. SEATO, destined for little, was born.

Attempts to buttress a European ally's international prestige thus eventually led Washington to place itself in opposition to Ho's national, Marxist-inspired Vietnamese revolutionary movement. Unfortunately, American efforts during the ensuing years to develop an effective, noncommunist popular alternative to Ho failed. And the United States, for at least a decade and a half after Geneva, remained committed to checking a presumed southward Chinese trust. Did Dulles, unlike the British, reject any idea that Ho's interests were distinct from China's and that he might emerge as an Asian version of Tito? Conclusive evidence, one way or the other, is not yet available. If Dulles did not distinguish much between Chinese and North Vietnamese interests, the obvious question is why, given the administration's perception of differences between Russia and China, was there not a similar understanding of separate national concerns among Communist parties in Asia. Perhaps official Washington's understanding of the foreign national interest had been reduced, at least in Southeast Asia, to simple anticommunism. Probably a paucity of knowledge about traditional

Chinese-Vietnamese antagonism also handicapped Dulles's understanding.

First Offshore Islands Crisis

For a brief period after the Korean armistice was signed and after Geneva, the cold war in the Far East seemed to take a peaceful turn. However, violence flared anew in early autumn 1954, when Chinese Communist gunners commenced bombardment of nearby Nationalist-held offshore islands. Reunification of Chinese territory undoubtedly was an important motive behind Communist attempts to assert sovereignty over Quemoy, the Tachen Islands, and Matsu. The threatening quality of American policy, as perceived in Peking, was also responsible for precipitating the crisis of 1954–55. From Peking's perspective, external security would be enhanced if the American-backed Nationalist forces were dislodged from their nearby offshore fortifications. The artillery attacks also demonstrated Chinese resolve not to be intimidated by increased American support of Taiwan. Peking had probably been alarmed in July 1954, when Washington revealed that plans to enter into a security pact with Taipei had been under study for some time and intimated that a mutual security treaty would shortly be signed. Chinese concern was certainly heightened in early September with the establishment of SEATO. The new pact must have seemed in Peking to strengthen the American-inspired ring of hostile states.

Capture of the offshore islands would end the Nationalist blockade, disruptive of Chinese shipping from Shanghai to Canton. The Nationalist guerrilla nuisance, operating from the islands, would also be eliminated. The New China News Agency explained: "Directed and protected by the aggressive junta in the U.S., the gang of Chiang traitors has been using these islands as an important base for plundering and seizing fishing boats and merchant ships on the seas, harassing the coastal areas of the mainland and menacing and undermining maritime shipping and the security of the people living along the coast."[38] Peking's control of the islands would also deprive the Nationalists of a staging area from which to launch their liberation campaign, imminent according to the recently "unleashed" Chiang.

Unaided, the People's Republic could not vanquish the apparent threat emanating from Quemoy and Matsu. Only with Soviet aid could China have forced an "imperialist" withdrawal to Taiwan. To Peking's disappointment, Moscow withheld support at the critical moment. Preoccupied with West German entry into NATO, Soviet leaders feared Sino-American conflict in the Pacific would distract from crucial European matters and posed a danger threatening to mix Russia with China in a hopeless war against the United States. Soviet support was limited to periodic verbal harangues against Washington.

Throughout the crisis China's leaders bravely maintained that they enjoyed unequivocal Soviet support. Inevitably, the fiction collapsed. In February 1955, as part of a program to develop nuclear warheads suitable for guided missiles, the United States initiated a series of H-bomb tests; these tests were also useful reminders to the Chinese of the odds against them. Peking responded by declaring that Moscow's support was substantial enough to check any American aggression, no matter how gruesome the struggle. Mao exclaimed, "We can all perceive the great cooperation between China and the Soviet Union. There are no aggressive plans of imperialism which cannot be smashed. Should the imperialists start a war of aggression we, together with the whole world, would certainly wipe them off the surface of the globe."[39] But a Soviet spokesman only blandly affirmed the great friendship between the Chinese People's Republic and the Soviet Union. Soon thereafter, American pressures combined with Soviet warnings to Peking evidently helped make China heed the risks, and in May Chinese air and artillery bombardments of the islands ceased. Significantly, during this episode the Soviets had not exploited American problems in Asia by taking aggressive moves in Europe. According to the administration, limited Soviet-American understanding was more important to Kremlin leaders than close cooperation with Peking.

At the peak of the offshore islands crisis, Khrushchev, Bulganin, and other members of the Soviet collective leadership met with Chinese leaders in Peking, an unthinkable gesture during Stalin's time. There the Soviets not only finally relinquished control of Port Arthur, but also dissolved the joint Sino-Soviet companies and pledged assistance to Peking's first five-year plan. Soviet aid to the new industrial and agricultural drives included a $130 million credit, technical advice, and help on a nonmilitary nuclear program. In exchange, the Soviets hoped to exact promises from the Chinese that they would exercise restraint in their dispute with Taipei and Washington over the offshore islands. To the Soviets, then, aid was essentially an inducement aimed at retaining Chinese obedience to Moscow.

The Mao-Khrushchev talks apparently caused considerable discomfort for the Soviet leadership. Khrushchev himself found direct dealing with his Chinese counterpart to be an ordeal, and in his memoirs he reveals a racialist predisposition, reflected and reinforced by his encounters with Mao. The tough Soviet party boss was partially overcome by an "atmosphere that was typically Oriental. Everyone was unbe-

lievably courteous and ingratiating, but I saw through their hypocrisy
. . . it was all too sickeningly sweet. The atmosphere was nauseating."
With respect to Mao, Khrushchev brooded: "I was never sure that I
understood what he meant. I thought at the time that it must have been
because of some special traits in the Chinese character and the Chinese
way of thinking."[40]

The Chinese, too, had reason to be less than delighted by their ally.
According to statements made by Mao in 1964, the Russians refused to
discuss Mongolia. Moreover, Chinese aid requests may have exceeded
Soviet capacity or generosity. Khrushchev relates in his memoirs that
during the 1954 meetings "when our country was still hungry and
poverty-ridden from the war, Chou En-lai asked, 'Perhaps you could
make us a gift of a university?' " To this Khrushchev replied that the
Soviet Union was also poor. "We may be richer than you, but the war
has just ended and we are still not back on our feet."[41]

Furthermore, at a time when Moscow was seeking to reduce international problems and yet China was skirmishing with American-
backed Nationalists off the coast, Mao and Khrushchev disagreed vi-
olently on the nature and probable outcome of war with the West.
Khrushchev preached the virtues of restraint and caution and admon-
ished the Chinese of the twin dangers of ridiculing the United States
and disparaging it as a paper tiger. Once home, Khrushchev, again
according to his memoirs, declared that Soviet conflict with China was
inevitable.

The American intelligence community was enormously impressed by
numerous "incredible reports" about a shocked Khrushchev and Bulganin, positively dazed by Chinese independence, intransigence, un-
controllability. Chinese demands for Soviet assistance against the
United States, it was also thought, went far beyond anything the sober
Russians would ever risk.[42] The NSC predicted that if the Chinese failed
to be satisfied with Soviet aid or if the Soviets should be disappointed
by Chinese misconduct, then Sino-Soviet relations would become precipitously a good deal rougher.[43] Subsequent security arrangements and
Russian-Chinese military coordination were, in any case, unimpressive.
One expert reports that joint military planning and maneuvers were
never conducted.[44]

Dulles and Eisenhower recognized from the outset of the offshore
islands crisis that Quemoy and Matsu were irrelevant to the security of
either Taiwan or the United States. Yet reasons both political and
diplomatic persuaded the administration to support Chiang's efforts to
retain the islands. Ceding more territory, no matter how insignificant,

would in the fall of 1954 be popularly regarded as still another victory for Moscow and Peking. To many critics, the administration had already acquiesced in the surrender of twelve million Vietnamese to communism. The China lobby was especially adamant in warning against renewed "appeasement" of totalitarianism in Asia. Henry Luce wrote to Eisenhower that "any slightest weakening in the position and posture of the United States as the forceful ally of all anti-Communists in Asia would . . . lead to disastrous consequences."[45] As for Chiang, the islands were vital to future plans; their loss would constitute a major reversal in his operations waged against the Mainland. He believed also that forfeiture of the islands would deal a severe psychological blow, albeit not directly endangering Taiwan, to the morale of his armed forces as damaging as a battlefield rout.

Anglo-American disagreement over Western policy toward China had been simmering long before the Communist bombardment of the Matsu and Quemoy islands sparked a minor crisis in the Atlantic Alliance. By promoting regular diplomatic and trade relations with Peking, London still hoped to safeguard Hong Kong and woo China away from Soviet influence, a policy viewed in late 1954 with pure dismay by Dulles. In any case, during the crisis Soviet restraint of China was paralleled by Britain's counsel to the Americans against actions that might instigate World War III. Macmillan wrote in his diary, "Indeed, both Moscow and London are working (somewhat paradoxically) on the same lines and are trying to restrain their friends."[46] Above all else, though, Eisenhower's natural caution ultimately prevailed over the recommendations of senior political and military advisors, notably Walter Robertson and Admiral Radford, urging him to embark on what Eisenhower later called "channels leading to war."

The Formosa Resolution authorizing the president to employ armed force in the defense of Taiwan, the Pescadores, and those island fortifications necessary for Taipei's defense was ambiguous regarding American commitments to Quemoy and Matsu. Would the Americans really act to save the inconsequential islands and risk full-scale war? The uncertainty enabled Washington to retain maximum flexibility toward a vulnerable Western salient. If necessary, the islands could be abandoned without loss of prestige by claiming that they were incidental to Taiwan's defense. On the other hand, a warning had been issued that military action would follow Chinese "recklessness." The resolution also placated Senator Knowland and Admiral Radford, who sought "decisive action" in support of the Chinese Republic. Finally, Rhee and Chiang—unable to conduct their "holy war" of liberation against the Mainland as they insisted they would, given American blessings and support—were reasonably satisfied by American commitments embodied in the resolution and in subsequent American actions.

Because Chiang's regime was unacceptable to most Asian governments—the price of recognizing it against the wishes of Peking was steep—the United States could not assure Taiwan's protection through a multilateral security pact. Consequently, the United States was forced to enter into a bilateral arrangement with Taiwan. In December, the United States and Taiwan signed a defense treaty pledging the parties to mutual aid in resisting "armed attack and communist subversive activities directed from without against their territorial integrity and political stability." Chiang and his congressional supporters were also gratified by the president's remarks at a news conference in March that the United States would employ atomic weapons against strictly military targets on the Mainland if Taiwan should be attacked. To his confidants, Eisenhower privately advised that there was no reason to fear China, at least not for a decade.[47] The country was poor, militarily weak, and heavily dependent upon a questionable ally.

Equivocal Soviet support of China, abundantly evident to American policy planners, indicated to them the validity of keeping pressure up along the Sino-Soviet periphery. Soviet caution may also have suggested to the United States that additional advantages could be gained by improving relations with Moscow. American intelligence reported during the first period of the offshore islands episode that Communist policy in Asia was developed through joint Sino-Soviet consultation, "not by the dictation of Moscow."[48] Despite Soviet preponderance, Chinese influence within the alliance was understood to be rising inexorably. Friction between the allies would steadily increase as China exerted greater independent authority. Nevertheless, leadership rivalry was not expected to debilitate the alliance, at least not in the immediately foreseeable future.

As for the Soviets, they were thought to be pursuing dual long-range goals. Theoretically at least, Moscow desired a Chinese ally both strong and reliable. Yet Russia, exercising Communist command in Asia, evidently hoped to keep China both economically and militarily dependent; the October accords were read in Washington as indicating Khrushchev's keenness for retaining Chinese compliance. Peking's aggressive proclivities especially disturbed the Soviets, who appreciated that "communist China possesses capability for some independent action, even action which the U.S.S.R. might disapprove but which it would find difficult to repudiate."[49] The nature and timing of attacks against Nationalist territory were precisely a case in point.

In March 1955, as the administration tested more H-bombs, American intelligence submitted the following assessment: In case of Sino-American clashes, both Peking and Moscow would try to contain the spread of hostilities, and the Soviet Union, although providing China with political and military support, would avoid direct military involvement. Intelligence analysts were divided, however, over the likely Soviet response should Moscow come to believe that American actions threatened Peking's survival. Possibly the Soviets would intervene while acting to limit hostilities to the Far East. Or perhaps Soviet armies would remain altogether aloof, as they had during the Korean War. In either case, the joint intelligence staff agreed that Soviet leaders—aware of their country's small nuclear stockpiles and inadequate delivery capabilities—would not hazard Russia's survival for China in war against the United States.[50] The analysts appreciated, moreover, that if Russia was unwilling to chance, or at least bluff, Moscow for Peking, the alliance's value to China was dubious indeed.

Dulles told the Advertising Club of New York in March that Chinese actions were more provocative of war than the Soviet Union's. The secretary also explained to newsmen—no doubt with his Kremlin audience in mind—that Soviet support for China in its confrontation with America was an expensive proposition and carried the risk of general war. He also emphasized the monumental expense to the Soviet Union of supplying weapons to China. Dulles thus played on Soviet fears of a Chinese bogey, expensive to maintain as an ally and dangerous if it should drag Russia into an unwanted war against the United States. Dulles accurately predicted to the president in May that "the Soviets may put increasing pressure upon the Chinese Communists to avoid war."[51]

Geneva 1955

Several months before the 1955 Geneva Summit Meeting, the NSC concluded that neither the Soviet Union nor China would within the next five years deliberately initiate or risk a war that might involve the United States. Even Chinese military probing of Taiwan and attacks against the offshore islands would be limited, lest the Americans were antagonized into full-scale fighting. And yet the NSC believed that by every means short of war the Mainland states would work to dislodge American influence from Asia and weaken by a blend of subversion and military pressure Washington's allies. At the same time, the NSC was confident that the Sino-Soviet bloc would confront problems aplenty, both strategic and political. For one thing, the Soviets had to police Eastern Europe, itself chafing as agricultural and consumer production lagged.[52] Further, the Kremlin, despite bonds of ideology with China and shared fears over the United States, was anxious about retaining Mao within the Soviet-led bloc. The NSC, therefore, resolved that Washington should be prepared, as ever, to exploit differences among the Communist states. Limited ad hoc negotiations with Chinese leaders might even serve American purposes in weakening Sino-Soviet ties.[53]

According to Prime Minister Eden, "The Geneva meeting was worthwhile if only for the discreet improvement it brought about in the Formosa Strait. By the end of the conference, the Foreign Secretary and I were convinced that all present would have been sincerely happy to see the offshore islands sunk under the sea."[54] Except for this particular slight advance, the July conference produced little tangible resolution of outstanding East-West problems. Behind solemn declarations about the desirability of peace in the nuclear age and the touting of a new Geneva spirit stood the stubborn fact: Europe was divided into two opposing military pacts. The discussion of various issues—the Soviet disarmament plan, Eisenhower's Open Skies scheme, German reunification, and the Soviet occupation of Eastern Europe—was predictably inconclusive. In rare understatement, Dulles told the press, "There are probably long arduous months ahead in which we must expect disappointments" before an "ultimate achievement of a secure peace."[55] Still, the conference was significant, for its convocation symbolized Soviet and American recognition of the dangers inherent in prolonged antagonism. If nothing else, the Geneva exercise in international amity caused a temporary deescalation in the violent Soviet-American war of words.

The peaceful sentiments expressed by Soviet and American leaders at Geneva were realized in subsequent limited political cooperation such as the establishment of cultural exchange programs. Superpower restraint was also advanced at the summit meeting. In 1956, when Soviet and Warsaw Pact forces "saved" Hungary from "capitalist counterrevolution," the United States responded simply by voicing disapproval in the United Nations and was prepared to do little else for Poland. Similarly, the Soviet reaction to the tripartite attack on Egypt by French, British, and Israeli forces was marked only by self-righteous denunciations. Although Khrushchev's language was particularly vitriolic and by innuendo he made a nuclear threat, it was American pressure, not Soviet, that forced the allies to end their offensive. And in 1958, Moscow's commitment to improved relations with the West again resulted in Soviet pressures on China to defuse the second offshore islands crisis.

Even before the Geneva meetings in July, the Americans seriously

doubted Peking's appreciation of Moscow as a trustworthy representative of Chinese interests. Dulles believed, moreover, that the Russian
leaders would have to push Chinese demands—U.S. troop withdrawal
from Korea, retirement of Seventh Fleet ships from the Taiwan Straits,
and UN membership—thereby demonstrating once and for all that the
Soviet Union was a loyal, useful ally.[56]

The British government, too, was alert. At the conference, Macmillan
discerned extreme Soviet nervousness about the People's Republic. He
noted on July 15 that the collective leadership was anxious about China
and made no effort to hide the fact from the British. "They (like us)
wish that Quemoy and Matsu could sink beneath the sea. They may
fear—in the long run—that China will be a danger to their eastern
flank."[57] He also felt that the Soviets would have preferred "a weak
nationalist or capitalist China which they could plunder to a Communist
China which they have to assist." After an Anglo-Soviet dinner meeting, Macmillan recorded that the Russians were not at all "keen" on
China, regarded it as a drain on both their industrial and military resources, and wondered when China would pose a threat to Russian
security in Siberia. Later, during his post-Geneva visit with Khrushchev
in Moscow, Chancellor Adenauer of Germany was quizzed by a plain-
tive-sounding chairman on how best to handle the Chinese problem.
The Soviet leader complained, "China already has 600 million inhabitants, who live on a handful of rice. Each year there are 12 million
more. How is that going to end? I beg you to help us to resolve our
difficulties with China."[58]

Dulles believed that, as indicated at Geneva, "the Soviet leaders did
not want reversion to sharp Russian-American antagonism and . . .
they will pay some appreciable price to avoid it."[59] If necessary, China
might even be expendable.

Shortly after the Geneva Conference, Nelson Rockefeller, special
assistant to the president, coordinated a study on "Psychological Aspects of U.S. Strategy." Rockefeller and his committee determined
among other things that the Chinese Communists were especially vulnerable on the basis of their militant nationalism. Contrasting Sino-
American enmity with decreased Soviet-American hostility, they also
stressed the importance of achieving a *modus vivendi* with Russia. After
all, the Soviet Union, not China, posed a strategic threat. Soviet actions
and press statements also revealed Moscow's fear of nuclear war and
her willingness to reject Chinese-inspired adventures.[60]

Beginning in July, American propaganda started to exploit Soviet
fears observed by Western leaders at Geneva. One VOA commentator
explained, "The cause of their [Sino-Soviet] conflict of interest lies in

one great fact—the fact that China suffers from chronic and increasing overpopulation, while the Soviet Union, relatively speaking, is underpopulated. What makes this contrast more striking is the fact that the most underpopulated areas of the Soviet Union are those closest to China."[61] Another American broadcast cited Adenauer's August remarks in the Swiss newspaper *Der Bund* to the effect that China had a yearly birth rate of millions. "In the near future the [Chinese] People's Republic will no longer have enough territory. It cannot expand to the South. It must move North in order to continue to live, and that means into the Russian Asiatic territories."[62] The commentator finished by prophesying almost cheerfully that a future "trouble spot" would develop along the Sino-Soviet border. At the same time, through varied other covert operations—their nature not now known—the United States continued efforts to impair relations between the U.S.S.R. and Communist China.[63]

America's Rebuff of Chinese Overtures

Twice, in 1954 and 1955, China emerged from isolation and joined in the Geneva Peace Conference and the Asian-African meeting at Bandung. During both conferences but especially at Bandung, Chinese prestige increased appreciably. There, under Chou En-lai, Peking's delegation affirmed support for Asian and African peoples struggling against imperialism. Khrushchev and Bulganin, perturbed that Russia had not been asked to send a representative to the conference, soon afterwards undertook a policy of cultivating relations with Egypt and India. The spectre, then, of Chinese-Soviet competition in Asia and Africa was evident as early as 1955.

The Bandung declaration of *panch shila*—the five principles were mutual respect for territorial integrity and sovereignty, nonaggression, noninterference in each other's internal affairs, equality and mutual benefit, and peaceful coexistence—provided the background for the launching of a strenuous Chinese campaign to improve relations with the United States. To begin with, as a gesture of good will, Radio Peking announced that the families of American servicemen in Chinese jails could visit their loved ones and stay in facilities sponsored by the Red Cross. Then Chou, whose virtuoso performance at Bandung set the conference's pace and style, declared on April 23, 1955 that "the Chinese people are friendly to the American people." Besides desiring peace, "the Chinese Government is willing to sit down and enter into negotiations with the U.S. government to discuss the question of relaxing tension in the Taiwan area."[64]

The State Department's initial conditions for Sino-American talks were plainly unacceptable to the People's Republic and indicated Washington's want of seriousness. The United States insisted that Taiwan should have equal representation with the United States and China at the proposed meetings; Peking was also expected to participate in UN Security Council meetings aimed at ending hostilities around Taiwan. The implied recognition of Taiwan as equal and legitimate was, of course, anathema to Peking. And the suggestion that Peking send representatives to an international body that had repeatedly denied her membership and condemned her as aggressor and in which her archrival played a significant role could not be sincere. Indeed, Dulles was suspicious that the friendly Chinese stance was merely a pose chiefly for propaganda purposes, and he feared that a conciliatory Chinese posture toward the United States was intended merely to demonstrate to Asian and African leaders the new moderate orientation of Peking's policy. An incensed Chou responded by scolding the State Department for cleaving to unsound principles and cautioned that China's willingness to negotiate with the United States did not deflect Peking from opposing imperialism or from plans to liberate Taiwan.

Sensing an opportunity, though, Dulles soon signalled that negotiations with Russia's increasingly burdensome ally might begin, and belligerent Chinese propaganda against the United States declined noticeably. At the same time, various governments that had diplomatic relations with Peking indicated to Dulles their belief that China was anxious to improve matters with Washington. The NSC was also entirely open to the idea that acceptable, enforceable agreements with China—over limited issues certainly, perhaps even over general ones—were possible. Consequently, the secretary declared that the United States could not forever "take a purely negative position" toward China and that limited negotiations between the two countries might be to their mutual advantage, especially in regard to such issues as the "citizens of the two countries held by the other."[65]

Dulles then stated that if a Taiwan cease-fire should be initiated, perhaps wider Sino-American negotiations could follow. Dulles also reported to some journalists that definite signs were appearing that suggested that China was beginning to exercise initiative independent of the Soviet Union. Yet for the sake of his conservative domestic constituency, the secretary emphasized that in any forthcoming discussions Taiwan's fate would not be decided "behind its back." Shortly thereafter, Eisenhower expressed hopes that productive discussions aimed at increasing Far Eastern stability might emerge. And, rather abruptly, the intensity of the Straits crisis subsided as both Peking and

Washington took actions to improve the climate for negotiations. Dulles announced that a cease-fire would not be viewed as Peking's renunciation of claims to Taiwan; in turn, Chou reiterated the desirability of acquiring Taiwan through nonmilitary means.

In late July, both governments simultaneously announced the beginning of Sino-American ambassadorial-level talks in Geneva. So-called practical matters and the problem of American prisoners in China were scheduled for discussion. Peking next proclaimed its intention to release captured American airmen incarcerated since the Korean War. In September, Ambassador Wang, Chinese representative to Czechoslovakia, and U. Alexis Johnson, American ambassador to Poland, announced an agreement that permitted all Chinese citizens in America and all American citizens in China to repatriate if they so desired. At roughly the same time, in August, the administration examined the possibility of exporting foods and cotton to China.[66]

For the Chinese, discussion of the repatriation issue was merely a pretext for initiating talks of a more comprehensive nature. Ambassador Wang announced on the first day of the meetings that China hoped to elevate them to the foreign-minister level as soon as possible. A few days later, he explained that once the nationals' problem was settled, the talks should concentrate on major topics such as establishment of diplomatic relations, cultural and trade exchanges, Peking's membership in the United Nations, American withdrawal of military forces on Taiwan, and so forth. However, with the exception of the prisoners' issue, the American negotiators did not express interest in exploring problems of underlying significance. From the administration's standpoint, the release of American POWs added to its popular standing, but substantive agreements with China were politically unfeasible. Dulles and Eisenhower were not about to try further the patience and good humor of their supporters, particularly Senators Knowland and Welker.

Prime Minister Eden and his government were especially disappointed. And Adlai Stevenson blamed the China bloc for once again thwarting Sino-American negotiations; he labelled this the "greatest political crime of our times." Indeed, Dulles had responded hastily to critics accusing him of softness, appeasement, retreat. In November, he submitted to the public that Peking's "use of U.S. hostages as pawns" demonstrated Chinese insincerity and treachery. The retention of nineteen remaining American prisoners apparently constituted an insuperable barrier between the two states.

By the end of the year, the Chinese again raised tensions in the Taiwan Straits by increasing propaganda activities and resuming limited artillery action. According to State Department intelligence, Peking was trying, rather clumsily, to force the United States into accepting a Sino-American foreign ministers meeting.[67]

In January 1956, the State Department suggested that the use of force in settling Sino-American disputes would not always remain a realistic option. Nothing, though, was mentioned of American interests in Taiwan. In a period of supposedly developing negotiations, few other American statements, implying continued involvement in internal Chinese affairs, could have more antagonized Peking. That same month, Dulles again reviewed his policy toward China for Britain's new foreign secretary, Selwyn Lloyd, and indicated that Western goals would suffer if London or Washington set out to win the good will of Chinese leaders or if British and American policies toward China continued to diverge.

Although discouraged, the Chinese determined to progress toward an understanding with Washington. Once more, Peking suggested that the ambassadorial-level talks should be elevated, to which Secretary Dulles vaguely replied that only a "meaningful renunciation of force" and release of all American prisoners could facilitate relations. As various analysts have argued, the return of prisoners could have been easily accomplished within the context of an overall agreement. Meanwhile, Chinese failure to return the prisoners was largely interpreted by the American public as reflecting Peking's bad faith. Even if the prisoners should be released, the administration could still claim that Peking had not made appropriate moves toward a true renunciation of force. As a result, the proposed foreign minister meetings, which if held would have constituted tacit recognition of the People's Republic, were undermined. The ambassadorial talks continued for years, but without major significance.

Both American political parties in 1956 included in their campaign platforms resolutions declaring hostility to future Chinese bids for UN admission and affirmed the soundness of nonrecognition. Respecting China's admission to the UN, the Democrats, despite Stevenson's private wishes, declared, "We pledge determined opposition to the admission of the Communist Chinese into the United Nations [and] urge a continuing effort to effect the release of all Americans detained by Communist China." The Republicans took a similar tough stand and piously promised "to oppose the seating of Communist China in the UN, thus upholding international morality." In the meantime, aid to Taiwan continued at ever increasing levels. Earlier auguries that a thaw in Sino-American relations might appear thus came to nothing. Dulles reminded his audiences in 1956 in one of his favorite adages, "One swallow does not make a summer." Nonetheless, the secretary must have been privately confident that his apparent receptiveness to Chinese overtures, no matter how qualified or hesitant, had startled and worried Russian leaders.

Conclusions

During the next few years the American government will release additional official documents that will make possible a more detailed account of the events and policies of the years 1953–56. Until then—frustrating though it is—we must content ourselves with the material now available, which shows two things. First, the concept that the United States could and should work to undermine Sino-Soviet cooperation was taken seriously by the Eisenhower administration during its first term and formed the basis for policy. Second, the Eisenhower administration was willing to consider more than one option. Arthur Dean, for example, strongly advocated improved relations with China as a means of weakening its exclusive reliance on Russia; Eisenhower and Dulles also seem to have at least flirted with such an idea. But to have pursued this course during the McCarthy period was very nearly impossible. Dulles was satisfied to retain Taiwan as a client and apply military and political pressure on China. He hoped, and subsequent events were to prove him correct, that both Chinese aid requirements of Russia for domestic modernization and support in foreign affairs would burden the Communist alliance beyond endurance.

During the second Quemoy crisis in 1958, China appears to have deliberately maneuvered the Soviet Union dangerously close to confrontation with the United States, perhaps again testing Soviet commitments to China. Still, the Soviets resisted Chinese pressures and took virtually no public position until after the crisis had passed. In 1963 a Chinese spokesman derided the feebleness of Soviet support. "Although the situation in the Taiwan Straits was tense, there was no possibility that a nuclear war would break out and no need for the Soviet Union to support China with its nuclear weapons. It was only when they were clear that this was the situation that Soviet leaders expressed their support for China."[68] Russian and American desires to resolve the German issue and reach an arms agreement remained intact during the crisis and demonstrated anew to China's leaders the waywardness of their fraternal ally. According to Edward Freers, former chief of the State Department's East European desk, Dulles knew about Soviet and Chinese differences during the 1958 crisis and fashioned his strategy accordingly.[69] A combination of military threat and diplomatic pressure toward the Communist states resulted in meager, marginal Soviet support of Peking.

During the last remaining years of the Eisenhower administration, the Communist alliance crumbled quickly, and attempts to salvage it were submerged by a crush of international events and by Russia's ambivalent support of Chinese modernization. In response to China's Great Leap Forward and the coincident campaign to develop modern military forces, the Soviets sent 1,400 technicians and advisors; according to Chinese accounts Khrushchev also promised, but did not supply, Chinese scientists with a sample atom bomb. Very likely, as at least one observer has stated, Soviet assistance during this period was an act of coalition diplomacy to insure Chinese support of Soviet leadership and to encourage them in a moderate foreign policy. The abject failure of this tactic was illustrated by the second Quemoy crisis and vociferous Chinese polemics against the policy of peaceful coexistence.

In 1959, amid speculations about Soviet-American detente and the trumpeting of a new "Camp David spirit," the Chinese leadership became deeply suspicious of superpower cooperation and even of their possible collusion against the People's Republic. The proposed 1960 Paris Summit Meeting between Eisenhower and Khrushchev precipitated a violent Chinese response significantly elevating the intensity of the Peking-Moscow quarrel. Chinese spokesmen warned against the dangers of negotiating with the still-murderous imperialists and claimed that while a peaceful resolution of global contradictions was a possibility, Socialist humanity would survive if war should occur and, with the debris of capitalism, could build an even greater, flourishing Communist society.

The U-2 incident in 1960, after which the Soviets cancelled the Paris conference, vindicated to the Chinese their long-held position on the treacherous nature of Western imperialism. Forsaking prudence, Chinese representatives openly criticized the Soviet party in various international Communist organizations and did so even at the 1960 Moscow conference of ruling Marxist parties. In turn, the Chinese criticisms were vigorously contested by Soviet polemicists, who stressed Lenin's advocacy of peaceful coexistence to assure socialist survival and prosperity. Later that same year, Khrushchev's indignation with Chinese criticisms, themselves becoming increasingly personal, and lack of cooperation led him to terminate all Soviet aid programs in China; he also withdrew all Soviet advisors, many of whom took blueprints with them of half-finished factories. Moscow probably hoped this unilateral action would force China to return to properly obedient and respectful behavior.

By late 1960 a conflict was fast developing between the two largest Communist states in which the magnitude of dispute was essentially greater than the sum of its parts. Foreign policy disagreements, mutual domestic interference, dissimilar domestic experiences, ideological confict, and to some extent American actions in the early 1950s was rending the Sino-Soviet partnership asunder.

Notes

The material in this essay is based on two chapters in my *Cracking the Monolith: US Policy Against the Sino-Soviet Alliance, 1949–1955* (Baton Rouge: Louisiana State University Press, 1986). I am very grateful to the editors of LSU Press for granting me permission to use this material again.

1. CIA Special Estimate, "Probable Consequences of the Death of Stalin and the Elevation of Malenkov to Leadership in the USSR," 10 March 1953, C. D. Jackson Papers.

2. C. L. Sulzberger, *A Long Row of Candles* (New York: Macmillan, 1959), 778–79.

3. Voice of America, "Ceremony at Harbin," 7 January 1953.

4. Voice of America, "Friendship Treaty Bargain Rates," 13 February 1954.

5. Voice of America, (title illegible), 16 February 1953.

6. Voice of America, "Time for Decisions in China," 6 March 1953.

7. Harold Stassen, memorandum: "Stalin's Death," 10 March 1953, C. D. Jackson Papers.

8. P. Bridgham, A. Cohen, L. Jaffe, "Mao's Road and Sino-Soviet Relations: A View from Washington, 1953," *China Quarterly* 52 (October-December 1972): 670–98.

9. Admiral Zacharias to Sherman Adams, 9 May 1953, OF 8-c/18-d (1), Eisenhower Library.

10. *Foreign Relations of the United States, 1952–1954*, 3: 640. Hereafter FRUS.

11. Karl Rankin, *China Assignment* (Seattle: University of Washington Press, 1964), 173.

12. *FRUS 1949*, 8: 412–13.

13. See Dulles's memorandum for Acheson, 30 November 1950, box 47 Dulles Papers and Dulles-Bowles correspondence, 23 April 1952 and 1 May 1952, box 58 Dulles Papers.

14. Dulles interview on "Meet the Press" transcript, 10 February 1952.

15. Dulles, memorandum of conversation with George Yeh and Dr. Wellington Koo, 14 November 1952, Dulles Papers.

16. NSC 166/1, 6 November 1953, NSC File, Modern Military Branch, NA.

17. *FRUS 1952–54*, 3: 711.

18. Ibid., 711.

19. Ibid., 712–13.

20. *Congressional Record*, 14 January 1954, 232–33.

21. Sulzberger, *Candles*, 1003.

22. Dulles, speech to Overseas Press Club of America, 29 May 1954, Dulles Papers.

23. *FRUS 1952–54*, 16: 4.

24. *FRUS 1952–54*, 3: 733.

25. *Providence Journal*, 3 January 1954.

26. *Congressional Record*, 14 January 1954, 232–33.

27. Melvin Gurtov, "China's Perceptions of the Indochina Crisis 1953–1954," in *Peking's Approach to Negotiation* (Washington: Government Printing Office, 1969), 21–25.

28. Ibid., 25.

29. *FRUS 1952–54*, 16: 435, 483, 520.

30. Anthony Eden, *Full Circle* (London: Cassell, 1960), 121; *FRUS 1952–54*, 16, 875.

31. Robert Sutter, *China Watch* (Baltimore: Johns Hopkins University Press, 1978), 334, 126.

32. Dulles to Senator Knowland, 30 June 1954, Dulles Papers.

33. Ibid.

34. Ibid.

35. *FRUS 1952–54*, 16: 621.

36. National Intelligence Estimate, "Communist China's Power Potential Through 1957," 3 June 1954, *Declassified Documents Quarterly* 3 (No. 1):5.

37. Sulzberger, *Candles*, 1004.

38. J. H. Kalicki, *The Pattern of Sino-American Crises* (London: Cambridge University Press, 1975), 137.

39. *New York Times*, 23 February 1955.

40. Nikita Khrushchev, *Khrushchev Remembers* (Boston: Little, Brown, 1970), 466.

41. Ibid., 465–66.

42. Robert Amory, address, "The Current World Situation," 29 March 1955, *Declassified Documents Quarterly* 5 (No.1): 25.

43. NSC 5429/5, 22 December 1954, NSC File, Modern Military Branch, NA.

44. Raymond Garthoff, *Sino-Soviet Military Relations* (New York: Praeger Publishers, 1966), 88.

45. Luce to Eisenhower, 22 January 1955, Eisenhower Papers.

46. Harold Macmillan, *Tides of Fortune* (London: Macmillan Press, 1969), 533.

47. Memorandum: "Discussion at the 271st Meeting of the NSC," 23 December 1955, Eisenhower Papers.

48. National Intelligence Estimate, "Communist Courses of Action in Asia Through 1957," 23 November 1954, *Declassified Documents Quarterly* 3 (No. 1): 3.

49. Ibid.

50. National Intelligence Estimate, "Communist Capabilities and Intentions with Respect to the Offshore Islands and Taiwan, 1955," 16 March 1955, *Declassified Documents Quarterly* 1 (No. 1): 1.

51. Dwight D. Eisenhower, *Mandate for Change, 1953–1956: The White House Years.* (Garden City, N. Y.: Doubleday, 1963), 479.

52. NSC 5440/1, 28 December 1954, NSC File, Modern Military Branch, NA.

53. Ibid.

54. Eden *Full Circle,* 311.

55. *New York Times,* 26 July 1955.

56. Soviet Goals at Geneva, April 1955, Dulles Papers.

57. Macmillan, *Tides of Fortune,* 619.

58. Andre Fontaine, *History of the Cold War,* 1 (London: Secker and Warburg, 1965), 133.

59. United States Post-Geneva Policy, 15 August 1955, Dulles Papers.

60. *Psychological Aspects of US Strategy: Source Book,* "Discrete Problems of the Far East," 67.

61. Voice of America, "China's Population and Soviet Empty Space," 18 July 1955.

62. Voice of America, "Peiping's Interest in Outer Mongolia," 25 August 1955.

63. NSC 5412/2, 28 December 1955, NSC File, Modern Military Branch, NA.

64. *New York Times,* 24 April 1955.

65. "Estimate of Prospects of Soviet Union Achieving Its Goals," April 1955, Dulles Papers.

66. "Potential Markets in the Sino-Soviet Bloc for US Surplus Agricultural Products," 12 August 1955, box 8, Clarence Francis Papers.

67. Office of Intelligence Research, Department of State: "Asian Communist Orbit," January 1956, RG 59, NA.

68. John Gittings, *Survey of the Sino-Soviet Dispute* (London: Oxford University Press, 1968), 92.

69. Edward Freers, Dulles Oral History, 13–14, Princeton.

Between the Unattainable and the Unacceptable
Eisenhower and Dienbienphu

Richard H. Immerman

"I finally had a talk with Radford," Donald Heath, United States ambassador to Vietnam, Laos, and Cambodia wrote to the State Department's Director of Philippine and Southeast Asian Affairs, Philip Bonsal, on America's Independence Day in 1954. "Radford told me that one afternoon last spring the Government was almost decided to intervene with aviation to save Dien Bien Phu. Radford said that he was convinced that throwing in our aviation would have saved Dien Bien Phu and our whole position in Southeast Asia would have been much stronger. His idea is that after intervening to save that fortress we could have withdrawn our aviation. He said unfortunately, however, the attitude of Washington toward our intervention was 'conventional'."[1]

The fall of the French fortress of Dienbienphu to the Communist-led Vietminh insurgents on May 7 dismayed many Americans in 1954, and Chairman of the Joint Chiefs of Staff Admiral Arthur Radford was but one of the key Washington actors who regretted that the United States had not provided France with more assistance, even if that assistance included direct military intervention. President Dwight D. Eisenhower himself confided to Heath that he continued to wonder "whether there was anything he might have done to have persuaded the French to internationalize the Indo-Chinese war."[2] In retrospect, however, after America's subsequent military involvement had resulted in the deaths of close to sixty thousand of its citizens, destroyed the lives of so many more, and nonetheless failed to prevent a Communist victory, the 1954 decision against active intervention took on a much more positive cast. Indeed, with increasing frequency it is cited to illustrate that far from being a bland, do-nothing president, Eisenhower was a shrewd, often devious leader whose perspicacity enabled him to avoid the pitfalls of his successors.[3]

Notwithstanding the prominent role played by the decision not to intervene in this "Eisenhower revisionism," the administration's handling of the Dienbienphu crisis remains shrouded in controversy and confusion. Owing to incomplete or misleading source material, ethnocentric bias, partisanship, or self-interest, scholars, journalists, and memoirists have advanced widely divergent and conflicting interpretations of the complex events.[4] An abundance of recently declassified documents clarifies many of the most salient issues and underscores that none of the previous accounts is wholly sufficient. Because Eisenhower's policy toward Indochina was such a significant episode of his presidency, the new documentation requires its reconsideration.

The situation in Indochina had not reached crisis proportions when Eisenhower took office, and his early national security agenda was crowded with such pressing issues as shaping the New Look defense posture and discussing means to settle the Korean conflict. Still, the administration neither neglected Indochina nor challenged its predecessor's commitment to support the French effort. Less than three weeks into the term Secretary of State John Foster Dulles clearly spelled out the government's position to appropriate representatives from the JCS and Mutual Security Administration. "If Southeast Asia were lost," Dulles explained, "this would lead to the loss of Japan. The situation of the Japanese is hard enough with China being commie. You would not lose Japan immediately, but from there on out the Japs would be thinking of how to get on the other side."[5]

By March, the JCS had recommended a strategy for keeping the Asian dominoes from falling. Outlining the military's position, Army Chief of Staff General Joseph Collins maintained in a memorandum ominously titled "Broadening the Participation of the United States in the Indochina Operation" that the United States need not become directly involved in the fighting. It would, however, have to provide the French with greater financial and material support. Most important, it must bring pressure on Paris to develop a more effective strategy, to augment the native troops, and to provide the natives with additional incentives by granting them increased autonomy.[6]

Implementing the JCS's recommendations proved extremely difficult. Not only was the budget- and Korean-conscious Congress threatening to cut current appropriations for Indochina, but Paris also resisted appeals to revise its strategy, expand the size and role of the indigenous forces, and agree to the Associated States's independence.[7] "If the

French were completely honest they would get out of Indochina,"
Dulles remarked on the administration's lack of leverage, "and we
certainly don't want that."[8] Yet if they continued to balk at the JCS's
suggestions, said Air Force chief General Hoyt Vandenberg in presenting the dilemma's other side, "we will be pouring money down a
rathole."[9]

Although not completely satisfied, Washington viewed developments
during the summer of 1953 as encouraging. To begin with, in France
Joseph Laniel succeeded Rene Mayer as prime minister and pledged to
"perfect" Indochinese independence. Concurrently, in Indochina
Henri Navarre replaced Raoul Salan as French commander. After consultations with an American advisory mission led by General John "Iron
Mike" O'Daniel, Navarre submitted a battle plan more in line with the
JCS's position. Paris, the French general proposed, would increase its
forces and accelerate its program to train native troops. Navarre would
then concentrate the resulting combination in the Red River Delta,
where it could overwhelm the Vietminh strongholds. The anticommunist Vietnamese could assume responsibility for pacification. According
to O'Daniel, this strategy promised to bring the war to a "successful
conclusion."[10]

On learning of the "Navarre Plan," neither the White House nor the
JCS was nearly as sanguine as O'Daniel. The price tag was $400 million,
and there was no guarantee that Navarre would pursue it aggressively.
Yet alternatives to accepting it were fraught with danger. Washington
had but two options from which to choose: back the Navarre Plan or
"begin to consider most seriously whether to take over in this area,"
opined the State Department policy planning staff.[11] Navy Chief Admiral Robert Carney was even more blunt: Either support the Navarre
Plan or Vietnam "is going to be right in our laps."[12]

Predictably but uncomfortably, therefore, on September 9 the National Security Council recommended that Washington extend to
France an additional $385 million in order to effect the Navarre Plan.[13]
Eisenhower immediately granted his approval, and after Paris publicly
reiterated its resolve to "perfect" independence and "make every effort
to break up and destroy" the insurgents, Congress voted the appropriation.[14] In December, nevertheless, Navarre responded to a Vietminh
incursion into Laos by revising his strategy. He launched an offensive
south of the Red River Delta and then collected some twelve thousand
of his elite troops at Dienbienphu in Vietnam's northwest corner. Com-
manded by Vo Nguyen Giap, the Vietminh circled back. Dienbienphu
was under siege.[15]

Eisenhower had hoped that by supporting the Navarre Plan he could avert deciding whether to commit U.S. forces. The five-star general fully understood that Vietnam was ill-suited to America's style of warfare. "The jungles of Indochina would have swallowed up division after division of U.S. troops. . .," he later wrote. "Furthermore, the presence of ever more numbers of white men in uniform would have probably aggravated rather than assuaged the resentment held by Asiatics."[16] In fact, as early as 1951 he had entered in his diary, "I am convinced no military victory is possible in that kind of theater."[17]

Yet the domino theory demanded that victory be denied the Vietminh, and the president needed to plan for a potential French defeat or withdrawal. He directed Robert Cutler and the NSC planning board to conduct a thorough review. Cutler produced a general statement of policy and objectives coupled with a special annex dealing with a French collapse or, perhaps equally bad, request for direct U.S. intervention. He presented the draft of NSC 177 to the full council on January 8.[18]

Although before the meeting Eisenhower had stipulated that the annex would be recalled once the day's discussion had concluded, indicating he was not yet prepared to make any decisions concerning military participation, he made certain that the deliberations focused squarely on that issue. "For himself," the president stated, "with great force" as soon as Cutler had completed his summary of the draft, "he simply could not imagine the United States putting ground forces anywhere in Southeast Asia, except possibly in Malaya which we would have to defend as a bulwark to our off-shore island chain. But to do this anywhere else . . . said the President with vehemence, [I cannot tell you] how bitterly opposed I am to such a course of action."[19]

Rather than stifle expressions of alternate viewpoints, Eisenhower's forceful statement sparked a wide-ranging yet detailed debate. All the NSC participants agreed that the fundamental policy objective must be "to prevent the countries of Southeast Asia from passing into the Communist orbit."[20] Disagreements immediately surfaced, however, regarding advisable methods to achieve the objective. Despite Eisenhower's apparent rejection of U.S. overt participation, the membership actively considered that option. Radford, avoiding mention of American troops, recalled that while Commander-in-Chief, Pacific Command (CINCPAC) he had had plans drawn up to provide U.S. air support. "He now felt that US should do everything possible to forestall a French defeat at Dienbienphu. Indeed, if necessary we should send an aircraft carrier to assist the French if they appear to be in danger of losing this strong point." Radford's implications alarmed Secretary of the Treasury George Humphrey. "When we start putting our men into Indochina, how long will it be before we get into the war? And," Humphrey continued, "can we afford to get into such a war?" Radford had a simple response. "We already had a lot of men in Indochina now, though none of them in combat operations. We are really in this war today in a big way."[21]

With the discussion now centered on the critical issue, Eisenhower again spoke out. He was no longer the unequivocal "dove" categorically opposed to U.S. involvement. Rather, he seemed to meet Radford half-way. "Even if we did not send pilots," he stated, "we could certainly send planes and men to take over the maintenance of the planes." Moreover, "It was certainly going to be necessary to work out some way by which our planes could be used. Obviously we couldn't just fly them into combat off the carrier." Repeating his earlier opinion, the president expressed his adamant desire to "keep our men out of the jungles." But this time he included a qualifier. "We could nevertheless not forget our vital interest in Indochina."[22]

At least to Cutler and Humphrey, the qualifier suggested that Eisenhower had shifted his position. Cutler made known his strong opposition to U.S. participation, and Humphrey asked Eisenhower point blank, "Suppose the French were to give up and turn the whole country over to the Communists. Would the United States then interfere?" The president replied no, but "we had better go to full mobilization." Speaking to Humphrey directly he continued, "What you've got here is a leaky dike, and with leaky dikes, it's sometimes better to put a finger in than to let the whole structure be washed away."[23]

Eisenhower, it seemed, had come full circle and had now aligned himself with Radford. When Cutler suggested that Washington place a French finger in the dike, the president and JCS chairman chorused in unison that the French had been the problem for all these years. "If we could put one squadron of U.S. planes over Dien Bien Phu for as little as one afternoon," Radford speculated, "it might save the situation. Weren't the stakes worth it?" Eisenhower had already asserted that they were. Musing about "a little group of fine and adventurous pilots," the president projected a scenario in which unmarked U.S. planes saved Dienbienphu without "involving us directly in the war, which he admitted would be a very dangerous thing." Radford posited that such an arrangement could be worked out.[24]

Because the debate illustrated the lack of accord within the NSC, and because no danger of an imminent collapse existed, Eisenhower directed the Defense Department in conjunction with the Central Intelligence Agency to undertake a study of additional steps Washington might take to assist the French effort.[25] The next week the NSC approved the general policy statement divorced from the controversial special annex. In order to prevent the fall of any Southeast Asian country to the Communists, NSC 5405 (it had been renumbered) read, the U.S. should, "without relieving France of its basic responsibilities for the defense of the Associated States, expedite the provision of, and if necessary increase, aid to the French Union forces, under terms of existing commitments . . . [and] encourage further steps by both France and the Associated States to produce a working relationship based on equal sovereignty within the general framework of the French Union.'"[26] Official policy, therefore, went little beyond Truman's NSC 124/2, approved in June 1952.[27]

More significantly, the same day Eisenhower approved NSC 5405 he held a meeting in the Oval Office with his chief national security advisors. Following its conclusion, he directed Undersecretary of State Walter Bedell Smith, Deputy Secretary of Defense Roger Kyes, Special Assistant to the President C. D. Jackson, Radford, and CIA Director Allen Dulles to form a special committee to "come up with a plan in specific terms, covering who does what and with which and to whom." "What was really lacking was an *area* plan," the president complained, "including possible alternative lines of action to be taken in case of a reverse in Indo China, or elsewhere in the area." Accenting the extraordinary nature of the committee's assignment, Eisenhower "specifically stated that he considered this group a self-contained one to recommend the necessary action, and that neither NSC nor OCB [Operations Coordinating Board, established September 3, 1953, to coordinate implementation] need be cut in on the deliberations."[28]

With Navarre's recent request that the United States send to Indochina more than twenty additional B-26s and four hundred mechanics to service them at the top of its agenda, the special committee met for the first time on January 29. None of the members objected to arranging for the aircraft, but sending in American personnel was another matter. Smith thought that two hundred technicians would be sufficient, but when Radford advised him that they would be stationed on air bases entirely secure from capture, the undersecretary changed his recommendation to support the full four hundred. Kyes, conversely, was wary of sending any Americans at all. Might this not be just the first step he questioned, so that the administration "must be prepared eventually for complete intervention, including use of U.S. combat forces?" Smith did not think so. "He felt, however, that the importance of winning in Indochina was so great that if worst came to worst he personally would favor intervention with U.S. air and naval forces— not ground forces." Not surprisingly, Radford immediately concurred with Smith's assessment. The committee compromised by agreeing to recommend the two hundred figure, and to leave it up to the president to make the ultimate decision. That same day Eisenhower signed off on the committee's recommendation.[29]

Also on that day's agenda was a report by General Graves B. Erskine, the Department of Defense's director of the Office of Special Operations. Kyes had requested Erskine to study "other general courses of action" to be used as "a point of departure for further work" by the committee. After the retired general read his report, Radford commented that although it covered many important areas, it was still too limited. He proposed that Erskine redraft the paper to include two parts. The first would continue along the lines of the present version, dealing exclusively with continuing support for the Navarre Plan. The second, however, would address "what should be done to prepare against the contingency where U.S. combat forces would be needed." After all, the Admiral explained, "The U.S. could not afford to let the Vietminh take the Tonkin Delta. If this were lost, Indochina would be lost and the rest of Southeast Asia would fall."[30]

The committee agreed with Radford's proposal. In addition, to assist Erskine it set up a special working group comprised of its members' representatives. But although the working group had revised part one of the Erskine paper by February 6, the special committee had had to delay reviewing it.[31] Several of its members were preoccupied trying to implement the decision to send the technicians. Eisenhower's announcement of the decision had elicited widespread concern from the press and Congress.[32] The president tried to quiet the opposition by being as candid as possible. "Don't think I like to send them there," he had told the legislative leaders on February 8, "but after all . . . we can't get anywhere in Asia by just sitting here in Washington and doing nothing. My God, we must not lose Asia—we've got to look the thing right in the face."[33] Still, to guard against another move to cut appropriations, Eisenhower promised to bring the technicians back by June 15. (He confided to Dulles, nonetheless, that if necessary he would recruit civilian technicians to take their place.)[34]

The pledge was necessary but not sufficient. Eisenhower realized that Congress's uneasiness was due to more than just the technicians. The technicians were a "symptom." The "disease" was the special committee. A February 4 CBS broadcast had divulged the committee's existence. Eisenhower was furious.[35] He was much too attentive to public opinion—and to congressional relations—to fail to connect the outcry over the technicians with the leak. For him to have any chance of obtaining future support for a commitment of more than U.S. maintenance personnel, he could not afford to let Congress think that the special committee was now plotting such a course in secret. The leak had undercut congressional confidence in the administration. Eisenhower sought to restore it.

Hence when they might otherwise have been studying the new Erskine report, Smith, Radford, and other top advisors were presenting lengthy testimony before the Executive Sessions of the Senate Foreign Relations and House Foreign Affairs Committees. At both hearings the fundamental question was the same: What would the administration propose if the French suffered a disastrous defeat at Dienbienphu and decided to pull out? At both hearings Eisenhower's representatives gave the same answer. To cite Smith only, the French would not pull out because such an action would undoubtedly lead to the slaughter of hundreds of innocent Frenchmen. Nevertheless, should "we see ourselves suddenly confronted with the loss of Indochina, and possibly the resultant loss of much of Southeast Asia to the Communists, there would be a situation created which would make it necessary for the President to come to the Congress and ask for its advice and consent to take more drastic means." Even if China intervened, Smith assured the congressmen, "We would not go into any all-out war . . . or even approach it without coming to Congress and asking for its decision."[36]

The hearings highlight that the decision to send the technicians and the leak over the special committee opened the Pandora's box of possible U.S. intervention. It was opened further still by changing international conditions. Dulles did not testify before Congress because even as the hearings were being held he was attending the Berlin Conference, suffering a serious diplomatic defeat. Dulles had gone to Berlin fully cognizant of and unalterably opposed to Paris's desire to place Indochina on the agenda of the forthcoming Geneva talks. Any negotiations at all, the administration felt, would provide the Vietminh with an added incentive and concomitantly erode French and noncommunist Vietnamese morale. Dulles had vigorously presented this position to French Foreign Minister Georges Bidault, threatening that the United States might refuse to attend Geneva if the agenda included Indochina. Bidault had retorted with equal vigor that the political situation in France required negotiations. To omit Indochina from the agenda would gravely jeopardize the viability of the Laniel government and, as a consequence, virtually assure France's rejecting the European Defense Community (EDC). Dulles had no choice but to give in. "If we had vetoed the resolution regarding Indochina," he explained to the NSC, "it would probably have cost us French membership in EDC as well as Indochina itself."[37]

The decision to discuss Indochina at Geneva represented another turning point in the mounting crisis. For the United States, it would no longer be enough just to develop policies to avert a French defeat at Dienbienphu in the hope that the tide could be turned later. As the situation currently stood, the Vietminh would hold most of the cards when the parties met to negotiate a settlement. "What is the plan if there is a negotiated peace in Indochina as a result of the Geneva Conference; where does this leave us?" Hubert Humphrey thus quite logically asked Dulles upon the secretary's return from Berlin. Undoubtedly Dulles was asking himself the same question. In the administration's view, America's objectives demanded a French military victory. He could only lamely respond to Humphrey that the Navarre Plan remained sound.[38] With only a few months left before Geneva, nevertheless, Dulles had to be more realistic. "Prospect of conference on Indo-China will increase Communist effort for knockout this season," he lamented to Smith the day Berlin adjourned, "and must be met with corresponding determination to win good negotiating position."[39] But how?

By the middle of March, it appeared that direct American intervention might be the only answer. Despite optimistic forecasts by O'Daniel, Navarre, and Radford, the outlook for maintaining a stalemate, let alone turning the tide, deteriorated precipitously.[40] On March 13, heavily reinforced Vietminh units launched an all-out assault on Dienbienphu, while a coordinated artillery barrage crippled the French air strips. "The fighters are fanatical, and the forts that were overrun had some of the best troops," Allen Dulles reported to his brother on the sixteenth. In the CIA's estimation, "there is a 50-50 chance we will hold."[41]

Of course, should the French fail to hold, should they not have "the stamina to stick it out," U.S. intervention might be the sole means to prevent the toppling of successive dominoes. Only two weeks before the Vietminh assault, Erskine's working group, upon completing the first part of its study, had recommended that the Department of Defense "develop . . . a concept of operations and considerations involved in the use of U.S. armed forces in Indo-China, should such involvement be determined upon."[42] Then, on March 12, the JCS wrote Secretary of Defense Charles Wilson on the ramifications of Geneva. According to the service chiefs, if the conference resulted in a negotiated settlement, it would "in all probability lead to the loss of Indochina to the Communists and deal a damaging blow to the national will of other countries of the Far East to oppose Communism." Thus, the "continuation of the fighting with the objective of seeking a military victory appears as the only alternative to acceptance of a compromise [i.e., unacceptable] settlement. . . ." To this end, the JCS recommended that the NSC consider now the extent to which the United States would be willing to commit its forces in concert with the French, other allies, or, if necessary, unilaterally.[43]

The NSC meeting of March 25 concentrated on the JCS memorandum. In doing so the participants found themselves confronted with the same problem that had been left unresolved in January. They were no closer to a solution. Wilson raised the possibility of "forget[ting] about Indochina for a while and concentrat[ing] on the effort to get the remaining free nations of Southeast Asia in some sort of condition to resist Communist aggression against themselves." Eisenhower put this idea to rest with the rejoinder that "the collapse of Indochina would produce a chain reaction which would result in the fall of all Southeast Asia to the Communists." Perhaps, he went on, "this might be the moment to explore with the Congress what support could be anticipated in the event that it seemed desirable to intervene in Indochina." Congress would "have to be in on any move by the United States to intervene in Indochina," the president flatly declared. "It was simply academic to think otherwise." The council responded to Eisenhower's unmistakable implication by directing the planning board once again to produce a detailed recommendation on intervention. Recalled on January 8, the special annex to NSC 177 was resurrected.[44]

The onrush of events, however, would not await NSC deliberations. General Paul Ely was already in Washington. Ely had been invited to discuss an increase in the flow of U.S. material to Indochina, but the Pentagon suspected that the French chief of staff would tell Washington that in light of the recent reversals Navarre could not hope to achieve victory in either 1954 or 1955, and for him to continue the United States would have to commit military forces. If this suspicion turned out to be correct, the administration's recurrent nightmare would become a reality. "I dreamt last night," Bonsal had written Heath apocalyptically a month before, "that Plevan [Ely] arrived in Washington and told us that the French had decided to get out of Indochina unless we are prepared to put in two or three divisions within ninety days."[45]

Conversations with Ely began on Saturday evening, March 20, over dinner at Radford's home. The subject of direct U.S. involvement did not arise.[46] Moreover, when Ely formally met with all the service chiefs the following Monday, he "dodged all questions of US troop participation in Indochina and on French plans in the event that peace is not obtained at Geneva."[47] Undoubtedly the general realized that he was engaged in a game of international cat and mouse. Neither Paris nor Washington wanted to reveal its future intentions until it received some type of indication about what the other was planning. Because the JCS did not have the authority to speak for Eisenhower, Ely had nothing to gain by answering their "broad political questions."[48]

That was not the case when Radford brought Secretary Dulles with him the next day. To most observers in the 1950s, Dulles reigned supreme over America's foreign policy. Hence Ely was more forthcoming. Apparently still unwilling to broach directly the question of America's plans should the French face imminent defeat at Dienbienphu, he brought up a less likely development. Could Dulles give him an idea of the administration's policy in the event the Chinese Communists intervened with MIGs? Would the United States respond in kind? Dulles adroitly circumvented the trap. The issue was an extremely important one, he replied, but one that involved too many factors for him even to venture an opinion. The secretary then turned the question around so as to serve his purpose, that of expressing America's disappointment over France's general conduct. "If the French wanted our open participation in the Indochina war. . . . they ought also to consider that this might involve a greater degree of partnership than had prevailed up to this time, notably in relationship to independence for the Associated States and the training of indigenous forces," he commented. "The United States would hesitate to participate in the fighting in Indochina on the basis of uncertainty as to the political relations necessary for a successful outcome." France had to keep in mind, Dulles concluded, "that if the United States sends its flag and its own military establishment—land, sea or air—into the Indochina war, then the prestige of the United States would be engaged. . . . We could not afford thus to engage the prestige of the United States and suffer a defeat which would have worldwide repercussion."[49]

Despite the diplomatic tone of Dulles's remarks, he had made his point unequivocally. The feeling of congeniality that Ely had sensed during his first days in Washington evaporated, and the meeting ended abruptly.[50] Early the next morning Dulles went to see Eisenhower. The president assured his chief foreign policy advisor that he "agreed basically" with what he had said. However, seemingly going beyond the position implied by the secretary's remarks, Eisenhower added that he would "not wholly exclude the possibility of a single strike, if it were almost certain to produce decisive results."[51] Moreover, from then on Radford conducted all the discussions. No more successful than Dulles in winning acceptance for a larger American role in training the Vietnamese and determining strategy, he convinced Ely to stay over an extra day in order to take up the general's memorandum on the question of U.S. policy in the event of Chinese intervention. "We should not answer their paper until we get a lot of answers from them," Dulles

advised the admiral. He would not like to see the United States intervene under any conditions "until we had better assurances from the
French that we can work effectively together." Any commitments, the
secretary maintained, would have far-reaching implications.[52]

The results of this March 26 Radford-Ely meeting remain murky.
They did exchange a nebulous "minute" agreeing that "it was advisable
that military authorities push through their planning work as far as
possible so that there would be no time wasted when and if our governments decided to oppose enemy air intervention over Indo-China if it
took place. . . ." But the minute referred only to Ely's memorandum,
and the discussion went much further. Rather than confine their talk to
the single contingency of Chinese intervention, the two addressed the
possibility of an American air strike to relieve the besieged fortress.[53]
The idea was not new. Both Ely and Radford unquestionably knew of
a plan—code name VULTURE—apparently conceived by French and
American military officers in Saigon that called for a massive nighttime
bombing attack on Vietminh positions. Ely later claimed that Radford
enthusiastically endorsed the plan and intimated that regardless of
Dulles's reservations he could obtain Eisenhower's support. Radford
admitted only that he told Ely he could arrange for U.S. aircraft to
reach Dienbienphu within two days of a formal request. Authorization,
nevertheless, could only come from the president and Congress.[54]

Possibly the two men simply misunderstood each other. This was the
only meeting at which they did not use an interpreter. They spoke in
English, in which Ely was conversant but hardly fluent.[55] It is also
possible that Ely heard what he wanted to hear, that in his eagerness
to receive assurances of overt U.S. support he overreacted to Radford's
hypotheses. Yet in all probability, Ely received the impression that
Radford intended. The JCS chairman personally favored an air strike,
and he may well have feared that Ely's unsatisfactory talk with Dulles
would adversely affect France's commitment to continue. His morale
needed a boost. In this regard, because the objective of NSC 5405 was
to prevent a Vietminh victory, because in conjunction with the military
the planning board was currently developing a concept of operations,
and because Eisenhower had frequently appeared to support Radford's
own position, the admiral had good reason to think he could obtain
approval for VULTURE. The president's conflicting remarks concerning U.S. intervention allowed his advisors sufficient latitude to interpret
them in a fashion consistent with their own predispositions. Radford
was predisposed toward VULTURE.

Whatever Radford did say to Ely, it had less effect on future U.S.
policy than a major address drafted by Dulles during this same period.

As was his custom, the secretary received background memoranda from his staff and then wrote the speech himself. He also talked it over with leading congressmen of both parties lest they "say they were not advised."[56] He did not, evidently, consult Radford. In fact, when Deputy Secretary of State for Political Affairs Robert Murphy briefly alluded to the speech at a March 26 State-JCS meeting, he dismissed it casually as containing "nothing new or startling in the way of policy."[57]

On one level Murphy was correct. Dulles's "United Action" speech, delivered to the Overseas Press Club on March 29, presented more of a guideline for policy than an actual statement of policy. Following the themes of the Monroe Doctrine, the secretary called for the formation of a coalition composed of the United States, Great Britain, France, Australia, New Zealand, Thailand, the Philippines, and the Associated States which could pledge collectively to defend Indochina and the rest of Southeast Asia against Communist aggression.[58] United Action was not "new or startling." It articulated and labeled a concept discussed for months within the administration. Moreover, Dulles was purposely vague in defining the scope of the coalition's potential responsibilities. His deputy Robert Bowie recalled that the secretary "definitely picked" his words to sound "menacing without committing anybody to anything." Dulles himself conceded that he intended the speech primarily "for consumption in France," hoping that it would "puncture the sentiment for appeasement" and encourage Paris not to take the easy way out of Geneva. The "menacing" language might also "have a deterrent effect" on the Chinese Communists, he thought, thereby possibly averting a development that would require U.S. intervention.[59]

Yet on another level the speech was "new and startling." Eisenhower had "carefully considered" the wording, and, without challenging Dulles's stated intention to bolster French morale and deter the Chinese, it is inconceivable that the president did not envisage United Action as a vehicle to prepare Americans for the possibility of intervention.[60] It could not have been a coincidence that he had Dulles publicly describe the situation in such menacing terms only four days after he had approved the planning board's resurrection of the special annex and suggested that the time might have come to explore "what support could be anticipated" if intervention seemed desirable.[61] Dulles and Eisenhower designed United Action to meet the many uncertainties of the Dienbienphu crisis. It left open the option of intervention in the event of a French defeat, Chinese intervention, or the collapse of Geneva while seeking to ensure that if such intervention did occur, it would be under favorable circumstances. The administration would have public and congressional support, the taint of French colonialism would be removed, and the United States could avoid fighting alone. America would provide air and naval support, allowing local and regional forces to bear the brunt of the ground action. Putting together a United Action coalition was a long shot; but given all the variables, to Eisenhower and Dulles it was the best shot they had.

Radford disagreed. An avid proponent of air power, he confidently predicted that a VULTURE-like strike could alter the military situation before Geneva, obviating the need to tie intervention to United Action. Therefore on March 29, the same day as Dulles's speech, Radford forwarded to the special committee a formal memorandum summarizing his talks with Ely. Point 15 read, "I am gravely fearful that the measures being undertaken by the French will prove inadequate and initiated too late to prevent a progressive deterioration of the situation in Indochina. If Dien Bien Phu is lost, this deterioration may occur very rapidly due to the loss of morale among the mass of native population. In such a situation only prompt and forceful intervention by the United States could avert the loss of all of South East Asia to Communist domination."[62]

New Army Chief of Staff Matthew Ridgway objected to the memorandum. Written on JCS stationery, it might easily be construed, he feared, "as the official expression of the corporate views of the Joint Chiefs, and even as advocating U.S. armed intervention."[63] Ridgway's fears were not without foundation. Apparently on his own, on March 31 Radford called a special meeting of the JCS in order to consider the "necessity or desirability" of recommending that "an immediate offer of assistance by U.S. Naval and/or Air Force units be made to the French."[64] Ridgway reacted negatively to both the question of intervention and the meeting itself. In his opinion, "Unless the question emanated from proper authority, any such recommended action—for or against—was clearly outside the proper scope of authority of the JCS." To advocate any policy "would be to involve the JCS inevitably in politics."[65] The other chiefs, however, agreed to consider offering the French combat support. Unanimously they recommended against it.[66]

Radford refused to give up. Two days later he called another meeting to take up the same question. This time each chief submitted a written memorandum with his recommendation. Opinions had not changed. Only Air Force chief Nathan Twining answered with a "qualified 'Yes'." If the French accepted U.S. command of air and naval units, if they accepted U.S. leadership of the training and deployment of troops, if they agreed to train and organize indigenous forces under indigenous leadership, and if they granted the Associated States "true" sovereignty, then, Twining advised, Washington should make the offer.[67] Radford's hope to use the JCS to exert influence had backfired.

Even had Radford succeeded, it is unlikely that Eisenhower's ultimate policy would have evolved differently. It was axiomatic to Eisenhower that policy decisions had to be formulated in the context of the political support they could engender. Consequently, the administration had from the beginning taken pains to keep Congress briefed on developments in Vietnam. Now, as the crisis neared its climax, the president told his party's leadership that "at any time within the space of forty-eight hours it might be necessary to move into the battle of Dien Bien Phu in order to keep it from going against us, and in that case I will be calling in the Democrats as well as our Republican leaders to inform them of the actions we're taking."[68]

In the event, Eisenhower called in the Republicans and Democrats before he took action. He instructed Dulles to schedule a special meeting with leaders of both parties for Saturday, April 3, and on April 2 the two men met with Radford, Wilson, and Cutler to plan for it. Despite Eisenhower's comment to the Republican leaders, not even Radford, who by now was isolated, proposed that the administration seek congressional authorization "to move into the battle of Dien Bien Phu." "Outcome there would be determined within a matter of hours," the admiral conceded, "and the situation was not one which called for any U.S. participation."[69] The issue at hand was what to do in the event of a complete French withdrawal or, with Geneva less than a month away, its acquiescence to a disastrous settlement. Thus, rather than request Congress's sanction for immediate intervention, the conferees opted to propose a broad, blank-check resolution that would grant Eisenhower discretionary authority to use American air and sea power to prevent the "extension and expansion" of Communist aggression in Southeast Asia and "to defend the safety and security" of the United States. The authority would terminate on June 30, 1954, and would in no way "derogate from the authority of Congress to declare war."[70]

The proposed resolution, therefore, was the logical follow-up to the United Action speech. Both were conceived as deterrents to Communist aggression and, concomitantly, morale boosters for the French and Vietnamese. Both could be used to strengthen the Allied position at Geneva. The resolution, moreover, would greatly increase the chances of forming a United Action coalition, for without prior assurances of America's participation no other ally would be likely to commit its forces. Finally, should the administration decide to intervene, there would be little time for consultation and deliberation. To satisfy all the policy objectives, Eisenhower needed congressional support, and he needed it rapidly.

Conversely, if Congress categorically rejected intervention regardless of the circumstances, United Action would be stillborn, and, according to administration thinking, the Communists would receive a virtual green light in Indochina and at Geneva. To minimize this risk, the conferees decided that Eisenhower should remain discreetly in the background, lest his involvement connote that he had decided to push for intervention. To further avoid the potential appearance of a setback, the president insisted that the "tactical procedure should be to develop first the thinking of Congressional leaders without actually submitting in the first instance a resolution drafted by ourselves."[71]

The next day Dulles and Radford followed the procedure he had advised; the resolution was never submitted. For Congress to approve intervention, the leaders of both parties expressed collectively, "satisfactory commitments" would have to be obtained from the British and other Allies to participate in a concerted effort and from the French to "internationalize the war and grant the Indochinese independence. . . ." "Once the flag is committed," they warned, "the use of land forces would surely follow." Dulles countered by affirming that the administration had no plans to request sending ground troops, but it required a guarantee of America's intentions in order to obtain the necessary commitments from France and Britain. The leaders would not be swayed. Put together United Action first, they remonstrated, and then they would pass the resolution.[72] Following the meeting Dulles confided to Eisenhower that although it "went pretty well," the outcome did "raise some serious problems."[73]

Ironically, at the very same time that Eisenhower was meeting with his chief advisors to affirm the conditions for U.S. intervention, the French were concluding that U.S. intervention could no longer be postponed.[74] On April 4, Navarre cabled frantically that only an air strike could save Dienbienphu, and even then it had to be carried out by the middle of the month. When the cable arrived, Laniel, Bidault, and Ely were gathered at Matignon listening to the report of their most recent military mission to Saigon. Summoning Ambassador Douglas Dillon, they immediately requested VULTURE. Dillon, who of course knew nothing of what had just transpired in Washington, said only that he would send the request on to the proper authorities.[75]

Dillon's telegram reached Dulles shortly after eight the next morning, his time. He phoned Eisenhower immediately. The president was markedly upset. "In the absence of some kind of arrangement getting support of Congress," he exclaimed, "we cannot engage in active war." Radford, he complained, should have done nothing, even in the strictest of confidence, to have left Ely with the impression that the United States was prepared to intervene militarily. Dulles assured Eisenhower that no commitments had been made by anyone connected with the administration and that Radford was "quite reconciled to the fact that it is political impossibility at present time—has no idea of recommending this action."[76] The secretary then directed Dillon to tell Paris, "As I personally explained to Ely in presence of Radford, it is not possible for US to commit belligerent acts in Indochina without full political understanding with France and other countries. In addition, Congressional action would be required."[77]

Not until a day later would the NSC meet to consider the planning board's recommendations concerning U.S. intervention. Cutler had circulated a draft in advance, affording Ridgway the time to submit his well-known report. Ridgway maintained that a military victory in Indochina could not be achieved through air and naval forces alone, regardless of whether atomic weapons were employed. The United States would have to commit ground troops, and in much greater numbers than suggested by the planning board. (The draft included a new annex estimating the requirements for intervention.) This commitment would severely tax mobilization capacities and seriously affect America's contribution to NATO. Ridgway claimed that his analysis played a determining role in Eisenhower's ultimate decision.[78]

The evidence does not support Ridgway's claim. Evidently informed immediately of Radford's unsuccessful effort to garner JCS support for VULTURE, Eisenhower had stated at the April 1 NSC meeting that not only Ridgway but also all the service chiefs save the chairman were "opposed to an airstrike using U.S. planes and pilots."[79] Furthermore, although Ridgway attended the April 6 meeting, the minutes indicate that Radford alone spoke for the JCS. No mention was made of Ridgway's position.[80] Instead, "with great emphasis" Eisenhower asserted from the outset that "There was no possibility of U.S. unilateral intervention in Indochina, and we had best face that fact. . . . We would have to take it to Congress and fight for it like dogs, with very little hope of success." Dulles explained the reason for Eisenhower's adamance by recapping the results of the April 3 meeting, adding that on the president's authority he had begun to work on satisfying the conditions necessary to get a resolution through Congress. He then remarked that although it would be difficult to meet all the conditions, it was not impossible. The immediate issue was not the efficacy of an air strike but the formation of a United Action coalition, which might make military intervention unnecessary. "We know that under certain conditions Congress is likely to back us up. We should therefore place all our efforts on trying to organize a regional grouping for the defense of Southeast Asia prior to the opening of Geneva. If we can do so we will go into that Conference strong and united, with a good hope that we would come out of the Conference with the Communists backing down."[81]

Richard Nixon challenged Dulles's analysis. If Indochina fell, he argued, a regional defense organization might be able to prevent subsequent overt aggression. Yet it would have little effect on Communist subversion of neighboring states, which to Nixon was much more likely. "At some point or other," the vice-president remarked, "the United States must decide whether it is prepared to take action which will be effective in saving free governments from internal Communist subversion." George Humphrey used Nixon's criticism to take on Dulles from the opposite perspective. If the secretary "succeeded in creating his proposed coalition and the United States adopted a policy of intervening every time that local Communist forces became strong enough to attempt to subvert free governments," he asked, "would this not amount to a policy of policing all the governments of the world?"[82]

Eisenhower could not let Humphrey's question go unanswered. No free government, he lectured "sharply," had ever chosen communism. "Certainly the United States could no longer say that internal Communist subversion, as opposed to external Communist aggression, was none of our business. We had [*sic*] got to be a great deal more realistic than that." Humphrey shot back that once the United States undertook "to prevent the emergence of Communist governments everywhere in the world," there would be "no terminal point in such a process." Eisenhower retorted, "Indochina was the first in a row of dominoes. If it fell its neighbors would shortly thereafter fall with it, and where did the process end?" But this time the president spoke "with great warmth." "George," he assured his friend, "you exaggerate the case." Neither Dulles, Nixon, nor anyone else was proposing that the United States become a global policeman. Yet there were certain areas that the free world could not afford to lose. "Dien Bien Phu itself may be just such a critical point. . . . We are not prepared now to take action with respect to Dien Bien Phu in and by itself, but the coalition program for Southeast Asia must go forward as a matter of greatest urgency."[83]

That was that, and the exhaustive meeting came to a close. The NSC agreed that Washington would supplement its nonmilitary support for the French, postponing a decision on direct intervention.[84] Nixon later claimed that by consenting to postpone the decision Eisenhower "backed down" considerably from his former position, that he "seemed resigned to doing nothing at all unless we could get the allies and the country to go along with whatever was suggested and he did not seem inclined to put much pressure on to get them to come along."[85] Nixon is wrong. Eisenhower was no less a believer than his vice-president in the need to defend Indochina, nor had he in any sense ruled out VUL-TURE. However, as Nixon would learn so dramatically, defending Indochina required more than just saving Dienbienphu. Military inter-vention without domestic, allied, and Indochinese support might be a temporary expedient; its long-range consequences, nevertheless, could be disastrous. Given his own views and those of his advisors, Congress, and the public, Eisenhower calculated that he could not risk these consequences. But he did not "back down," and he certainly was inclined to use "pressure." It was on the day following this NSC meeting that Eisenhower first spelled out the " 'falling domino' prin-ciple" to the American people."[86] And three days later, Dulles em-barked on one of the most concentrated periods of diplomatic arm twisting in the nation's history.

As he had acknowledged, before the NSC had met Dulles had begun to sound out the Allies on United Action, even going so far as to leak the results of the "secret" meeting of April 3.[87] On April 10, the sec-retary left for London and Paris on "a mission of peace through strength."[88] The obstacles he encountered shuttling between the two capitals are well known. After extensive diplomatic haggling, all Dulles managed to accomplish was to persuade each government to agree obliquely to join in preliminary discussions of a collective security system for Southeast Asia.[89] Worse, Dulles had hardly arrived back in Washington on April 15 and extended invitations for an allied meeting when the very foundations of United Action were shaken. For Dulles to have any chance of turning Britain and France around he had to assure them that the United States would participate actively in any coalition and, paradoxically, the coalition would decrease the need to "internationalize" the war. A remark by Nixon on April 16, however, conveyed the impression of American saber rattling which, in turn, called into question the administration's ability to acquire congressional approval for United Action. Speaking before the American Society of Newspaper Editors, the vice-president answered a "hypothetical" question on how the United States would respond to a French collapse in Indochina by affirming that "we must take the risk by putting our boys in." The universal reaction was immediate and negative. Hence, at the very time that the administration was attempting to calm both congressional and allied fears concerning the administration's belligerence while simultaneously convincing the Communists that it was, in fact, belligerent, the statement and reaction threatened to elicit precisely the opposite effect.[90]

Conventionally regarded at the time and since as a trial balloon, Nixon's comments had not been authorized. Press Secretary James Hagerty described them as "foolish"; Dulles, as "unfortunate."[91] In an effort to minimize the damage and embarrassment, Eisenhower had the State Department issue a vague statement to "clarify" U.S. policy without "cutting the ground from under Nixon."[92] But two days later Dulles received a more serious setback when Britain declined his invitation to attend a meeting to discuss collective security arrangements for Southeast Asia. The secretary was furious, speculating that Foreign Secretary Anthony Eden had been influenced by India's neutralist Prime Minister Jawaharlal Nehru. London may also have been alarmed by the implications of the Nixon statement, thus fearing that attendance at the meeting would signify its endorsement of military intervention. Whatever the cause, Washington lost a prime opportunity to implement the policy of United Action. Having no choice but to accommodate himself to the situation, Dulles hastily altered the meeting's agenda so that it would deal in general terms with both the Korean and Indochinese phases of Geneva. He still presented his pitch for United Action, arguing that "The best hope for peaceful solution seemed to lie in creating such conditions that the Communists would realize their ambitions would encounter an obstacle so formidable as to oblige them to write off the area." The meeting, nonetheless, had lost its significance.[93]

With the opening of Geneva less than a week away and Allen Dulles predicting that "The chances are we are going to lose it [Dienbienphu]," Eisenhower and his secretary of state gamely tried one more time to obtain French and British support for the collective defense of Indochina.[94] Returning to Europe for the NATO conference scheduled for April 23, Dulles placed Washington's case before Anthony Eden. "We might be faced at Geneva with a sudden collapse of French will *re* Indochina," he reported to the foreign secretary. "If we took no steps and had no alternatives at Geneva our chances of achieving anything were very slight." Eden replied that he might consider private discussions concerning a regional defense coalition, but he had in mind a coalition to defend the region *after* Indochina fell. In any event, he wanted to get a better idea of what France planned to do before he made any recommendations.[95] The news Dulles received from France's Bidault was, if anything, more dismaying. "The situation in Dien Bien Phu was virtually hopeless," Bidault confirmed, and nothing could save it "except perhaps 'massive' air intervention which the US would have to supply." If Dienbienphu fell, he continued, the French would have little interest in United Action and would probably "want to pull out entirely from Southeast Asia . . . and the rest of us would have to get along without France in this area. He urged that our [the United States] government should give most serious consideration to armed intervention promptly as the only way to save the situation."[96]

To Dulles, the French minister appeared "totally exhausted mentally." By the next afternoon, he seemed "close to the breaking point." Bidault had shown Dulles an "urgent" cable from Navarre indicating that in the absence of U.S. flown bombing raids he would have no alternative but to arrange a cease-fire throughout Indochina. Consequently, Paris again requested VULTURE. According to Bidault's memoir, Dulles "looked glum." He did not even promise to support the request in Washington. Indeed, Bidault claimed that instead Dulles offered to give the French two atomic bombs.[97]

Bidault's assertion is highly implausible. No other evidence of the alleged offer exists in available French or American sources. Dulles had displayed little interest in discussing a JCS contingency plan which called for the dropping of three tactical atomic weapons *if the U.S. intervened*. After the administration had become resigned to losing Dienbienphu, Cutler and Eisenhower had considered *possibly* offering Paris atomic weapons; the record suggests nothing came of it. Dulles was at that time in Europe.[98] Throughout the crisis the secretary exhibited caution and restraint. The notion of using nuclear devices ran antithetical to his concern for world opinion, his fear of widening the war, and his objective of enlisting British support. It was one thing to threaten massive retaliation; it was another to retaliate massively.

What Dulles did do was tell Bidault that U.S. intervention was "out of the question under existing circumstances."[99] The first step in altering those circumstances was to get Britain's acceptance of United Action. Hence, for the next two days the secretary, along with Radford (who had just arrived in Paris), pressured Eden relentlessly. They warned him that without assurances of British and American support a French collapse was inevitable. The mere knowledge that a "common defense system was in prospect" would deter the Communists and strengthen the allied hand at Geneva. All the British would have to do, the Americans suggested, was to commit a few air squadrons from Malaya and Hong Kong. This would enable Eisenhower to receive the necessary authorization for VULTURE, which might just "stabilize the situation." Eden doubted that an air strike would stabilize Indochina; moreover, it would greatly increase the risk of Chinese intervention and, as a result, World War III. Radford responded that China's capacity for effective intervention was "very low" and posed no threat that could not be "dealt with." It would mean "hell at home" if Britain went along, Eden said in conclusion. Nevertheless, he promised to take the matter up in London with Churchill and the cabinet.[100]

Dulles assiduously reported the conferences to Eisenhower. The frustration that had been building up within the president over the past months boiled over. Upon learning of Eden's obstinance, he had Smith instruct Radford to follow the foreign secretary to London, suggesting that the admiral ask the British "baldly why they would prefer to fight after they had lost 200,000 French." Eisenhower then ordered Smith to begin drafting the message he would deliver when Dienbienphu fell.[101] Radford did fly to London, where he dined with Churchill at Chequers. Instead of obtaining the prime minister's endorsement for United Action, however, he received a lecture on how the British had lost India. He for one, Churchill exclaimed, was certainly not going to risk a nuclear holocaust to save Indochina for the French. "Before very long," he added, "he would have to render an account to his maker."[102] Radford also met with Eden and the British chiefs of staff. Whether he asked them Eisenhower's "bald" question cannot be determined. Apparently he was quite blunt. Eden complained to journalist Marquis Childs that the British were "very much disturbed and angered by Radford's coming over to London and trying to pressure the Cabinet and the Chiefs of Staff to come into Indochina with sea and air power. . . . The British had a suspicion that Radford wanted to use this as a means of launching what Eden said was 'Radford's war against China.'"[103]

On April 24 Eden flew to Geneva for the conference. He confronted Dulles with London's verdict. Britain would give the French "all possible support" at Geneva and, if a satisfactory settlement could not be achieved, it would join with the United States in exploring the possibilities for United Action. For the time being, however, "None of us in London believe that intervention can do anything," and it would be a "great mistake" in terms of world opinion. "It was definite that they were not prepared to fight in Indochina," Dulles cabled Washington the next day, "and they were not willing to have any conversations that assumed that premise." Not surprisingly, Dulles found the news "most disheartening."[104]

With the Geneva Conference opening, the administration could no longer postpone a decision on intervention. Either it would have to face what it feared would be a military, ergo diplomatic, disaster, or, it seemed, at least temporarily shelve United Action and intervene unilaterally, which would probably mean without congressional authorization. Indeed, the French pressed for "armed intervention by action" or some other "constitutional way to help."[105] Dulles advised that because U.S. security was not directly threatened, intervention "is not warranted." Further, "There would be no time to arrange proper political understanding with France with reference to independence of Associated States and training of indigenous forces, and once our prestige was committed, our negotiating position in these matters would be almost negligible. . . . We would almost surely be confronted by a demand to replace French forces with our own, and refusal to do so would confirm French view that we were merely trying to keep them stuck in the fight."[106]

Still, neither Dulles nor Eisenhower were willing to throw in the towel. They quickly devised an alternative plan by which a United Action coalition could be arranged among France, the ANZUS countries, and the Associated States. Dienbienphu would be lost, but the French could withdraw to defensible enclaves where they could be supported by American air and sea power. The British could join the coalition later.[107] Eisenhower sounded out the Republican leaders. "There are plenty of people in Asia," he explained, "and we can train them to fight well. I don't see any reason for American ground troops to be committed in Indo China, don't think we need it, but we can train their forces and it may be necessary for us eventually to use some of our planes or aircraft off the coast and some of our fighting craft we have in that area for support." The essential point was, Eisenhower concluded, "Where in the hell can you let the Communists chip away any more [sic]. We just can't stand it."[108]

Acting upon Dulles's suggestion, Smith held a similar session with the leaders of both parties immediately thereafter. The administration's scrupulous attention to Congress paid off. "I was actually surprised by the restrained gravity of all who participated," the under secretary reported to Dulles. "With no carping questions or criticisms, there appeared to be a full realization of the seriousness of the situation . . . and there was open discussion of the passage of resolution authorizing use of air and naval strength following a declaration of common intent, with or possibly without British participation."[109]

On April 29 Eisenhower remarked at his press conference that U.S. policy toward Indochina must steer "a course between two extremes, one of which . . . would be unattainable, the other unacceptable."[110] Later that day the NSC met to decide precisely what that course should be. The discussion began routinely enough, with Allen Dulles, Smith, and Radford briefing the council on recent developments. "A brief interval of silence" followed; the debate erupted. Arguing the case for intervention, MSA administrator Harold Stassen asserted that the United States had no choice but to "go in alone." Congress and the public would support intervention "if the Commander-in-Chief made it clear to them that such a move was necessary to save Southeast Asia from Communism." Eisenhower heard Stassen out, and then accused him of not only misdiagnosing the national temper but also making assumptions that "leaped over situations of grave difficulty." The position of the United States as the leader of the free world necessitated associates. Without allies "the leader is just an adventurer like Genghis Khan." Further, "We would in the eyes of many Asiatic peoples merely replace French colonialism with American colonialism . . . [and] be everywhere accused of imperialistic ambitions." Unilateral intervention, the president continued, "would mean a general war with China and perhaps the USSR, which the United States would have to prosecute separated from its allies." Accordingly, perhaps the NSC should be examining the "great question:" "If our allies were going to fall away in any case it might be better for the United States to leap over the smaller obstacles and hit the biggest one with all the power we had."[111]

Eisenhower had laid it on the line. The United States did have to steer a course between the "unacceptable and the unattainable." Prudence required a trade-off. To Roger Kyes, "The President was as sound as anyone could be. The people of the United States would rather hit Soviet Russia than put a single man to fight in Indochina." Stassen, now joined by Nixon and Smith, remained unconvinced. America had to draw the line somewhere. A single air strike might not be decisive at Dienbienphu, they rebutted, but it would signify to the Communists "This is as far as you go, and no further." Once that line had been drawn, France could reassume responsibility. There would be no need for a U.S.-USSR confrontation.[112]

Eisenhower did not disagree. France was the key. If he could be assured that with American and regional support France would reassume responsibility for continuing the war, Eisenhower declared, he would request Congress's authorization. He had not decided against intervention, only against intervention under the present circumstances. Without further controversy, therefore, the Council agreed that "despite the current unwillingness of the British Government to participate at this time and without awaiting developments at the Geneva Conference, the United States should continue . . . to organize a regional grouping, including initially the U.S., France, the Associated States, and other nations with interests in the area, for the defense of Southeast Asia against Communist efforts by any means to gain control of the countries in this area. . . .''[113] Lest any responsible official misunderstand, Cutler elaborated upon the decision at the planning board meeting later that afternoon. "Intervention by US combat forces," he emphasized, "would still depend on invitation of indigenous nations; a sufficient regional grouping so that it would not appear that the U.S. was acting alone to bail out French colonies and to meet Congressional sentiment, and on Congressional authority. *No intervention by executive action*" (added emphasis).[114]

Dienbienphu fell on May 7, the hopelessly outmanned defenders finally surrendering after fifty-five days of heroic resistance. Under the policy guidelines established by Eisenhower and Dulles and confirmed by the NSC, nevertheless, the administration's endeavor to prevent the loss of Indochina, by intervention if necessary, progressed. The State Department drafted another joint congressional resolution authorizing the president to employ air and naval forces in Asia to assist friendly governments "to maintain their authority against subversive and revolutionary efforts fomented by Communist regimes."[115] Discussions were held with the French to plan for military collaboration, the JCS developed a comprehensive concept of operations, and interagency planning continued.[116] Officials even drew up a working paper outlining day-by-day measures that would be taken.[117] In the end, the conditions Eisenhower had deemed essential for intervention to be viable were never met. He never received Paris's necessary assurance that it would maintain responsibility for the war, with or without United Action. Instead, the Laniel government set conditions of its own. If Eisenhower wanted France to continue, he was informed, he would have to make a prior commitment to use ground forces and promise full-fledged intervention if China entered the war. The president conceded a willingness to deploy a limited number of Marines, but he would formally agree only to use air and naval forces. To Washington, Paris's refusing to "internationalize" the war unless the U.S. acceded to its conditions was like "holding a sword of Damocles over our heads."[118]

On June 10, Dulles wrote "As regards internationalization, it should be made clear to the French that our offer does not indefinitely lie on the table to be picked up by them one minute before midnight. . . . I believe we should begin to think of a time limit on our intervention.[119] The limit was one week. On June 16, Dulles told the Senate Foreign Relations Committee that when the administration first proposed United Action, "It then seemed that intervention with some sea and air power, with possibly only a token show of a few marines on land, might be enough to change and alter the situation. . . . Now the situation has become such that successful intervention would be a much more momentous affair from a military standpoint. . . . The French are perfectly well aware that they don't have in any sense any call upon the United States to join the war, even if the war goes on as a result of what happens at Geneva."[120] On June 17, Pierre Mendes-France was elected France's prime minister. Committed to a negotiated settlement, he had no intention of calling upon the United States to join the war. Dulles remarked at that day's NSC that "he thought it best to let the French get out of Indochina entirely and then to try to rebuild from the foundations." Eisenhower agreed and suggested that the council move on to the next item on the agenda.[121]

Before Mendes-France's election, the administration had already prepared itself for a French withdrawal from Indochina and the probable loss of all of Vietnam. Within a week of the fall of Dienbienphu Dulles, in contrast to his previous statements, testified, "We do not want to operate on what has been referred to as the domino theory, where the loss of one area will topple another and another. . . . I think there is a good chance, if we can get some cooperation, to prevent that situation from continuing and that we can, through some collective security or united defense arrangement, which I hope would still include Indochina, prevent the loss of vital areas in Southeast Asia. This is what I am working on at the present time."[122]

Hence, while the administration sought United Action in Indochina, it simultaneously sought what would become the Southeast Asia Treaty Organization (SEATO). Ironically, the major unanticipated development was the partition of Vietnam. In a carefully prepared briefing to Congress on May 5, Dulles had maintained that "The most hopeful formula for peace in Vietnam was for an agreement with the Vietminh on the withdrawal of all foreign troops, the establishment of a coalition government, and the holding of elections in six months, all of which would probably result in the loss of Vietnam to the communists. Partition was not a likely solution because either side agreeing to partition of the country would lose the support of the people of the area."[123] The evidence reveals that the administration held to this view and acquiesced to partition only in order to prevent prolonging the Geneva negotiations, a circumstance, it feared, that could lead to further deterioration.[124] Once partition had been effected, however, and Ngo Dinh Diem emerged as a seemingly capable leader, it decided to include South Vietnam, albeit informally, in SEATO. In hindsight this proved to be a gross mistake. Despite his own rationale for not intervening in 1954, Eisenhower did "Americanize" the region and commit U.S. prestige to defend a government which, to use Dulles's phrase, "would lose the support of the people." It had been Eisenhower himself who predicted the consequences. It would be Eisenhower's successors who would have to face them.

Notes

1. Ambassador Donald Heath to the special adviser to the United States Delegation, 4 July 1954, *Foreign Relations of the United States, 1952–1954,* 16: 1282. Hereafter cited as *FRUS 1952–54.*

2. Ibid.

3. For example, see David Halberstam, *The Best and the Brightest* (New York: Random House, 1972); Robert Divine, *Eisenhower and the Cold War* (New York: Oxford University Press, 1981); Alexander George, *Presidential Decisionmaking in Foreign Policy: The Effective Use of Information and Advice* (Boulder, Colo.: Westview Press, 1980); Melanie Sue Billings-Yun, "Decision Against War: Eisenhower and Dien Bien Phu, 1954" (Ph.D. diss., Harvard University, 1982).

4. The historiography on Eisenhower's policy toward Indochina is too extensive to cite exhaustively. In addition to the above sources, representative literature includes Chalmers Roberts, "The Day We Didn't Go to War," *Reporter* 11 (September 1954): 31–35; "Did U.S. Almost Get into War?" *U.S. News & World Report* 19 June 1954, 35–38; Matthew Ridgway, *Soldier* (New York: Harper, 1956); Dwight D. Eisenhower, *Mandate for Change 1953-1956: The White House Years* (Garden City, N.Y.: Doubleday, 1963); *From Pearl Harbor to Vietnam: The Memoirs of Admiral Arthur W. Radford,* ed, Stephen Jurika, Jr., (Stanford: Hoover Institution, 1980); Richard Nixon, *RN: The Memoirs of Richard Nixon* (New York: Grosset & Dunlap, 1978); Henri Navarre, *Agonie de l'Indochine* (Paris: Plon 1956); Joseph Laniel, *Le drame Indochinois: De Dien-Bien-Phu au pari de Geneve* (Paris: Plon 1957); Paul Ely, *Memoires: L'Indochine dans la tormente* (Paris: Plon 1964); Georges Bidault, *Resistance,* trans., Marianne Sinclair (New York: Praeger Publishers, 1967); Anthony Eden, *Full Circle* (Boston: Little, Brown, 1960); Ellen Hammer, *The Struggle for Indochina, 1950–1955* (Stanford: Stanford University Press, 1955); Bernard Fall, *Street without Joy: Indochina at War 1946–1954* (Harrisburg, Pa.: Stackpole, 1961); *idem., Hell in a Very Small Place: The Siege of Dienbienphu* (Philadelphia: Lippincott, 1967); Joseph Buttinger, *Vietnam: A Dragon Embattled* (New York: Horizon Press, 1967); Melvin Gurtov, *The First Indochina Crisis* (New York: Columbia University Press, 1967); Philippe Devillers and Jean Lacouture, *End of a War: Indochina, 1954* (New York: Praeger Publishers, 1969); Robert Randle, *Geneva 1954* (Princeton: Princeton University Press, 1969); Ronald Irving, *The First Indochina War: French and American Policy, 1945–1954* (London: Croom Helm, 1975); Leslie Gelb with Richard Betts, *The Irony of Vietnam: The System Worked* (Washington, D.C.: Brookings Institution, 1979); George Herring, *America's Longest War: The United States and Vietnam, 1950–1975* (New York: John Wiley, 1979).

5. Substance of discussions of State—DMS-JSC meeting, 28 January 1953, *FRUS 1952–54,* 13: pt.1, 361.

6. Memorandum for the secretary of defense, 13 March 1953, U.S. Congress, House, Committee on Armed Forces, *United States-Vietnam Relations, 1945–1967: A Study Prepared by the Department of Defense* (Washington, D.C.: Government Printing Office, 1971), book 9, 11–14.

7. John Foster Dulles telephone conversation with William Knowland 26 July, 1953, John Foster Dulles Papers, Telephone Conversation Series, July 1–August 31, 1953(3), Dwight D. Eisenhower telephone conversation with Wilton (Jerry) Persons, 27 July, 1953, Dwight D. Eisenhower Papers as President of the United States, 1953–1961 (Whitman File), Diary Series, Phone Calls—July-December 1953, Dwight D. Eisenhower Library, Abilene, Kansas (hereafter cited as Whitman File); *Congressional Record,* 83rd Cong., 2nd sess. (29 July 1953), 10,234–10,235.

8. Memorandum of discussion at the 141st meeting of the National Security Council, 28 April 1953, *FRUS 1952–54,* 13: pt.1, 519.

9. Substance of discussions of State-Joint Chiefs of Staff meeting 24 April 1953, Ibid., pt.1, 497.

10. Lieutenant General John W. O'Daniel to the commander in chief, Pacific (Radford), 30 June 1953, Ibid., pt.1, 626. According to Navarre, the French defined "successful conclusion" as creating conditions necessary for a political solution, not a military victory. See Navarre, *Agonie,* 71–72.

11. Report to the National Security Council by the Department of State, 5 August 1954, *FRUS 1952–54,* 13: pt.1. 714–17.

12. Substance of discussions of State-Joint Chiefs of Staff meeting, 4 September 1953, Ibid., pt.1, 756.

13. Memorandum of discussion at the 161st meeting of the National Security Council, 9 September 1953, Ibid., pt.1, 787–89.

14. The secretary of state to the president, 29 September 1953, with attached annex, Ibid., 810–12; Eisenhower, *Mandate for Change,* 169.

15. Ambassador at Saigon (Heath) to the Department of State, 5 December 1953, *FRUS 1952–54,* 13: pt.1, 899–900; Herring, *America's Longest War,* 26–27.

16. "Indochina—Master copy of JSDE Draft," 109; Dwight D. Eisenhower Papers, Post Presidential 1961–69, "Drafts and other Material re *White House Years,*" Dwight D. Eisenhower Library, Abilene Kansas. For publication, Eisenhower substantially condensed the draft, initially written by his son, John S.D. Eisenhower. See Eisenhower, *Mandate for Change,* 373.

17. Entry for 17 March 1951, *The Eisenhower Diaries,* ed., Robert Ferrell (New York: W. W. Norton, 1981), 196.

18. NSC 177, "United States Objectives and Courses of Action with Respect to Southeast Asia," and attachments, 30 December 1954, *Documents of the National Security Council* (microfilm collection) (University Publications of America).

19. Memorandum by the assistant secretary of state for Far Eastern affairs (Robertson) to the secretary of state, 6 January 1954, *FRUS 1952–54,* 13: pt.1, 944, n.2; memorandum of discussion at the 179th meeting of the National Security Council, 8 January 1954, Ibid., pt.1, 949.

20. Ibid., pt.1, 947–54; NSC 177, 8.

21. Memorandum of 8 January 1953 NSC, *FRUS 1952–54,* 13: pt.1, 951.

22. Ibid., pt.1, 952.

23. Ibid.

24. Ibid., pt.1, 953.

25. Ibid., pt.1, 954.

26. Memorandum of discussion at the 180th meeting of the National Security Council, 14 January 1954, Ibid., pt.1, 961–64; NSC 5405, "United States Objectives and Courses of Action with Respect to Southeast Asia," 16 January 1954, U.S. Congress, Senate Subcommittee on Public Buildings and Grounds (Senator Mike Gravel, chairman), *The Pentagon Papers* (Boston: Beacon Press, 1971) 1: 434–43. Hereafter cited as *Pentagon Papers (Gravel).*

27. NSC 124/2, "United States Objectives and Courses of Action with Respect to Southeast Asia," 25 June 1952, Ibid., 384–90.

28. Memorandum by C. D. Jackson, special assistant to the president, 18 January 1954, *FRUS 1952–54,* 13: pt.1, 981–82.

29. Office of the assistant secretary of defense, memorandum for the record, 30 January 1954, *Pentagon Papers (Gravel)* 1: 443–47; memorandum by the deputy secretary of defense (Kyes) to the secretary of the Air Force (Talbott), *FRUS 1952–54,* 13: pt.1, 1007.

30. Memorandum for the Record, 30 January 1954, *Pentagon Papers (Gravel)* 1: 445–46.

31. The Erskine Report, pt.1, Ibid., 90–91; director of the Office of Philippine and Southeast Asian Affairs (Bonsal) to the ambassador at Saigon (Heath), 12 February 1954, *FRUS 1952–54,* 13: pt.1, 1041–43.

32. For example, see the *New York Times,* 6–11 February 1954.

33. Quoted in James C. Hagerty Diary, 8 February 1954, James C. Hagerty Papers, Dwight D. Eisenhower Library (hereafter cited as Hagerty Diary). See also memorandum by the assistant staff secretary (Minnich) to the president, n.d., *FRUS 1952–54,* 13: pt.1, 1023–25.

34. Eisenhower telephone conversation with Charles Wilson, 8 February 1954, Whitman File, Diary Series, "Personal Diary January-November 1954"; Eisenhower to Dulles, 10 February 1954, attached to W. K. Scott memorandum for General Paul Carroll, 11 February 1954, Whitman File, Dulles-Herter Series, "Dulles—February 1954(2)."

35. Memorandum of discussion at the 183rd meeting of the National Security Council, 4 February 1954, *FRUS 1952–54,* 13: pt.1, 1016.

36. For Smith's testimony as well as that of Radford and other administration representatives, see the 18 February 1954 hearing, *Selective Hearings of the House Committee on Foreign Affairs 1951–56* (Historical Series) (Washington, D.C.: Government Printing Office, 1980) 8: pt.2, 99–123; and the 16 February 1954 session, *Executive Sessions of the Senate Foreign Relations Committee 1954* (Historical Series) (Washington, D.C.: Government Printing Office, 1977) 6: 107–46.

37. Memorandum for the record by the counselor (MacArthur), 27 January 1954; secretary of state to the president, 6 February 1954; memorandum of

discussion at the 186th meeting of the National Security Council, 26 February 1954, all in *FRUS 1952–54*, 13: pt.1, 998–1000, 1020–21, 1081.

38. Dulles testimony, 24 February 1954, *Executive Sessions. . . . Foreign Relations Committee 1954* 6: 165–82.

39. Dulles to Smith, 18 February 1954, attached to Smith to Eisenhower, n.d., Whitman File, Dulles-Herter Series, "Dulles—February 1954 (1)."

40. Report of the special U.S. mission to Indochina, 5 February 1954, White House Office, "Project 'Clean Up,' Indochina," Dwight D. Eisenhower Library, Abilene, Kansas; ambassador at Saigon (Heath) to Department of State, 22 February 1954, *FRUS 1952–54*, 13: pt.1, 1064–67; Radford testimony, 18 February 1954, *Executive Sessions. . . Foreign Relations Committee 1954* 6: 106–16.

41. Dulles telephone conversation with Allen Dulles, 16 March 1954, JFDP, Telephone Conversations Series, March-April 30, 1954 (3).

42. Eisenhower to Everett "Swede" Hazlett, 18 March 1954, Whitman File, Diary Series, "March 1954;" memorandum by the chairman of the Operations Coordinating Board (Smith) to the president with attached annex, 11 March 1954, *FRUS 1952–54* 13: pt.1, 1108–16.

43. Memorandum for the secretary of defense, 12 March 1954, *Pentagon Papers (Gravel)* 1: 448–51.

44. Memorandum of discussion at the 190th meeting of the National Security Council, 25 March 1954, *FRUS 1952–54*, 13: pt.1, 1167–68.

45. Ely, *Memoires*, 59; memorandum by the counselor (MacArthur), 19 March 1954, *FRUS 1952–54*, 13: pt.1, 1133–34; director of the Office of Philippine and Southeast Asian Affairs (Bonsal) to ambassador at Saigon (Heath), 12 February 1954, Ibid., pt.1, 1042. Minister of National Defense Rene Pleven had been invited along with Ely, but declined.

46. Ely, *Memoires*, 61–63; memorandum for the record by Captain G. W. Anderson, 21 March 1954, *FRUS 1952–54*, 13: pt.1, 1137–40.

47. Memorandum by the director of the Office of Western European Affairs (Jones) to the assistant secretary of state for European affairs (Merchant), 23 March 1954, Ibid., pt.1, 1144–45.

48. Ibid.

49. Ely, *Memoires*, 65–67; Dulles's quote is a composite taken from two memoranda of the meeting. See memorandum of conversation, 23 March 1954, 751G.00/3-2354, Department of State Records, Record Group 59, National Archives, Washington, D.C.; and memorandum for the president, 23 March 1954, Whitman File, Dulles-Herter Series, "Dulles—March 1954 (1)."

50. Ely, *Memoires*, 64–67; memorandum of conversation, 23 March 1954.

51. Memorandum of conversation with the president, 24 March 1954, Lot 64 D 199, Box 222, Department of State Records.

52. Ely memorandum for Admiral Arthur W. Radford, 23 March 1954, *Pentagon Papers (Gravel)* 1: 458–59; Dulles telephone conversation with Admiral Radford, 25 March 1954, JFDP, Telephone Conversations Series, March-April 1954 (2).

53. Memorandum for the president's Special Committee on Indo-China, 29 March 1954, *Pentagon Papers (Gravel)* 1: 455–58.

54. Laniel, *Le Drame Indochinois,* 83–88; Ely, *Memoires,* 67–83; *Radford Memoirs,* 391–401.

55. Author's interview with Admiral George W. Anderson, 17 April 1981.

56. Memorandum by the director of the Policy Planning Staff (Bowie) to the secretary of state, 23 March 1954, and memorandum by Charles C. Stelle of the Policy Planning Staff, 23 March 1954, both in *FRUS 1952–54,* 13: pt.1, 1145–48; Dulles telephone conversations with Carl McCardle, 27 March 1954, and Walter Judd, 29 March 1954, both in JFDP, Telephone Conversations Series, March-April 30, 1954 (2).

57. Substance of discussions of State-Joint Chiefs of Staff meeting, 26 March 1954, *FRUS 1952–54,* 13: pt.1, 1172.

58. Memorandum of conversation with the president, 24 March 1954; "The Threat of a Red Asia," *Department of State Bulletin* 30 (12 April 1954): 539–40.

59. Dulles telephone conversation with Judd, 29 March 1954; author's interview with Robert Bowie, 29 October 1981; Dulles telephone conversation with William Knowland, JFDP, Telephone Conversations Series, March-April 30, 1954 (2); memoranda of conversations, 27 March and 2 April 1954, both in *FRUS 1952–54,* 13: pt.1, 1180, 1214–15.

60. Chronology of action on the subject of Indochina prior to the Geneva meeting on Korea and Indochina in the spring of 1954, JFDP, Subject Series, "Indochina 1954(3);" Dulles telephone conversation with James Hagerty, JFDP, Telephone Conversations Series (White House), January 1-June 30, 1954 (2); memorandum of conversation, 2 April 1954, *FRUS 1952–54* 13: 1214–17.

61. See note 43.

62. Memorandum for the President's Special Committee on Indo-China, 29 March 1954, 458.

63. Matthew Ridgway, memorandum for the record, 29 March 1954, Matthew Ridgway Papers, U.S. Army Military History Institute, Carlisle, Pennsylvania.

64. Ridgway, memorandum for the Joint Chiefs of Staff, 2 April 1954, Ridgway Papers.

65. Ibid.

66. Memorandum by the Joint Chiefs of Staff to the secretary of defense (Wilson), 31 March 1954, *FRUS 1952–54,* 13: pt.1, 1198, n.1.

67. Memorandum by the chief of staff, United States Air Force (Twining) to the chairman of the Joint Chiefs of Staff (Radford), 2 April 1954, Ibid., pt.1, 1222. All the service chiefs' memoranda are in Ibid., pt.1, 1220–23.

68. Quoted in Nixon, *RN,* 150.

69. The president's appointments, 2 April 1954, Dwight D. Eisenhower Records as President, Daily Appointments 1953–61, Dwight D. Eisenhower Library, Abilene, Kansas; Dulles memorandum of conference with Eisenhower, 2 April 1954, JFDP, White House Memoranda Series, "Meetings with the President 1954 (4)."

70. Draft joint congressional resolution, attached to Dulles memorandum of conference, 2 April 1954.

71. Dulles memorandum of conference, 2 April 1954.

72. Dulles memorandum of conference with congressional leaders, 3 April

1954 (dated 5 April 1954), JFDP, Chronological File, "April 1954." See also Richard Russell's notes of the meeting, "Red-Line File," Richard B. Russell Papers, University of Georgia, Athens.

73. Dulles telephone conversation with Eisenhower, 3 April 1954, JFDP, Telephone Conversations Series (White House), January 1-June 30, 1954 (2).

74. Eisenhower affirmed that his policy would conform to the conditions set by Congress on the evening of April 4, 1954. President's daily appointments, 4 April 1954; Sherman Adams, *Firsthand Report: The Story of the Eisenhower Administration* (New York: Harper, 1961), 122.

75. Dillon to secretary of state, 5 April 1954, *Pentagon Papers (Gravel)* 1: 461–62; Ely, *Memoires,* 84–88; Laniel, *Le drame Indochinois,* 84–86.

76. Eisenhower telephone conversation with Dulles, 5 April 1954, Whitman File, Diary Series, Phone Calls—January-May 1954.

77. Dulles to American embassy, Paris, 5 April 1954, *Pentagon Papers (Gravel)* 1: 476.

78. NSC Action No. 1074-a, 5 April 1954, Ibid., 462–71; Army Position on NSC Action No. 1074-a, Ibid., 471–72; Ridgway, *Soldier,* 276–78. See also Ridgway memorandum for Joint Chiefs of Staff, 6 April 1954, and Radford memorandum for secretary of defense, 22 April 1954, both in Ridgway Papers.

79. Memorandum of discussion at the 191st meeting of the National Security Council, 1 April 1954, *FRUS 1952–54,* 13: pt.1, 1201.

80. Memorandum of discussion at the 192nd meeting of the National Security Council, 6 April 1954, Ibid., pt.1, 1250–66.

81. Ibid., pt.1, 1253–56.

82. Ibid., pt.1, 1258–60.

83. Ibid., pt.1, 1260–61.

84. Ibid., pt.1, 1264–65.

85. Nixon, *RN,* 151.

86. *Public Papers of the Presidents of the United States: Dwight D. Eisenhower, 1954* (Washington, D.C.: Government Printing Office, 1960), 383.

87. Memoranda of conversations, 2 April and 4 April 1954, and memorandum by the counsellor (MacArthur) to secretary of state, 5 April 1954, all in *FRUS 1952–54,* 13: pt.1, 1214–17, 1231–35, and 1244–45.

88. The secretary of state to the embassy in France, 10 April 1954, Ibid., pt.1, 1301.

89. Chronology of Action . . . Indochina; memorandum of conversation by the assistant secretary of state for Far Eastern affairs (Robertson) and the counsellor (MacArthur), with attached annexes 1 and 2, Ibid., pt.1, 1311–13; memorandum of conversation, 14 April 1954, Whitman File, Dulles-Herter Series, "Dulles-April 1954 (2)."

90. Hagerty Diary, 16 April 1954; the *New York Times,* 17 and 18 April 1954; *Congressional Record,* 83rd Cong., 2nd sess. (19 April 1954), 5289–98.

91. Hagerty Diary, 16 April 1954; Dulles telephone conversation with H. Alexander Smith, 19 April 1954, JFDP, Telephone Conversations Series, March-April 30, 1954 (1).

92. Hagerty Diary, 16, 17, 19 April 1954; the *New York Times,* 18 April 1954.

93. Memorandum of conversation by the secretary of state, 19 April 1954, *FRUS 1952–54,* 16: 532–34; author's interview with Eleanor Lansing Dulles, 9 October 1979; memorandum of conversation by Elizabeth Brown of the Office of United Nations Political and Security Affairs, 20 April 1954, *FRUS 1952–54,* 16: 536.

94. Dulles telephone conversation with Allen Dulles, 19 April 1954, JFDP, Telephone Conversations Series, "March–April 30, 1954 (1).

95. The secretary of state to the Department of State, 22 April 1954, *FRUS 1952–54,* 13: pt. 1, 1362–63.

96. Dulles to Department of State, 22 April 1954, Whitman File, Dulles-Herter Series, "Dulles-April 1954 (2)."

97. United States minutes of a tripartite foreign ministers meeting, 22 April 1953, *FRUS 1952–54* 16: 544, n.2; Dulles to Department of State, 23 April 1954, Whitman File, Dulles-Herter Series, "Dulles—April 1954 (2);" Bidault, *Resistance,* 196–97.

98. Memorandum by the counselor (MacArthur) to the secretary of state, 7 April 1954, *FRUS 1952–54,* 13: pt.1, 1270–72; memorandum by the special assistant to the president for national security affairs (Cutler) to the under secretary of state (Smith), 30 April 1954, Ibid., pt.1, 1446–48. See also Dulles memorandum of conversation with Eisenhower, 19 May 1954, JFDP, White House Memoranda Series, "Meetings with the President 1954 (3)."

99. Dulles to State Department, 23 April 1954, Whitman File, Dulles-Herter Series, "Dulles-April 1954 (2)."

100. Memorandum of conversation, 24 April 1954 (dated 26 April 1954), JFDP, Subject Series, "Mr. Merchant Top Secret (Indochina) (2)."

101. Eisenhower telephone conversation with Smith, 24 April 1954, Whitman File, Diary Series, Phone Calls—January–May 1954.

102. *Radford Memoir,* 408–9; author's interview with Admiral Anderson.

103. Memorandum by the assistant secretary of state for public affairs (McCardle) to the secretary of state, 30 April 1954, *FRUS 1952–54,* 16: 629–30.

104. The secretary of state to the Department of State, 26 April 1954; memorandum of conversation, by the secretary of state, 25 April 1954, both in Ibid., pt.1, 570–71, 553–57.

105. Dulles to State Department, 25 April 1954, Whitman File, Dulles-Herter Series, "Dulles-April 1954 (1); *Radford Memoirs,* 407; the acting secretary of state to the secretary of state, 26 April 1954, *FRUS 1952–54,* 16: 569–70.

106. Dulles to State Department, 25 April 1954, Whitman File, "Dulles-Herter Series, "Dulles-April 1954 (1)."

107. Memorandum for the files by the president, 27 April 1954, *FRUS 1952–54,* 13: pt.2, 1422–23; Dulles to State Department, 29 April 1954, Whitman File, Dulles-Herter Series, "Dulles-April 1954 (1)."

108. Memorandum by the assistant staff secretary (Minnich) to the president, n.d., *FRUS 1952–54,* 13: pt. 2, 1412–14; acting secretary of state to secretary of state, 28 April 1954, Ibid. 16: 599–600; Hagerty Diary, 26 April 1954.

109. Dulles to State Department, 25 April, Whitman File, Dulles-Herter

Series, "Dulles-April 1954 (1);" acting secretary of state to secretary of state, 26 April 1954, *FRUS 1952–54*, 16: 569–70 and 574.

110. *Public Papers of the President . . . 1954*, 427–28.

111. Memorandum of discussion at the 194th meeting of the National Security Council, 29 April 1954, *FRUS 1952–54*, 13: pt.2, 1431–41.

112. Ibid., pt.2, 1441–43.

113. Ibid., pt.2, 1443–45.

114. Memorandum by the special assistant to the president for national security affairs (Cutler) to the under secretary of state (Smith), 30 April 1954, Ibid., pt.2, 1445–48.

115. Draft joint resolution, 17 May 1954, JFDP, Subject Series, "Indochina May 1953–May 1954 (4)."

116. Examples of discussions with Paris include memorandum of conversation by the secretary of state, 8 May 1954; the secretary of state to the embassy in France, 11 May 1954; the secretary of state to the embassy in France, 15 May 1954; all in *FRUS 1952–54*, 13: pt.2, 1516–17, 1534–36, 1569–71. On military operations, see *Radford Memoirs*, 417–13; *Pentagon Papers (Gravel)* 1: 122–32; memorandum by the Joint Chiefs of Staff to the secretary of defense, 20 May 1954, *FRUS 1952–54*, 13: pt. 2, 1590–92. For interagency planning, see memorandum prepared in the Department of State, 11 May 1954; memorandum by the executive secretary of the National Security Council (Lay) to the secretary of state, 18 May 1954; memorandum by the acting assistant secretary of state for Far Eastern affairs (Drumright) to the counsellor (MacArthur), 24 May 1954; memorandum by the director of the Policy Planning Staff (Bowie) to the secretary of state, 27 May 1954; note by the executive secretary to the National Security Council on studies with respect to possible U.S. action Indochina, 1 June 1954; all in Ibid., pt.2, 1533–34, 1581–82, 1606–07, 1624–26, 1649–52.

117. "Procedural Steps for Intervention in Indochina," n.d., JFDP, Subject Series, "Indochina May 1953–May 1954 (4)."

118. Substance of discussions of State-Joint Chiefs of Staff meeting, 10 June 1954, *FRUS 1952–54*, 13: pt.2 1675–78; See also Dillon to secretary of state, 17 May 1954, Whitman File, Dulles-Herter Series, "Dulles-May 1954 (2);" memorandum of conversation between the president and General Cutler, 1 June 1954, *FRUS 1952–54*, 13: pt.2, 1647–49.

119. The secretary of state to the Department of State, 10 June 1954, Ibid. 16: 1117–18.

120. Dulles testimony, 11 May 1954, *Executive Sessions . . . Foreign Relations Committee 1954* 6: 639–40.

121. Memorandum of discussion at the 202nd meeting of the National Security Council, 17 June 1954, *FRUS 1952–54*, 13: pt.2, 1717.

122. Dulles testimony, 11 May 1954, *Select Hearing . . . Foreign Affairs Committee 1951–56* 18: 134.

123. Secretary's briefing for members of Congress, 5 May 1954, JFDP, Subject Series "Indochina 1954 (3)." Briefing papers are located in JFDP, Subject Series, "Indochina May 1953–May 1954."

124. Memorandum of conversation by Paul J. Sturm of the Office of Philippine and Southeast Asian Affairs, 12 May 1954, *FRUS 1952–54,* 13: pt.2, 1538; the secretary of state to the United States delegation, 12 May 1954, the United States delegation to the Department of State, 7 June 1954; the coordinator of the United States Delegation (Johnson) to the head of the delegation (Smith), 6 June 1954; all in Ibid. 16: 778–79, 1054–55, 1047.

Eisenhower's Foreign Economic Policy
The Case of Latin America

Thomas Zoumaras

In the most comprehensively researched study of United States foreign economic policy in the 1950s, Burton I. Kaufman argues that President Dwight D. Eisenhower made the American government "more attentive to the problems of Third World countries" while "assum[ing] greater responsibility for meeting the [less developed countries'] economic needs." Eisenhower, we are told, came to this conclusion with experience as the nation's chief executive. Simply stated, he entered office in 1953 intent upon pursuing a policy of "trade not aid" only to learn that "trade and aid" were inseparable instruments of economic warfare designed to blunt the Soviet economic offensive launched in 1954. Eisenhower, according to this interpretation, oversaw a transition away from reliance on the private sector for third-world development to a strategy that provided public capital whenever trade and private investments proved incapable of satisfying the less-developed countries' (LDCs) aspirations for economic growth.[1]

Kaufman challenges the thesis that Eisenhower's policy transformation was a grudging and half-hearted response to a series of crises, especially the growing Soviet economic offensive in the LDCs, Vice-President Richard M. Nixon's disastrous South American tour in May 1958, and the January 1959 victory of Fidel Castro's revolutionary forces over the pro-American Cuban dictator, Fulgencio Batista. As R. Harrison Wagner has written, only international turmoil allowed "momentarily centraliz[ed] decision making" to overcome a lack of presidential leadership and ideological inertia. It was at such junctures that the administration's foreign policy specialists were able to enlist Eisenhower's influence to overcome resistance by more budget conscious policymakers and use "ad hoc procedures" to force "comprehensive reviews" of U.S. foreign economic policy.[2] Each policy revision took years to gain high-level acceptance. This essay will show that innovation in United States' foreign economic policy came slowly, haphazardly, even reluctantly, and that the changes were inadequate responses to cold-war challenges rather than a reasoned and comprehensive plan to overcome structural underdevelopment in Latin America.[3]

Eisenhower's foreign policy convictions impelled him to run for the presidency in 1952. The only other Republican party candidate of consequence was Ohio Senator Robert A. Taft, a reputed isolationist. Eisenhower had little complaint with Taft's domestic politics and outlook, but the ex-general's foreign policy positions were based upon his perception that Americans lived in an interrelated world. Eisenhower opposed anything that established barriers between the United States and its trading partners, particularly the resource-rich but economically fragile LDCs. The general feared that an isolationist president would succumb to protectionism. In Eisenhower's estimation, this was tantamount to suicide, because "aggressive" Communists would turn the trade-starved LDCs into vassals of the Soviet bloc.[4]

Eisenhower advised Republican leaders that free access to raw material sources and trade markets was not only "necessary to the health, strength and development of our economy," but it was also the most effective and least expensive way to promote "collective security" in "our own enlightened self-interest."[5] Eisenhower hoped that world trade and foreign aid, during periods of economic and military crisis, would strengthen the anticommunist alliance system enough to guarantee peace and allow reduction of the U.S. defense budget. Therefore, Eisenhower intended to become president, in part, to protect the Mutual Security Program (MSP), that is, foreign aid and free trade, from devastation by the Taft Republicans so that the free world would not have to risk nuclear confrontation.[6]

Eisenhower wanted security, but he knew that foreign assistance could be expensive. His "natural conservatism" mandated "fiscal morality."[7] In effect, he wanted to maintain internationalism and to control the cost of foreign policy programs at the same time. These goals led him to give Secretary of the Treasury George M. Humphrey a permanent seat on the restructured National Security Council (NSC) with the tacit power to veto any foreign relations program that violated sound fiscal policy. Eisenhower selected the perfect man to wield the fiscal ax.[8] Humphrey had been president of the Cleveland-based holding company M. A. Hanna & Co. His self-described mission was to eliminate government influence in the private sector, to shrink the size of the federal budget, and to replace foreign assistance with private investment and trade at every opportunity.[9] He was convinced that a vibrant U.S. economy was a prerequisite to a free world able to combat communism. Eisenhower endorsed Humphrey's formula. Five years would pass before Eisenhower realized that Humphrey's policies did not address the realities of United States-Latin American economic relations and the desires of Hispanic statesmen impatient to see their countries modernize with the help of public capital provided by the United States.

Attention was called to the MSP even before Eisenhower took his oath of office. Paul G. Hoffman, industrialist, first Marshall Plan director, and an early advocate of Eisenhower's presidential candidacy, proposed that a commission on foreign economic policy be formed on inaugural day to study and report within 120 days on trade, the balance of payments, economic growth and stability, the potential for private foreign investment, and the impact of these factors on foreign assistance programs, namely, whether trade and investment could replace economic aid. Hoffman felt that expeditious review was needed because the Reciprocal Trade Agreements Act was up for renewal in June, and because Eisenhower faced mounting pressure to cut President Harry S. Truman's $7.6 billion Mutual Security (aid) budget request. Eisenhower and his advisors decided that Hoffman's proposal was premature. They did not expect Congress to oppose the president's foreign economic program, and they agreed with some of the criticisms leveled at the Democrats (Eisenhower's first budget reduced the aid request to $5.1 billion).[10]

The president presented his foreign economic program to the nation in his first State of the Union Message. Besides a three-year trade extension, he sought government promotion of overseas private investment, purchase of foreign products for American defense, stepped-up raw materials acquisitions, and a more stable and open free-world economic system. By early April, Eisenhower realized that Hoffman's advice was appropriate; it was apparent that Congress would not pass his program. He convinced the legislative leaders to extend the existing bill another year while a bipartisan presidential commission considered all facets of national foreign economic policy.[11] This would give the president the opportunity to remove international economic programs from the congressional chopping block until he could generate support for the MSP.

Eisenhower chose Clarence B. Randall, chairman of Inland Steel Company, to head the commission, on the strength of recommendations by Commerce Secretary Sinclair Weeks and Humphrey. They promoted Randall because he was a revered conservative who also advo-

cated freer trade.[12] Randall's already difficult assignment was complicated when congressional leaders appointed three of their most
conservative colleagues to the commission. In an attempt to achieve a
consensus, if not a unanimously endorsed report, Randall and his staff
boiled the report down to the "low[est] common denominator." Randall
orchestrated the testimony and evidence to underline the need for freer
trade, but he recommended mechanisms to placate protectionists, for
example, higher tariffs if overseas competition threatened domestic
industries. The January 1954 Randall Commission Report still provoked
opposition from the protectionist legislators who issued a minority
report. The message was clear: Eisenhower's foreign economic policy
would face stiff opposition in Congress if it was based upon the Randall
Report.[13]

The report advocated little more than modifications to existing policies and legislation. Its major point of departure was to endorse Humphrey's recommendation to terminate, at the earliest opportunity, all
aid to developed countries and economic grant assistance to LDCs.
Private investment, trade, and occasional high-interest loans were to
be the prime engine for free-world economic development. This was to
be promoted through tax relief for overseas profits made by U.S. firms,
freer trade so that investors would have markets for goods produced
overseas, offering foreign producers an equal chance to bid on U.S.
government contracts, and pressure on foreign governments to avoid
statism. The Randall Commission Report recommended a minimum
extension of three years for the trade act. The commission also urged
that the president have the power to reduce tariffs 5 percent in each
year of the act's existence, and that efforts be undertaken to achieve
currency convertibility to further the stated goal of turning to private
investment and trade. Finally, the report implied that privately funded
diversification, not price stabilization schemes, was the way to alleviate
economic difficulties facing countries dependent upon one or two ex-
portable products. Despite frequent representations by State Department (DOS) officials, this and opposition to development assistance
were the only significant references to the development problems and
aspirations of the Third World. [14]

The report triggered the first major foreign economic policy debate
within the administration. Free-trade advocates in the DOS decried
Randall's lukewarm endorsement of liberalized trade provisions; however, Commerce Secretary Sinclair Weeks opposed even these modest
trade proposals. He noted that 70 percent of the corporations surveyed
feared the cheap labor available to foreign firms. American tariffs had
been reduced by 68 percent since 1937.[15]

Although Weeks was unable to sway Eisenhower from his determination to accept the report as the basis for administration policy, he and other protectionist-minded senior advisors convinced the president that his report to Congress should not "take a far-advanced position which would endanger support already gained from somewhat reluctant groups." Thus, Eisenhower rejected DOS advice that he seek greater authority to reduce tariffs. There was little resistance to the proposal to limit economic aid grants, but Secretary Humphrey suffered a setback when Foreign Operations Administration (FOA) and DOS officials prevented elimination of all development assistance. Finally, to facilitate movement of the three-year extension through Congress, the administration agreed to downplay foreign policy considerations and to stress economic self-interest.[16]

On March 30, Eisenhower outlined his foreign economic policy in a special message to Congress. He stressed that trade was essential to overcome the dollar gap that prevented foreign marketing of United States goods. The president asked Congress to renew the trade act for three years, to authorize the president to make tariff cuts of up to 15 percent, and to encourage overseas investments by lowering corporate taxes some 14 percent below the domestic rate on income earned through foreign subsidiaries of U.S. businesses. Eisenhower summed up by identifying four interrelated parts to his new policy: "Aid—which we wish to curtail; Investment—which we wish to encourage; Convertibility—which we wish to facilitate; and Trade—which we wish to expand."[17]

Congress passed a diluted version of the three-year trade agreements act in June 1955. Eisenhower labelled his victory a "milestone" in the nation's foreign economic policy; however, the goal of liberalized trade within the free world was undercut when Congress refused to authorize membership in the Organization for Trade Cooperation (OTC). In fact, throughout the remainder of his presidency, Eisenhower was content to prevent further encroachment by protectionists.[18]

Eisenhower's compunction to proceed cautiously on free-trade legislation and his readiness to cut economic assistance grants did not bode well for United States-Latin American economic relations. Up to 49 percent of Latin American export trade went North.[19] Eisenhower knew any diminution in free-trade policies would be particularly painful given the monocultural nature of Latin American economies and the cutback in public assistance from Washington.[20] Therefore, the president sent his brother, Milton, to South America in the summer of 1953 to glean information required to understand Latin American complaints about their economic relations with the United States and to symbolize Washington's interest in a hemispheric partnership. Milton Eisenhower was a logical choice. The two brothers were extremely close, and Milton doggedly refused to associate himself with special interests. Latin American leaders were impressed with the gesture, but they expected more than high-level goodwill tours or study groups designed, according to Secretary of State John Foster Dulles, "to pat them a little bit."[21]

The thrust of Milton Eisenhower's report asserted that "Economic improvement . . . and economic cooperation is without question the key to better relations between the United States and nations to the South. Everything else . . . must take secondary [sic] place . . . ." He specifically emphasized that Latin America's economic well-being rested primarily with internal self-help programs, sound fiscal policies, and an open door policy for private investments; nevertheless, he challenged ideological dependence on free enterprise. Most important, Milton Eisenhower strongly endorsed resumption of Export-Import Bank of Washington (Exim) economic development loans to build the infrastructure projects necessary to attract investors. The report placed considerable weight upon free trade and enlargement of the government's overseas purchases for the strategic stockpile program given the administration's ideological distaste for price stabilization via international commodity agreements.[22]

Milton's rapport with his brother did not counterbalance the influence of fiscal conservatives. Stepped-up stockpiling of strategic raw materials faced opposition from most cabinet-level reviews because the added expense would unbalance the budget, and new purchases would exceed security needs. Humphrey was particularly vehement that free enterprise should not be replaced by a return to economic development through government-financed assistance programs.[23]

Milton Eisenhower's defeat at the hand of economic conservatives undermined United States-Latin American relations. First, he also decided to distance himself from Secretary Humphrey's anti-loan policy in order to preserve what was left of his influence among the leaders of the other American republics. This would preclude his playing a major on-the-scene role at the Organization of American States (OAS) economic conference in 1954. Second, Washington's trade and stockpile policies caused Latin Americans to wonder whether their commodities would find sufficient markets and stable prices. Debate over the report hardly ended when slumping prices for Chilean copper followed by lead and zinc from Peru and Mexico threatened to derail whatever goodwill Milton Eisenhower had compiled in his South American tour during the summer of 1953.[24]

By early 1954, the Chilean government faced a budget crisis thanks to an accumulation of more than one hundred thirty thousand tons of copper. The surplus developed because the Chileans refused to accept declining prices when the Korean War ended. Chilean officials warned that they might sell the excess holdings to the Soviet bloc unless the United States agreed to make purchases for its strategic stockpile. Milton Eisenhower opposed surrendering "to political or economic blackmail" in principle, but he confidentially urged purchase of the backlogged commodity at the existing low market price if the Chilean government prohibited sales to bloc countries and legislated "removal of present exchange inequities" facing American copper corporations.[25] Once again Secretary Humphrey opposed Eisenhower's advice because the purchases threatened his commitment to fiscal responsibility and free enterprise. This time however, the secretary of state decided to vigorously support Eisenhower. Dulles concluded that "we can't prevent them [the Chilean government] from selling to the Russians if we refuse to buy. . . . No matter how stupid they may act we must remember that we have to deal with them."[26]

The administration agreed to purchase one hundred thousand short tons of copper at the prevailing market prices of 30 cents per pound rather than the 36.5 cents sought by Chile. The sale was contingent upon a pledge, in writing, from the Chilean government, not to trade with Soviet bloc countries and to assist American copper companies settle disputes with labor unions and return control of copper sales to the private sector. Other requirements included shifting levies from duties on production levels to less onerous taxes on income. Secretary Humphrey still feared the impact upon domestic producers, but he was convinced to end his opposition after being assured that the stockpile purchases would isolate surplus copper from the world market. More important, Humphrey and the president were unwilling to stand firm behind economic purity given Dulles's dire prediction that a Soviet-Chilean trade relationship would be the byproduct of United States inaction.[27] There was an important lesson from this confrontation. Fiscal conservatives would be suspended, if only temporarily, when cold-war imperatives threatened national security.

Eisenhower had little time to relish closing Chile to Soviet influence. In mid-1954, responding to pressure from western miners and their congressional representatives, the Tariff Commission ruled that foreign producers were dumping lead and zinc in this country, thereby endangering an industry important to national security. The commission raised the duty on lead and zinc by 1.5 and 1.4 cents per pound, respectively. The lead and zinc issue prompted communiques from ten countries (including Bolivia, Mexico, and Peru) warning of apocalyptic consequences for their export-dependent economies if their commodities were made uncompetitive thanks to higher United States' duties. Moreover, they did not understand how new tariffs could be allowed given Eisenhower's March 30, 1954, foreign economic policy message to Congress.[28]

Dulles and Eisenhower worked out their course of action over a two-and-a-half month period beginning in mid-June. At the outset, Eisenhower was informed that the strategic stockpile program could not absorb much more lead and zinc. The president preferred to subsidize domestic producers rather than to curtail foreign imports, but the Interior Department lobbied strongly for higher tariffs.[29] Once again Humphrey expressed reservations about engaging in state subsidies for marginal producers, but, as with the Chilean copper matter, he would avoid driving allies into the Communist camp as long as the solution did not impose "a lot of bugaboos" upon the free-enterprise system.[30]

Eisenhower was most interested in maintaining friendly relations with Mexico where he "[knew] that the possibility of her turning communist would mount rapidly" if new trade barriers were erected. Dulles had already warned "The Boss" that duties would counteract the anticommunist momentum initiated by the successful Guatemalan coup. These "grave consequences" for hemispheric solidarity led Eisenhower to accept Dulles's recommendation that there be no subsidy or tariff increases for six months. Stockpile purchases would be accelerated, as in the earlier case of copper, to stabilize prices by removing surpluses from the marketplace. To justify contravention of the Tariff Commission's judgment, the administration required foreign producers to sign gentlemen's agreements that froze export levels.[31] This at least allowed the fiction that our allies were curtailing exports voluntarily instead of being forced to do so by the self-interested actions of a hegemonic power.

The gambit worked in the short run. Import levels were "virtually stationary" one year later, and domestic production was on the rise as prices began to climb.[32] Thus, potential Communist advances prompted Dulles to mobilize the president's influence against the economic conservatives. Eisenhower reluctantly acted when the threat to hemispheric tranquility overrode his concern for sound fiscal management. He knew that he had to find a satisfactory solution to the trade problems that troubled Latin American leaders. He was not ready to significantly increase development assistance at that time, but capital subsidies were the only viable option if protectionism was allowed to resume. This was the reason why the export-import sector was used to ameliorate Latin American economic difficulties.

The administration temporarily quieted Latin American remonstrances regarding U.S. foreign trade policy even though the lead and zinc issue would boil over again, but it could not silence the growing chorus calling for liberalized trade credits and more development assistance.[33] Latin American statesmen and businessmen decried the fact that they were "forced" to buy European finished products. The common complaint was that durable goods from the United States were more reliable and desirable, but that their higher price tag made them too expensive to purchase without long-term trade credits. Representatives of American exporters, manufacturers, and overseas corporations such as American and Foreign Power, Inc. (the largest foreign utility investor in Latin America), testified to the validity of this claim. Up to four-fifths of Latin American purchases from Europe in 1953 and 1954 were attributed to low-deposit, low-interest, long-term credits subsidized by European governments. During the Truman administration, Exim loans helped American traders compete with the aggressive Europeans. The bank also served as the primary source of development capital for the southern republics, which were denied an aid program akin to the $13 billion Marshall Plan for Western Europe.[34]

Secretary Humphrey convinced the president to reverse his predecessor's policy barely a month after the inauguration. The changes were devised by the Humphrey-chaired National Advisory Council on International and Financial Problems (NAC). The Exim's membership on the NAC and its independent board of directors were terminated; the bank's loan activities were limited to short-term export credits; long-term credits were to be made only in unusual circumstances dictated by national security considerations; and the International Bank for Reconstruction and Development (IBRD) became the long-term lender of first resort and could veto or preempt all loans the Exim might extend to an IBRD member. The impact on credit and development loans to Latin America was instantaneous. The authorizations for new purchases dropped from an annual average of $264 million in 1951 and 1952 to only $17 million in 1953.[35] The policy change reflected Humphrey's faith in the ability of free enterprise to develop economically aspiring countries.

Throughout 1953 State Department officers responsible for relations with Latin America unsuccessfully tried to counteract Humphrey's lending policy and his influence over the Exim. National Security Council policy paper 144/1 supported "accelerating and increasing" loans to supplement private investment, but Secretary Dulles was unwilling to use the power of his post to aid his underlings in their battle with Humphrey. The DOS Policy Planning Board's review of relations with Latin America had the impact of a dull thud without support from Dulles. The report warned that widespread anti-American "social revolution" might evolve unless the government maintained "a public lending institution empowered to make development loans . . . responsive to the requirements of U.S. policy."[36] Dulles refused to use his resources to support economic policies designed to improve relations with other American republics until he thought they were targeted by the Soviet bloc.

The catalyst for a more forthcoming review of Exim lending policies came from a coalition of exporters and congressmen interested in trade with Latin America, and two OAS conferences held in 1954: the Tenth Inter-American Meeting of American Foreign Ministers at Caracas in March, and the November gathering of economic ministers at Rio de Janeiro. A conservative Republican from Indiana, Homer E. Capehart, the chairman of the Senate Banking and Currency Committee (B&C), led a congressional mission to Latin America in late 1953 and held hearings to explore the development and trade enhancement capabilities of the Exim and IBRD. The 131-member Citizens Advisory Committee (CAC), representing nearly every industry from the private sector, assisted him.

The Capehart studies concluded that European competition, subsidized by government credit corporations, endangered the United States trade position in Latin America. They identified the Exim as the preferred institution among Latin American and U.S. exporters because the IBRD demanded time-consuming surveys and world-wide contracts for contracts it funded. But Capehart learned that the Exim's short-term policy forced Latin Americans to buy less-desirable European goods augmented by low-interest, long-term, low-deposit credits. The studies concluded that liberalized Exim lending policies were needed to counter the European advantage. On June 11, 1954, Capehart introduced legislation to liberalize bank policies by reestablishing an independent board of directors, renewing Exim representation on the NAC, and raising the bank's $4.5 billion lending authority by $500 million.[37] Capehart's bill received broad support on Capitol Hill. Clearly the Eisenhower administration would have to review its Exim lending policies.

As might be expected, Humphrey was less than elated with Capehart's interference. He told Eisenhower that the CAC was "packed by those who want to use Government money." The secretary believed that the additional $500 million threatened his quest for a balanced budget. He also realized that Capehart intended the authorization to signal a congressional mandate for more development financing.[38] On the other hand, Assistant Secretary of State for Latin American Affairs John Moors Cabot hoped that Capehart's efforts would help him convince Secretary Dulles that he would have to satisfy the economic expectations of the Hispanic delegates at the Caracas Conference. Cabot was disconsolate because Dulles believed that the Guatemalan government was infiltrated by Communists; thus, his only goal was to get the other American republics to go on record against communism as alien to the region before the Central Intelligence Agency (CIA) unleashed a coup by Guatemalan exiles.[39]

The Randall Commission Report crushed Cabot's hopes for true free trade and raw material stabilization agreements, but Cabot and Milton Eisenhower did persuade Dulles, Eisenhower, and even Humphrey that the secretary of state could not go to Caracas empty-handed if he wanted an anticommunist resolution. This realization led to a review of economic relations with Latin America. Time prevented a major reexamination before the Caracas Conference convened; therefore, the president authorized Dulles to tell his counterparts that the United States was amenable to a separate economic meeting at Rio de Janeiro later in the year. In the meantime, Dulles told the delegates that the Exim would consider sound loan applications not considered by the IBRD, provided that the requests fell "within the prudent loaning capacity of the bank." As this passage implied, policy had not changed all that much. Dulles's actions underscored this point. He tried to keep the Caracas agenda free of secondary issues like creation of a regional development institution. He left the conference immediately after obtaining his anticommunist resolution. The Latin Americans, Cabot, and Milton Eisenhower were disappointed by Dulles's early departure. They also knew that the Dulles statement did not alter the parsimonious Exim lending policy, but they hoped that Capehart's bill and preparations for Rio would yield liberalized development policies.[40]

Capehart also thought the administration was still trying to make the Exim "the little fellow" in comparison to the IBRD. He relentlessly lobbied the president. Finally, in June, Eisenhower decided that there was no alternative to the Capehart Bill given the number of influential businessmen who supported the legislation. He also hoped that Latin Americans would abandon their resolutions for commodity price stabilization agreements, preferential trade concessions, and creation of an inter-American development bank funded in large part with monies from the United States Treasury, if the Exim's independence was assured and its lending capacity was increased.[41]

Cabinet officers heralded the new Exim lending policy and the creation of the International Finance Corporation (IFC). The latter would promote investment by using equity holdings to attract private business ventures to otherwise marginal portfolios. The IFC was authorized to lend funds without host government guarantees, something the IBRD required. This was supposed to entice businessmen into making investments in LDCs. According to the NSC, the "*more liberal* lending policy" was designed to stop Communist gains in the region.[42]

Humphrey announced the new policy at the Rio Conference on November 22, 1954. His counterparts interpreted the changes as a symbolic victory. The president's brother refused to attend the conference because the package was much too stingy, and more important, he suspected that operational lending mechanisms, controlled by Humphrey, would prevent liberalized lending practices. The president chose to accept these reactions rather than undertake more costly programs.[43]

Exim authorizations averaged $200 million per year between May 1954 and March 1956.[44] This was well below the $500 million demanded by Humphrey's critics because the NAC reviewed every loan to keep operations within "fiscally responsible" limits. Even the president expressed disappointment with Humphrey's tactics as late as March 1955; however, he did nothing more than ask for an in-house study to ascertain the facts.[45] This timid leadership style failed to budge Humphrey until September 1956, when the NSC adopted new lending guidelines stating that closer association with the Latin American people required "essentially complementary" IBRD and Exim development loan policies. The change occurred after the Soviets began to penetrate Latin American markets with unsupervised low-interest, long-term credits and concessionary trade agreements.[46] As with the earlier commodity crises, the Exim lending issue illustrated that Eisenhower refused to abandon fiscal conservatism unless domestic pressure groups and cold-war concerns threatened to disrupt his Latin American policy. It would take another cold-war challenge before the president endorsed a modest but comprehensive regional development program.

Aside from the Exim decision, United States-Latin American relations were relatively uneventful between 1955 and 1957. There was only one significant change in foreign economic policy, and it was administrative. President Eisenhower created the interagency Council on Foreign Economic Policy (CFEP) in July 1954 to formulate, coordinate, and monitor foreign economic policy.[47] The new bureaucracy altered very little policy in this period, although it increased the influence of domestic-oriented fiscal conservatives, who sat on the CFEP at the expense of foreign policy specialists. For example, the CFEP opposed the $4 billion World Economic Program (WEP) proposed by C. D. Jackson, Eisenhower's first psychological warfare advisor, who wanted a 1 percent annual increase in the LDCs' per capita income for ten years. The Eisenhower administration decided that the proposal was too costly, that it duplicated existing programs, and that it might intensify congressional opposition to the MSP.[48] The administration also rejected United Nations Ambassador Henry Cabot Lodge's campaign to get support for a Special United Nations Fund for Economic Development (SUNFED). Humphrey and the CFEP convinced the president that SUNFED's low-interest, long-term loans for nonliquidating projects would undercut the commercial rates and standards of the Exim and IBRD. Their argument that American funds were more secure in American institutions rather than a body with Communist members also swayed Eisenhower. Finally, Humphrey thought a soft-loan UN fund might set a precedent for regional soft-loan agencies. Secretary Dulles originally supported both proposals, but he failed to lobby for either out of fear that funding for them would be at the expense of existing bilateral programs or that Congress would emasculate the entire MSP.[49]

Eisenhower was not prepared to embark upon a massive new economic policy like that ensconced in the WEP, and he frowned upon sharing control of taxpayers' money with the UN. The cases indicated that he would expand bilateral economic assistance if rational justifications were developed and if there was public support for development aid. Before 1957, Eisenhower preferred to use low-keyed tactics to get support for his aid programs. He held weekly meetings with Republican congressional leaders and regularly covered foreign policy matters during bipartisan legislative meetings. He frequently defended the MSP at stag dinners, press conferences, and his speeches. Eisenhower and his advisors usually argued that the MSP was the least expensive way to avoid the tragedy and cost of a war, and that public assistance, supervised by United States' personnel, was an effective way to transmit American values and meet the development aspirations of impatient LDCs. He was not predisposed to publicly harangue his legislative opponents, nor did his perception of presidential decorum incline him toward hawking national security programs by a public exhibition like the whistle-stop Woodrow Wilson used to seek support for the League of Nations. Unfortunately, his dignified reliance on logic and patriotism did not work as well as he had expected.

By mid-1956, repeated slashes to his "minimal" aid requests moved

Eisenhower to reconsider his tactic of jaw-boning congressmen for their support on MSP bills. For fiscal year 1957 alone, Congress cut mutual security appropriations from $4.8 billion to $3.8 billion. Concurrently, Dulles became receptive to formation of a flexible, multiyear, soft-loan development agency. He worried that aid reductions were too deep, and he was frustrated that so much of his time was required for planning and testimony during the annual budget battles on Capitol Hill. Finally, Dulles reached the conclusion that Soviet trade and aid programs were a significant challenge to his far-flung collective security system.[51]

Both men were beginning to realize that their foreign policies were endangered by the United States' apparent unwillingness or inability to meet the LDCs' calls for public assistance on terms easier than could be obtained from either the IBRD or the Exim. It became evident that trade and private investment were not adequate for Latin Americans interested in creating national industries that could diversify exports and reduce dependence on imported capital goods. Just as the administration was about to reevaluate its foreign economic policy, both the House Foreign Affairs Committee and the Senate Foreign Relations Committee indicated that they were going to examine whether foreign assistance was necessary, and the magnitude, duration, and goals that aid programs should operate under if continuation of mutual security was in order.[52]

The White House gradually decided that it was more important to form the right kind of citizens board even if that risked the "disorderly" prospect of "competing" congressional and presidential committees.[53] In late September, Eisenhower appointed a sympathetic bipartisan committee headed by Benjamin F. Fairless, former chairman and president of United States Steel Corporation, to study the purposes, scope, operations, and impact of the entire aid program, especially the relative roles of military and economic aid, "in relationship to the foreign policy and national interest of the United States." Eisenhower expressed particular interest in knowing their opinions about the appropriate size and duration of the program given the nation's resources, how flexibility and continuity might be achieved, and how public lending institutions might improve their efforts to stimulate private investment overseas. They were instructed to file their recommendations by March 1, 1957, in order to give the administration sufficient time to incorporate the committee's findings into the FY 1958 aid budget.[54]

In late October, the International Development Advisory Board (IDAB) of the International Cooperation Administration, which replaced the FOA as the aid agency, undertook a review of foreign economic policy. Its chairman, the maverick Eric Johnston, president of the Motion Picture Association, was a holdover from the Truman administration. He wanted to provide a reasoned alternative to the Fairless Report should the latter prove to be a tirade against development assistance. The IDAB justified its undertaking by trying to develop "a well-defined and clearly articulated rationale underlying U.S. economic development assistance." Specifically, the IDAB asked: "Is our long term goal economic development [and how] does this promote our position versus [the] Soviets."[55] All three studies assumed that aid could be justified if it were an effective cold-war weapon, but the Fairless and Johnston committees conducted their hearings as if it was their duty to discredit the congressional study if the legislators released an anti-aid report.

The Fairless Report was delivered to the president on schedule. The need to maintain economic assistance for the foreseeable future as a complement to private investment was accepted by the advisors given the challenges mounted by traditional Soviet imperialism and their expanding economic offensive. The report advocated larger economic assistance programs. The committee advocated segregation of economic and military aid so that the Department of Defense administered and paid for the latter. They called for larger economic assistance programs but could not agree how much bigger. Two-year authorizations were recommended to provide operational continuity, flexibility in the event of unforeseen crises, and to avoid the annual budget confrontation with Congress. The advisors advocated virtual elimination of all economic grant assistance and guaranteeing the soundness of dollar loans by prohibiting repayment in soft currencies. Reflecting the cold-war orientation of the Fairless Committee, the report urged the president to favorably allocate limited resources to members of the "collective security system."[56]

The Johnston Report presented a clear justification for the administration's foreign aid program; the Fairless Committee could not agree that aid was more than a tool against Soviet aggression. The IDAB emphasized the interdependence of all free-world nations and the United States' unique responsibility and capacity to use its limited but substantial resources to facilitate economic expansion necessary for free enterprise. The IDAB assumed that aid would pay for the infrastructure that third-world countries required to attract foreign investors. The accent on economic development hinged upon a "substantial increase" in nonmilitary aid and separating economic programs from those designed to prop up the alliance system. Long-term economic aid was seen as a prerequisite for the flexibility needed in an unstable world and the continuity necessary to kindle third-world confidence in the

United States. Most important, the Johnston Report called upon the administration to charter an International Development Fund (IDF) to make long-term, low-interest loans in dollars and local currencies. The fund's autonomy from Congress was to be assured by providing it with a replenishable no-year authorization; an independent director would possess sufficient power to insure responsiveness to unforeseen loan requests.[57]

The CFEP exhaustively reviewed the Fairless and Johnston reports.[58] The Citizens Report did not elicit much enthusiasm. The most favorable comments were from Treasury officials who claimed that the Fairless Report balanced the nation's limited means and international economic development. The DOS and the ICA opposed the elimination of economic grants and restrictions on soft loans on the assumption that poorer countries were unable to repay loans. State condemned preferential treatment for military allies; thus, ICA and DOS urged allocation of economic assistance be linked to a nation's development needs and the feasibility of its project applications. Only IBRD president Eugene Black totally denigrated the report for its negative national security "tone and approach in so far as economic aid is concerned." He thought the advisors treated development aid "as the tail of the dog," the direct consequence, he concluded, of an almost nonexistent analytical framework. There was general agreement that aid would continue indefinitely, but no consensus emerged on the value of separate military and economic assistance programs or how to administer two independent but related forms of aid. Therefore, the CFEP concluded that further study of each issue was appropriate before administration policy could be stated with authority.

The Johnston Report elicited hearty endorsement from the DOS and the Council of Economic Advisors. They were attracted by the conceptual justification for development assistance and the IDF proposal. State Department officials did not believe it was "realistic" to expect Congress to approve a "substantial" fund free from legislative review. Instead, Dulles preferred to establish a multiyear, replenishable, soft-loan institution in 1957 and then try to enlarge the fund once Congress accepted the concept. The fiscal agencies objected to the open-ended financing provisions and the attempt to remove annual congressional oversight from the aid program; the ICA director denounced any attempt to establish an aid agency outside his influence. Once again the CFEP was forced to conduct an evaluation of the IDF concept even though most department and agency comments liked the flexibility and long-term planning intrinsic in the IDAB proposal. In short, neither report provided detailed proposals innocuous enough to be incorporated into Eisenhower's 1957 mutual security message to Congress.[59] The two Executive Branch reports were both a disappointment and a boon to the president. They failed to develop a dynamic pro-aid consensus that Eisenhower could rely on to muster public support in behalf of new programs; however, they agreed that aid was a valuable cold-war tool. This conclusion made it highly unlikely that the threat to terminate the MSP would be carried out by Congress.

Dulles was not about to wait another year to present the IDF to Congress. He understood the relationship between international stability and the unfulfilled aspirations of less-developed peoples, but he did not feel comfortable trying to drag Eisenhower away from his traditional faith in private investment, reciprocal trade, and supplemental capital loaned by cautious hard-money institutions. His diffidence disappeared by 1956, when Dulles and Eisenhower had established a symbiotic relationship based on mutual respect and trust.[60] Dulles and Eisenhower were convinced "trade, not aid" had not lived up to expectations, that is, to develop the Third World while maintaining popular and congressional support for a modest assistance program that would reinforce free trade and private-sector initiative. The Fairless and especially the IDAB reports convinced Dulles that he would have at least a few allies in the coming legislative battle. Therefore, Dulles decided to press for the enactment of the Development Loan Fund (DLF) in 1957. He captured Eisenhower's support by pointing out that flexible and consistent development policies necessitated asking Congress to create an institution authorized to draw (directly from the Treasury) $750 million annually for three years. Dulles delivered his proposal to the Congress on April 8, 1957.[61]

The DLF and the 1958 aid package did not fare well even though the White House mounted its first determined public relations campaign on behalf of the MSP. The fund faced opposition from Humphrey and Exim officers, who questioned whether hard lending institutions could maintain sound banking practices in the face of more liberal lenders. Humphrey condemned the attempt to remove a spending agency from the annual congressional review process. Eisenhower let his treasury secretary know that he was "completely dedicated and committed" to the DLF and chided Humphrey for allowing his ideological biases to obscure the value of a flexible tool responsive to "the particular moment and situation."[62] For the moment, rigid fiscal conservatism was not allowed to supersede the administration's foreign economic goals. This shift in emphasis did not mean that Eisenhower abandoned interest in Humphrey's *cause célèbre*. Therefore, as congressional opposition mounted against the DLF concept and the amount of unregulated capital, Eisenhower convinced Dulles that a two-year authorization of $500 million and $625 million was the best possible compromise.[63]

Interdepartmental committees drafting the DLF charter made every effort to encourage private investment activities. On paper, the terms of reference minimized the difference between loan terms offered governments and private applicants (other institutions favored government requests), even though the latter received preferential consideration by the DLF loan board. One rationale for this policy was the assumption that Congress might be more sympathetic to future appropriation requests. In fact, Dulles invoked Eisenhower's pledge to ask Congress for more money in April when he learned that loan requests were four times greater than DLF resources authorized by Congress in 1957.[64] But in late 1958 and early 1959 Dulles and Robert Anderson, Humphrey's replacement, were frustrated when Eisenhower hesitated to lead a new request for at least $700 million in fiscal years 1959 and 1960.[65]

Actually, support for the DLF began to abate as soon as Dulles, the administration's most vigorous proponent of multiyear funding, died from cancer in May 1959, because Eisenhower preferred more traditional hard-loan agencies like the Exim and the IBRD. Besides insufficient appropriations and official neglect, the DLF's value to developing countries was limited when the administration decided to apply Buy American restrictions to DLF loans. The CFEP, in November 1959, ruled that DLF credits must be spent in the United States in an attempt to force European governments to expand their share of the development assistance burden, and to combat declining gold reserves caused by the first prolonged postwar debit in the nation's balance of trade.[66]

The DLF reflected the administration's readiness to employ liberalized lending techniques in response to the aspirations expressed by LDCs and the competition posed by less belligerent Soviet tactics. It was the only substantive change in the aid programs traceable to the 1956–57 aid studies. The institution was a significant departure from Humphrey's antidevelopment financing policies, but Eisenhower, at best, proved he was reluctant to support the kind of DLF advocated by Dulles. The president was unable to divorce himself from economic conservatism until international crises compelled a more forthcoming response to third-world demands for more development assistance. For Latin America, the fund was never a windfall. The lending criteria emphasized aid to countries formed after World War II, especially India and other Asian states. By the end of 1961, Latin America received only $337 million, or 15 percent of the DLF's total expenditures.[67]

Something other that the DLF was needed to maintain a special relationship with the American republics.

Latin Americans were rarely satisfied with Eisenhower's foreign economic policies before 1958. They frequently charged that the United States lavished aid on nations along the Soviet Union's periphery and ignored the more tranquil southern republics. The Exim ceiling was increased to $7 billion, and the annual authorization rate within the hemisphere rose to about $500 million by 1958, but the credits carried high interest rates and required repayment in dollars.[68]

Latin American leaders continued to ask for a regional soft-loan institution without a Buy American policy. Hispanics voiced dissatisfaction with United States' reliance upon private investment for economic development. American firms had some $9 billion in direct investments in Latin America by 1960, but most of that was concentrated in extractive industries, and, of that, more than 25 percent went to locate and remove petroleum from Venezuela. Even President Eisenhower conceded that foreign private investors were either too hesitant or too selective to further the kind of infrastructure and industrial development called for by the NSC. Finally, government trade policies were unraveling by 1958. For instance, Latin Americans noted that commodity prices had fallen 12 percent over ten years.[69] Although sensitive toward Latin American complaints, the administration did not undertake real policy reformulation until it was confronted by anti-Nixon mobs in South America and the advent of Castroism in Cuba.

In mid-1957, the administration's five-year trade extension proposal rekindled debate over the best way to promote economic development and friendly relations in the hemisphere. Eisenhower worried that Congress might subvert his entire trade program unless domestic lead and zinc producers were protected from cheaper suppliers in Latin America by the Tariff Commission. Dulles and Eisenhower were worried about the repercussions if the United States appeared to be limiting trade opportunities for countries already experiencing depressed commodity prices. Peruvians complained that the United States ignored their requests for aid. Moreover, the proposed tariff policy would undercut their self-financed development efforts. Peruvian legislators threatened to open trade relations with the Soviet bloc if they did not receive more satisfactory treatment. Eisenhower was sympathetic, but he was paralyzed by the surge of congressional protectionism.[70]

Mexican president Adolfo Ruiz Cortines was, if anything, more anxious than the Peruvians, because 50 percent of Mexico's mining production, 32 percent of its exports, and 6 percent of its tax revenues came from lead and zinc trade with its northern neighbor. Ruiz Cortines appreciated Eisenhower's decision to hold firm on his call for a five-year extension of the reciprocal trade program. Nevertheless, reflecting an uneasiness about Eisenhower's fortitude, he called for "a multilateral solution that would make . . . individual measures unnecessary" and help to insure hemispheric friendship and solidarity. Eisenhower replied that it was premature to act before a ruling was issued by the Tariff Commission.[71]

The decision was sent to the president on April 24, 1958. The report recommended maximum tariffs under the Reciprocal Trade Act to prevent "serious injury" to the domestic lead and zinc industry. Eisenhower desperately searched for a solution. Fiscal considerations ruled out economic aid. Instead, he suspended the commission's findings and proposed to subsidize domestic producers without curtailing imports.[72] In September, the legislators rejected the Mineral Stabilization Plan. The administration unilaterally invoked a temporary 20 percent quota reduction to forestall protectionist measures. Peruvian and Mexican officials were informed that this alternative to the Tariff Commission report "was a stop-gap measure pending a multilateral solution" which would take time to negotiate. Latin Americans criticized the independent trade action, but they hoped Washington's new attitude toward multilateralism would be fruitful.[73] In effect, the Eisenhower administration found it was being forced to enter negotiations from which a commodity agreement was the logical end product.

Opposition to international commodity agreements was endemic within the Eisenhower administration. The Randall Commission rejected the concept of artificial price stabilization in 1954. Randall, who became the CFEP chairman in 1956, endorsed the committee's 1955 decision not to engage in commodity arrangements except in rare circumstances. His belief that they would lead the free world "toward socialism" reflected the consensus within the administration. The CFEP reconfirmed this policy, at the NSC's behest, on May 20, 1958.[74]

Under Secretary of State C. Douglas Dillon, who did not want to antagonize friendly governments, reopened the issue when he refused to publicly reject possible membership in any lead and zinc settlement as a prerequisite to attendance at the Geneva Commodity Agreements Meeting beginning on November 6, 1958. The CFEP authorized DOS participation in exploratory talks after Thomas Mann pledged that State would obtain the council's approval before it signed an agreement that conflicted with government prohibitions against commodity agreements. At Geneva, Mann fended off criticisms of the United States' unilateral quotas, then he agreed to convene a lead and zinc study group at the United Nations in January 1959. The CFEP began to reconsider the quota policy and explore ways to purchase surplus commodities through barter programs as pressure for participation in an agreement mounted. The issue languished for the remainder of Eisenhower's presidency except for the four-year extension of reciprocal trade in August 1960. Administration officials were pleased that "excessive" tariff increases on lead and zinc were defeated before the bill passed; however, free traders and Latin Americans were angered by provisions that prevented tariff reductions and made it easier to invoke tougher penalties when foreign competitors threatened domestic industries.[75]

The Eisenhower administration would not subsidize the production of surplus raw materials, but Washington realized that it could not continue to dismiss petitions for assistance by telling Hispanics to rely upon private investments and existing hard-loan agencies. The administration reexamined the relationship between economic aid and its investment policies in the spring of 1958 under the impetus of Vice-President Nixon's admonitions about the mounting Soviet threat in the LDCs. Eisenhower wanted to know if a coordinated program of private capital and public funds could effectively compete against a Soviet system able to operate "without regard to profits." The study was conducted by the Committee on World Economic Practices (CWEP), chaired by Harold Boeschenstein, president of Owens-Corning Fiberglass Corporation, under the auspices of the Commerce Department's Business Advisory Council (BAC).[76]

The Boeschenstein Report, like the Johnston Report, decided that economic aid was necessary and that aid agencies were already doing all they could to promote foreign investment. The CWEP cited $1 billion in Soviet aid to LDCs to justify making more loans to United States' businesses operating overseas, to establish local development banks and savings associations, and to fund turnkey projects begun by host governments. Committee members believed that progress required patience; nevertheless, they concluded that the administration underestimated how reluctant domestic corporations were when it came to overseas capital ventures. Foreign policy specialists were also informed that denying aid did not promote a favorable foreign investment climate when governments believed multilateral corporations were inconsistent with their development aspirations.[77] It was becoming evident that another weapon was needed to combat the Soviet challenge during Eisenhower's last two years in office, especially in crisis-ridden Latin America.

In May 1958, Vice-President Richard M. Nixon made a goodwill trip to South America. His hosts politely but insistently demanded commodity agreements and establishment of a multi-billion dollar regional development bank. His hosts conveyed the impression that social revolution was seething just below the surface of the growing urban blight, and, as if to highlight the gravity of the appeals, Nixon and his wife were confronted by life-threatening anti-American mobs in Lima, Peru, and Caracas, Venezuela.[78] The vice-president reported to the Cabinet that the organized nature of the riots certainly was evidence of Communist involvement, but he went on to explain that the outbursts represented pent-up frustrations against the United States for supporting dictators and unresponsive elites instead of popular organizations, for appearing to foist foreign corporations upon poor countries, and for withholding the kind of assistance demanded throughout Latin America. The treatment meted out to Nixon, and his report, added a new sense of urgency to the reevaluation of hemispheric economic relations already underway.[79]

Even before the riots, Milton Eisenhower planned a fact-finding mission to the region to evaluate the accuracy of statements made by Pedro Beltran, the publisher of *La Prensa* and the future Peruvian minister of the economy and prime minister, and other leading Latin Americans who felt that revolution was on the horizon unless new social development programs and more traditional development projects were quickly launched by a regional bank. Besides traditional requests for commodity agreements, stable trade relations, and more economic aid to industrialize, Latin American leaders made special pleas for a flexible development bank ready to make soft loans to the region for traditionally unbankable projects in fields like health, education, and housing.[80]

Milton Eisenhower reported his findings to the president in December 1958. He recommended initiation of social development programs within the limitations of United States' resources if host countries expanded efforts to attract private investment capital. He called for a variation of the soft- and hard-loan regional development bank that received approval, in principle, by the administration in August. He also endorsed participation in commodity agreements, efforts to prevent closing the United States to foreign exports, and creation of a Central American Common Market. The sense of pending crisis, the combined influence of officials like Dillon, and the resignation of Humphrey in 1957 assured a much more sympathetic review of this report than Eisenhower's 1953 version. Nevertheless, the report went through significant revision after a cabinet-level review in November to, in the president's words, "achieve concurrence among those most interested." In the final draft, dated December 28, 1958, most of Milton Eisenhower's innovative ideas were diluted or removed, for example, "rapid industrialization" became "requires industrialization"; social development proposals like low-cost housing for Canal Zone employees were tabled; and the CFEP scuttled his commodity agreement recommendation.[81] The Cabinet supported his common-market concept, but development bank negotiations proceeded in a deliberate fashion as the administration attempted to find an inexpensive alternative to Brazilian President Juscelino Kubitschek de Oliveira's Operation Pan America (OPA).

Kubitschek had been pressing the OPA upon the Eisenhower administration ever since 1956. The plan envisioned a $5 billion development bank and up to another $35 billion in aid over twenty years. To redress Latin America's relationship with industrialized nations, Kubitschek also sought commodity price stabilization and lower tariffs for poorer OAS countries. Kubitschek reintroduced the proposal after Nixon's ill-fated trip.[82] Eisenhower expressed delight at Kubitschek's initiative to further regional unity. He sent Assistant Secretary of State R. R. Rubottom and Secretary Dulles on separate missions to Brazil to ascertain what the OPA proposal entailed and to signal the administration's receptiveness. Dulles concluded that "unreasonable" antipathy toward a worldwide development approach mandated reorganization of "our Latin American operations so as to make them seem somewhat more regional.[83] Eisenhower and Dulles reluctantly decided that it would be too risky to ignore Kubitschek given Nixon's May reception and hemispheric support for OPA.[84]

The State Department hoped to narrow the scope of what Dulles termed an "essentially constructive idea."[85] In a November meeting with Latin Americans, Dillon proposed an Inter-American Development Bank (IADB) plan and select projects (most of the technicians would come from the United States). The Hispanics would have voting control of a $700 million hard-loan fund, but Dillon insisted that the U.S. government possess majority interest in the more flexible $150 million soft-loan fund.[86]

Latin American officials "generally favored" the draft because it gave life to a regional bank, even though they knew that the bank was a hollow alternative to the OPA. Brazilians complained that the soft-loan component would be controlled by the United States and that its budget fell well below the $5 billion Kubitschek proposed. Confident the Latin American governments would not jeopardize their aspirations for a regional bank, Treasury Secretary Anderson's Final Proposal added only $150 million to the initial hard-loan capitalization. The

United States' $450 million contribution meant that Washington controlled 42.8 percent of the bank's hard-loan voting stock. Eisenhower approved Anderson's ultimatum for it avoided "imping[ing] too heavily upon" the operations of the existing institutions, it was small enough to satisfy fiscal conservatives, and it prevented a significant loss of "influence" over the government's foreign expenditures. On April 8, 1959, Latin American economic ministers reluctantly signed the IADB enabling agreement proposed by Anderson. They were pleased that their twenty-year-old dream was a reality, but United States' influence on the loan board and the small soft-fund account soured the accomplishment.[87]

Establishing the IADB in early 1959 was a seminal development in United States-Latin American relations, but the Eisenhower administration was unable to gloat once Eisenhower and his advisors convinced themselves that the Cuban Revolution was turning toward the Soviet bloc. Fidel Castro's coalition of Constitutionalists, Socialists, and Communists triumphantly entered Havana on January 1, 1959, after three years of fighting against Fulgencio Batista's dictatorial regime. At first, Castro was an unstable "enigma" to Washington sages.[88] Eight months later, policymakers concluded that leftist "Zealots" were plotting, with Soviet assistance, revolutions in neighboring countries. By early January 1960, Eisenhower actively sought Latin American support for an economic embargo against Cuba and a replay of the Guatemalan coup of 1954. Meanwhile, Latin American presidents aroused Washington with stories of guerrilla warfare fueled by the masses' growing discontent over their economic plight.[89]

The ferment convinced President Eisenhower to visit Brazil, Argentina, Chile, and Uruguay early in 1960. He knew other Latin American presidents including Llezas of Colombia, Beltrán of Peru, and Betancourt of Venezuela resented his absence from the area since his two-day 1956 stay in Panama.[90] Seeing Latin Americans working to improve their standard of living, such as residents of Santiago building their own homes, moved President Eisenhower to accept the need for "historic measures designed to bring about social reforms for the benefit of all the people of Latin America." Eisenhower tried to tie departures from existing public assistance policies with "repudiat[ion of] dictatorship in any form." But he was exasperated to learn that South American leaders declined to denounce Castro until they had an olive branch to offer constituents who had begun to turn the Cuban revolutionary into a folk hero.[91]

Eisenhower did not abandon the idea that those living in depressed areas had the greatest responsibility for their future; however, Latin

American leaders insisted he grant "more reality to Operation Pan America" if he wanted to foster anticommunist unity. Even Milton Eisenhower exhorted his brother to lend substance to the 1960 trip by increasing hard and soft loans before "left-wing governments" sprang up and forced "vast expenditures" that probably would be too late to overcome United States' identification "with the existing order. . . ."[92]

To cultivate better relations with Latin American governments, the president substituted the IADB for the DLF as the preferred soft-loan agency in the hemisphere. The decision was relatively easy because the $150 million Fund for Special Operations was already planned for the IADB. With this revision, the American bank would increase its lending by up to $200 million per year. This policy reflected preparations for an OAS conference to be held in Bogotá, Colombia, at summer's end. The CFEP had already cleared the way for soft-loan agencies to engage in social development programs in October 1959, when it endorsed the financing of private home ownership projects overseas. In March 1960, the DLF authorized its first housing loan to Latin America—$2 million to assist a Peruvian savings and loan association to extend mortgages to middle-class residents of Lima.[93] Facing the prospect of a Cuban social development model and Latin American hostility toward the right-wing dictatorship in the Dominican Republic, Eisenhower decided to make social development and reform the hallmark of his Bogotá policy in lieu of the more costly OPA proposal.

On July 8, 1960, in a prepared statement, Eisenhower noted the "aspirations" for homes, land, and a better life as well as economic growth conveyed to him during the four-nation tour. He articulated a new emphasis on "practicable ways" to promote self-development and to create conditions that would accelerate the formation of democratic governments. As an example of effective cooperation in this venture, the president cited the opening of more land to settlement and cultivation and beginning housing programs to further "individual ownership of small homes." Eisenhower concluded with the promise to seek a special although modest program for Latin America from Congress before the Bogotá Conference convened.[94]

The July 8 statement did not garner unrestrained approval from the other OAS members, in part because it was seen for what it was—the second of a two-pronged attack against Castroism. The first was the decision, announced July 6, to cut the amount of sugar that Cuba could export to the United States by seven hundred thousand tons. The aid was candy coating to make the embargo palatable to Latin Americans wary about the United States' economic power.[95] In addition, the presidential package fell far short of OPA. The Brazilian government's response was representative. It termed Eisenhower's proposal an "unsatisfactory" and "timid" compromise incapable of stopping the "cold war already clearly unleashed in this hemisphere."[96]

Eisenhower was not prepared to make more significant concessions to the American republics. Concern about the nation's fiscal integrity and the fear that Congress would defeat a large new program stiffened his resolve. Secretary Anderson opposed using a presidential message to give special emphasis to the Latin American program. He thought the proposal might become a bottomless pit for American capital; therefore, he wanted to avoid another foreign assistance layer by using existing aid funds in Latin America. Encouraged by Milton Eisenhower and preoccupied with Cuba and the coming meetings in San Jose, Costa Rica (to unite the OAS against Cuba) and Bogotá, the president overrode Anderson on the message to Congress, but he agreed to limit the program's size to prevent destabilization of the American economy. On August 5, he asked Congress to authorize a special social development fund of $500 million before the Bogotá meeting began on September 5.[97]

Adding to Eisenhower's dilemma were congressional complaints that the authorization bill was being rammed through the legislature. DOS officials wondered if Congress would act before the Bogotá Conference convened. Congress sent the bill to Eisenhower on September 8 after an intense but brief debate. The opposition was vocal, but after Castro's success most legislators apparently agreed with Senator Capehart, who charged that the legislation was several years too late.[98] With funds in hand, Dillon told the Latin American delegates that the new United States' policy was designed to "bring fresh hope to the less privileged people . . . of Latin America. . . ." The under secretary promised that the United States was prepared to stand by a long-range program; he cited President Eisenhower's recommendation that Congress appropriate the authorized funds in 1961. The OAS adopted the Act of Bogotá on September 13, 1960. It stressed land reform, the building of housing and community facilities, and improved education. Social development was to be made possible through tax reforms and modernized credit institutions. A $500 million inter-American social development fund, to be administered by the IADB, would help defray the local costs for development projects. Finally, the United States would help the OAS strengthen its development planning capacity so that fruitful projects could be identified and started at the earliest possible moment.[99]

By proposing the Act of Bogotá, President Eisenhower and his advisors tacitly recognized the shortage of development capital and the need for social development programs in Latin America. The real significance of the Bogotá agreement was not that the United States government agreed to spend more money in its own backyard; rather, it was whether the transition away from the trade, not aid policy was "too little and too late."[100] Inherent in this question posed by the CFEP was why it took seven years for the administration to adopt the spirit and implement the programs favored by Milton Eisenhower in his 1953 report to the president and the October 1953 position paper by the State Department Policy Planning Board. The answer lies largely with the ideological baggage of Dwight Eisenhower, and especially of Secretary Humphrey. Both men pursued fiscal responsibility even though they were aware that serious capital shortages undermined the LDCs' ability to diversify monocultural economies. Thus, before 1956, Humphrey had little difficulty convincing Eisenhower to rely upon free-enterprise solutions to development problems. Even when international problems like the Chilean copper crisis of 1953–54 required the government to intervene in the marketplace, every attempt was made to minimize statism.

This crises indicated that free trade was always an illusion for Latin America in the 1950s. The Eisenhower administration rejected Latin American calls for commodity agreements in the name of free markets only to compromise reciprocal trade in order to appease protectionists at home. The one remaining option was to increase foreign assistance on concessionary terms to promote conditions conducive to private investors. This was a modest improvement, but the program suffered from the administration's failure to realize that corporate interests often had nothing in common with the foreign policy concerns of the United States' government, and that Latin Americans distrusted any endeavor designed to extract profits from their struggling economies.

Humphrey's influence gradually declined as the cold war threatened to impinge upon relatively tranquil relations between the American republics. Every policy innovation can be traced to the fear of either Soviet economic encroachment in the area or "communist-inspired" revolutions like the one in Cuba. Even before such threats, Humphrey's ideological commitment to free enterprise appeared dated, even obstructionist, to advisors like Milton Eisenhower, who tried to convince the president that fiscal conservatism would have an unhealthy effect on United States-Latin American relations. President Eisenhower was receptive to such counsel at times, after all, like Dulles, he was an internationalist. Both men were committed to containing communism, but each was hampered in this crusade. Much of their energies went into explaining to Humphrey the United States' changing geopolitical obligations. In the meantime, Eisenhower continually hesitated to undertake sizeable spending programs. Dulles found it difficult to press for new foreign economic policies for fear of undermining his working relationship with the president. Eisenhower was a decisive leader once policy options were presented to him; however, policy formulation by staff consensus reduced the choices from which he could select. This hindered and even defeated innovation, especially innovations that might incur substantial financial obligations for the United States government.

It is ironic that Eisenhower, who deeply believed in the Mutual Security Program and reciprocal trade, failed to take a consistent and a strong leadership position on these issues. For example, liberalized Exim lending was mandated by legislation, endorsed by the NSC, and promised to Latin Americans. Humphrey continued to restrict the bank's operations through his position as chairman of the NAC. Eisenhower's leadership amounted to the commissioning of another study, which did not bring about a significant increase in lending activity until intelligence reports indicated that the Soviets were launching their own programs to help the LDCs. Eisenhower was rarely able to maintain the kind of leadership necessary to see innovations through a hostile Congress, even after consigning his prestige and influence to the fray. Eisenhower gave his total support to the DLF and the entire aid package in the budget battle over fiscal year 1958 appropriations, but his commitment to the DLF waned when Dulles died and fiscal priorities reemerged. Then again, the president's leadership could be decisive and consistent whenever he perceived a clear threat to national security. This was the case when Eisenhower willingly employed his political capital to get a special development program for Latin America after Castro came to power.

Only crises or unrelenting pressure from Latin American leaders provided foreign policy specialists with the leverage needed to overcome the resistance of interdepartmental committees like the CFEP, where representatives from domestically oriented and fiscally concerned agencies could veto proposals by the State Department. This fact helps explain why officials concerned with Latin American affairs had to settle for one change at a time even though they knew sweeping revisions in foreign economic policies were in order. This ad hoc approach to United States-Latin American relations eventually led to the Act of Bogotá. OAS nations were promised more public assistance in the form of hard and soft loans, but there was no attempt to redress the structural trade problems inherent in the exchange of goods and services between developed and underdeveloped countries. That is, modest increases in temporary capital transfers were preferred to more fundamental correctives like international commodity agreements. This was the policy that John F. Kennedy inherited in 1961 and popularized as the Alliance for Progress.

Notes

1. Burton I. Kaufman, *Trade and Aid: Eisenhower's Foreign Economic Policy, 1953–61* (Baltimore: Johns Hopkins University Press, 1982), 7, 58–73.

2. R. Harrison Wagner, *United States Policy toward Latin America: A Study in International and Domestic Politics* (Stanford: Stanford University Press, 1970), 104–5, 150–51.

3. See *Trade and Aid,* 207–9.

4. The best illustration of Eisenhower's free-trade outlook is DDE Diary, 2 July 1953, Diary—Copies of DDE Personal—1953–54 (2), box 9, Dwight D. Eisenhower Diary Series (hereafter DDE Diary S.), Ann Whitman File, Dwight D. Eisenhower Papers as President of the United States, 1953–61 (hereafter (AWF), Dwight D. Eisenhower Presidential Library, Abilene, Kansas. All documents are from the DDEL unless otherwise noted.

5. Eisenhower to John Foster Dulles, letter, 20 June 1952, Dulles, John F. Prior to Inauguration, box 1, Dulles-Herter Series (hereafter Dulles-Herter S.) (AWF).

6. See Ann C. Whitman (Eisenhower's personal secretary), memorandum of conversation between the president and Senator Styles Bridges, 21 May 1957, May 1957 Miscellaneous (2), box 24, DDE Diary S. (AWF).

7. Herbert S. Parmet, *Eisenhower and the American Crusades* (New York: Macmillan, 1978), 37.

8. Emmet John Hughes, *The Ordeal of Power: A Political Memoir of the Eisenhower Years* (New York: Atheneum, 1963), 60, 71–72.

9. For Eisenhower's budget consciousness, see his letter to National Policy Association Chairman Frank Altschul, 25 October 1957, DDE Diary S. (AWF). For a representative sample of Humphrey's economic philosophy and policies, see Humphrey to Clarence Randall, letter, 20 March 1957, Foreign Aid, 1953–57, folder 5, box 4, George M. Humphrey Papers, Western Reserve Historical Society (hereafter GMHP).

10. Hoffman to Dwight D. Eisenhower, letter and memorandum, 31 December 1952; and Eisenhower to Dulles, memorandum, 15 January 1953, both in Paul Hoffman (5), box 21, Administration Series (hereafter Admin. S.) (AWF).

11. Eisenhower to Richard M. Nixon, letter, 1 May 1953, Reciprocal Trade Agreements, box 32, Admin. S. (AWF); and Annual Message to Congress on the State of the Union, 2 February 1953, *Public Papers of the Presidents of the United States: Dwight D. Eisenhower, 1953* (Washington, D.C.: Government Printing Office, 1960), 15–16 (hereafter *PPPUS, 1953*).

12. See Randall's *A Creed for Free Enterprise* (Boston: Little, Brown, 1952);

and Parmet, *American Crusades*, 289–90. A commendable treatment is available in Kaufman, *Trade and Aid*, 18–26.

13. Quoted from C. D. Jackson to John Foster Dulles, memorandum, 9 April 1954, Economic Policy (1), box 2, Subject Subseries, Dodge Series, U.S. Council on Foreign Economic Policy, Office of the Chairman: Records, 1954–61 (hereafter Subj. Subs., Dodge S., CFEP, Chair.).

14. The President's Commission on Foreign Economic Policy, *Report to the President and the Congress* (Washington, D.C.: Government Printing Office, 1954) (hereafter Randall Commission Report), 1–89, passim.

15. For instance, Weeks to the president, letter, 15 March 1954, Sinclair Weeks—1952–55 (1), box 42, Admin. S. (AWF).

16. See L. Arthur Minnich, Jr. (cabinet secretary), minutes of Cabinet meeting, 19 March 1954, 10:05–11:55 a.m., Cabinet Minutes 20 November 1953–17 December 1954, box 26, White House Office, Cabinet Secretariat: Records, 1953–60, (hereafter WHO, Cab. Sec.).

17. Special Message to Congress on Foreign Economic Policy, 30 March 1954, *PPPUS: Dwight D. Eisenhower, 1954* (Washington, D.C.: Government Printing Office, 1960), 352–64.

18. Statement by the President upon Signing the Trade Agreements Extension Act, 21 June 1955, *PPPUS: Dwight D. Eisenhower, 1955* (Washington, D.C.: Government Printing Office, 1959), 615; and Dwight D. Eisenhower, *The White House Years: Mandate for Change, 1953–1956* (Garden City, N.Y.: Doubleday, 1963), 498–99. For an example of how protectionists frustrated the administration, see John Foster Dulles to Clarence B. Randall, telephone call, 12:50 p.m., 31 August 1954, Telephone Memos (Except to and from White House) 1 July 1954–31 August 1954 (1), box 2, Telephone Conversations, General, Subseries (hereafter Telcon., Gen., Subs.), Telcon. S., JFDP.

19. Roy R. Rubottom, Jr. (assistant secretary of state for Inter-American affairs, 1957–60), address, "Basic Principles Governing United States Relations with Latin America," 21 March 1958, *Department of State Bulletin* (hereafter *DSB*) 38 (14 April 1958): 608–14.

20. Eisenhower, *Mandate for Change*, 421; and Milton Eisenhower, *The Wine Is Bitter: The United States and Latin America* (Garden City, N.Y.: Doubleday, 1963), 188–89.

21. Eisenhower, *Mandate for Change*, 148; and memorandum of John Foster Dulles telephone conversation with the president, 26 February 1953, White House Telephone Conversation January–April 1953, box 10, White House Telephone Calls Subseries (hereafter W.H. Tel. Calls Subs.), Telcon. S., JFDP. Dulles is quoted from this document.

22. Eisenhower, *Wine Is Bitter*, 197–99. His recommendations and quote are drawn from "United States-Latin American Relations: Report to the President." *DSB*, 29 (23 November 1953): 695–717.

23. See Ezra T. Benson (secretary of agriculture) to the president, letter, Humphrey for the president, memorandum, and Weeks to the secretary of state through the president, letter, all dated 15 January 1954, all in Eisenhower, Milton So. Am. Rpt. 1953 (1), box 13, Names Series (hereafter Name S.) (AWF).

24. The administration also dealt with a complex tin crisis undermining Bolivian stability as it emerged from a revolution.

25. Milton S. Eisenhower to Dwight D. Eisenhower, letter and report, "Specific Country Problems," 11 January 1954, Eisenhower, Milton So. Am. Rpt. 1953 (1), box 13, Name S. (AWF).

26. Dulles to Humphrey, telephone call, 4 p.m., 25 August 1953, Telephone Memos (Except to and from White House) July–October 31, 1953 (3), box 1, Telcon., Gen., Subs., Telcon. S., JFDP.

27. Smith to Arthur S. Flemming (director, Office of Defense Mobilization (ODM)), letter, 1 March 1954; and ODM, "Summary Memorandum on Chilean Copper Proposal," 11 March 1954, both in Stockpiling (2), box 7, WHO, Cab. Sec.

28. Walter Bedell Smith for the president, memorandum, "Recommended Action for Relief of Lead and Zinc Producers," 19 May 1953, John F. May 1953, box 1, Dulles-Herter S. (AWF).

29. Eisenhower to Dr. Gabriel Hauge (special assistant to the president for economic affairs), telephone call, 10:49, 14 June 1954, Phone Calls—June–December 1954 (3), box 7, DDE Diary S. (AWF).

30. Dulles to Humphrey, telephone call, 6:32 p.m., 6 July 1954, Telephone Memos (Except to and from White House) 1 July 1954–31 August 1954 (5), box 2, Telcon., Gen., Subs., Telcon. S., JFDP.

31. Eisenhower is quoted from his 20 July 1954, letter to Captain E. E. (Swede) Hazlett, Hazlett, Swede (1), box 18, Name S. (AWF). Also see Dulles, memorandum for the president, "Foreign Policy Aspects of Increased Lead and Zinc Duties," 17 August 1954, White House Correspondence 1954 (2), box 1, Chronological Subseries (hereafter Chron. Subs.), White House Memoranda Series (hereafter W.H. Memo. S.), JFDP.

32. Dulles for the president, memorandum, 25 August 1955, White House Correspondence—General 1955 (1), box 3, Ibid.

33. For example, Dulles to Eisenhower, letter, 24 August 1954, Dulles, John Foster August 1954 (1), box 3, Dulles-Herter S. (AWF).

34. Report on meeting of the New York Export Managers Club, *New York Times* (hereafter *NYT*), 15 July 1953, 35 and 38; U.S. Congress, Senate, Banking and Currency Committee (hereafter B&C), *Legislative History of the Export-Import Bank of Washington*, 83rd Cong., 1st sess., 10 September 1953, Committee Print, 2–16. Data from Export-Import Bank of Washington, 12th through 17th *Semiannual Report to Congress* for the periods January 1951 through December 1953 (Washington, D.C., 1951–54).

35. Ibid., B&C, *Legislative History*, 19; and *PPPUS, 1953*, 222–25.

36. NSC, statement of policy, "United States Objectives and Courses of Action With Respect to Latin America," NSC 144/1, 18 March 1953, NSC 144—Latin America (2), box 4, Policy Planning Subseries, NSC Series, White House Office, Office of the Assistant for National Security Affairs: Records, 1952–61 (hereafter PPS, NSC, OSANSA), 4; and Policy Planning Board, Department of State, report, "Latin America: A Study of US Problems and Policy," 14 October 1953, Study of U.S. Problems and Policy toward Latin

America, box 59, U.S. President's Commission on Foreign Economic Policy (Randall Commission), Records, 1953–54.

37. U.S. Congress, Senate, B&C, *Hearings, Export-Import Bank Amendments, 1954*, S. 3589, 83rd Cong., 2d sess., 14, 15, 16, and 17 June 1954; *Hearings, Study of the Export- Import Bank and the World Bank*, 83rd Cong., 2d sess., rpt. 1, 25, 27, 28, 29 January, 1, 2 February, and rpt. 2, 14 June 1954; and B&C, *Interim Report, Study of Latin American Countries*, 83rd Cong., 2d sess., rpt. 1082, 1954.

38. Ann Whitman, memorandum of items brought up by secretary of the treasury in discussion with Dwight D. Eisenhower on 26 October 1953, ACW Diary Aug.-Sept.-Oct. 1953 (1), box 1, ACW Diary S. (AWF).

39. Cabot to Samuel C. Waugh (assistant secretary of state for economic affairs, 1953–55), memorandum, 3 February 1954, folder 52, 1954, Washington D.C. Embassy Correspondence; and Cabot diary entry for 11 January and 11 February 1954, folder 54B, both from the John Moors Cabot Papers, Edwin Ginn Library, Fletcher School of Law and Diplomacy, Tufts University (hereafter JMCP).

40. Cabot Diary, 12 and 21 January 1954, JMCP. Dulles is quoted from "The Spirit of Inter-American Unity," *DSB*, 30 (15 March 1954): 382.

41. Capehart to Eisenhower, telephone call, 12:05, 30 March 1954, Telephone Calls—January–May 1954 (2), box 5, DDE Diary S. (AWF).

42. Henry F. Holland (Cabot's successor) to the under secretary of state, memorandum, "Export-Import Bank Policy in Latin America," 29 March 1955, Export-Import Bank Policy in Latin America, box 1, series 361, Central American Trip, 1955, Richard M. Nixon Pre-Presidential Papers, Los Angeles (Laguna Niguel) Federal Archives and Records Center; the quote, including emphasis, is from a handwritten note in James S. Lay, Jr., (NSC secretary) to the NSC, note, "U.S. Policy Toward Latin America," sending "Major Points in Proposed Revision of NSC 144/1, 'U.S. Objectives & Courses of Action with Respect to Latin America,' " 18 August 1954, NSC 5432/1—Policy Toward Latin America, box 19, PPS, NSC, OSANSA; and S. Everett Gleason (NSC secretary) to NSC, note, "U.S. Policy Toward Latin American Policy (NSC 5432/1)," September 1954, Ibid., especially 1–2, 5.

43. Gabriel Hauge for Mrs. Whitman, memorandum, 10 November 1954, ACW Diary November 1954 (4), box 3, ACW Diary S. (AWF).

44. Data is drawn from Operations Coordinating Board (OCB) Progress Reports on U.S. Objectives and Courses of Action with Respect to Latin America (NSC 5432/1), 19 January 1955, 12–13; 10 August 1955, 3; and 28 March 1956, 5, all in NSC 5432, box 13, PPS, NSC, OSANSA. The IFC committed only $37 million to Latin America between 1956 and 1960.

45. Dulles, memorandum of conversation with the president, 10:30 a.m., 7 March 1955, Meetings with the President 1955 (7), box 3, Chron. Subs., White House Memoranda Series (hereafter W.H. Memo. S.), JFDP. The assertion that the two banks achieved parity in Latin America only after a Soviet threat was perceived is based on OCB Progress Report on NSC 5432/1, 28 March 1956, box 13, PPS, NSC, OSANSA, 9; and NSC Statement of Policy, "U.S.

Policy Toward Latin America: General Considerations,'' NSC 5613/1, 25 September 1956, revised 27 September 1956, NSC 5613/1—Policy Toward Latin America (2), box 18, PPS, NSC, OSANSA, especially 7.

46. For an example of the Soviet threat, see Aldo César Vacs, *Discreet Partners: Argentina and the USSR since 1917*, trans., Michael Joyce (Pittsburgh: University of Pittsburgh Press, 1984), 15–18.

47. Need for the CFEP is drawn from Scott Moore and Ed Hutchinson to William F. Finan (all Bureau of the Budget officials), memorandum on replies to Dodge Questionnaire on Foreign Economic Policy and Report, 7 September 1954, Foreign Economic Policy (3), box 2, Subj. Subs., Dodge S., CFEP, Chair,; and Dodge to the president, letter and report, ''The Development and Coordination of Foreign Economic Policy,'' 22 November 1954, Economic Report January 1955, box 15, Admin. S. (AWF).

48. Discussion of the meeting is based upon a 284-page transcript, ''Proceedings of the OFF-THE-RECORD CONFERENCE Held under the Auspices of *Time*, Inc.,'' Princeton Inn, Princeton, N.J., May 15–16, 1954, *Time* Inc. File-Princeton Eco. Conf. 5/54 Transcript, box 68; and Paul T. Carroll to the president, memorandum, undated (13 August 1954), Jackson, C. D. 1954 (1), box 24, Admin. S. (AWF); Eisenhower to Jackson, letter, 16 August 1954, *Time* Inc. File—Eisenhower, Dwight D.—Corres. thru 1956 (1), box 41, both in C. D. Jackson Papers.

49. See Lodge, undated memorandum, ''Multilateral Aid Under the United Nations,'' transmitted to Clarence B. Randall on 17 July 1956, SUNFED (2), box 12, Subj. Subs., Randall S., CFEP, Chair. For the concession by Dulles and Humphrey's persistence, see Dulles, memorandum of conversation with the president, 1 May 1956, Meetings with the President January 1956 through July 1956 (3), box 4, Chron. Subs., W.H. Memo. S., JFPD.

50. For instance, Stephen E. Ambrose, *Eisenhower: The President* (New York: Simon & Schuster, 1984), 119.

51. Dulles, memorandum of conversation with Nelson Rockefeller, 2 p.m., 2 December 1955, Nelson Rockefeller, box 6, Alpha. Subs., Subj. S.; and Senate Minority Leader William F. Knowland to Dulles, telephone call, 5:29 p.m., 12 January 1956, Memoranda of Telconv. General 3 January 1956–30 April 1956 (7), box 5, Telcon., Gen., Subs., Telcon. S., both in JFDP.

52. See Eisenhower's diary entry for 19 January 1956 regarding a 5 p.m. meeting including Dulles, Humphrey, and Dodge to coordinate a survey of overseas economic relations in January 1956 Diary, box 12, DDE Diary S. (AWF).

53. Dulles, memorandum of conversation with the president, 18 June 1956, Meetings with the President January 1956 through July 1956 (3), box 4, Chron. Subs., W.H. Memo. S., JFDP.

54. Eisenhower to Whitelaw Reid, letter, 22 September 1956, Terms of Reference, box 10, U.S. President's Citizen Advisers on the Mutual Security Program (Fairless Committee): Records, 1956–57.

55. William C. Schmeisser, Jr. (IDAB executive director) to Johnston, memorandum, ''I.D.A.B. Program—Final Quarter, 1956,'' 28 September 1956, In-

ternational Development Advisory Board, box 7, Ibid.; and IDAB, discussion outline for October 30 meeting, 22 October 1956, International Development Advisory Board (ICA) (3), box 7, Subj. Subs., Randall S., CFEP, Chair. The last quote is a longhand notation in pencil from the back of page 2.

56. *Report to the President by the President's Citizen Advisers on the Mutual Security Program* (Washington, D.C.: Government Printing Office, 1957), passism, 15.

57. IDAB, *A New Emphasis on Economic Development Abroad* (Washington, D.C.: Government Printing Office, 1957), 2–19.

58. This is probably the best example of how the council collated departmental and agency evaluations of reports and major policy issues. Scholars can review point-by-point comparisons of these and other economic reviews. Comments on the Fairless Report from the DOS, 9 March 1957; the Council of Economic Advisors (CEA), DOD, Robert Cutler for the NSC, Agriculture Department, BOB, and Eugene R. Black on 11 March 1957; DOC, ICA, Cutler again for the NSC, 12 March 1957; and the DOT, 20 March 1957, are located in Fairless Report (2–4), box 5, Subj. Subs., Randall S., CFEP, Chair. Similar comments on the IDAB report by Cutler for the NSC, 15 March 1957; DOS, 16 March 1957; ICA, Agriculture, DOC, and DOD, 18 March 1957; BOB, DOT, and CEA on 19 March 1957, are in International Development Advisory Board (1–2), box 7, Ibid. Discussion of the administration's position is based upon this documentary treasure.

59. A more exhaustive treatment of the CFEP reviews is in Kaufman, *Trade and Aid,* 98–99, 101–3.

60. For the Dulles-Eisenhower relationship, see Dwight D. Eisenhower, *The White House Years: Waging Peace, 1956–1961* (Garden City, N.Y.: Doubleday, 1965), 365; Ambrose, *Eisenhower,* 21–22; and Robert A. Divine, *Eisenhower and the Cold War* (New York: Oxford University Press, 1981), 19–23.

61. Dulles, memorandum for the president, "Possible Revisions in the FY 1958 Mutual Security Program," 25 March 1957, Dulles, John Foster March 1957, box 6, Dulles-Herter S. (AWF); and U.S. Congress, Senate, Special Committee to Study Foreign Aid Program, *Hearings, Foreign Aid Program,* 85th Cong., 1st sess., 1957, 394–407.

62. Joseph Rand (CFEP staff), memorandum, "Export-Import Bank Position on Economic Development Fund," 3 May 1957, Development Loan Fund (5), box 1, Agency Subs., Randall S., CFEP, Chair.; Humphrey to Dulles, letter, 8 May 1957, George M. Humphrey—1957–58 (3), box 23, Admin. S. (AWF); and Eisenhower to Humphrey, letter, 7 May 1957, May '57 Miscellaneous (4), box 24, DDE Diary S., Ibid.

63. See Eisenhower to Dulles, telephone call, 4:30 p.m., 8 May 1957, Memoranda Tel. Conv.—W.H. March 1957 to 30 August 1957 (3), box 12, W.H. Tel. Calls Subs., Telcon. S., JFDP.

64. For example, see Charles B. Warden (finance advisor to the ICA director) to Walter Schaefer (assistant to the ICA director for finance, and chairman, DLF steering committee), memorandum and "Final Report of the Private Enterprise Study Group," 15 November 1957, Development Loan Fund [November–December 1957], box 5, Staff S., CFEP.

65. Dulles to Anderson, telephone call, 4:30 p.m., 5 November 1958, Memoranda of Tel. Conv.—Gen. 2 November 1958 to 27 December 1958 (2); and Anderson to Dulles, telephone call, 2:55 p.m., 23 January 1959, Memoranda of Tel. Conv.—Gen. 4 January 1959 to 8 May 1959 (3), both in box 9, Telcon., Gen., Subs., Telcon. S., JFDP.

66. See Paul H. Cullen, Approved Minutes of 95th Meeting of CFEP—19 November 1959, undated, Balance of Payments—Procurement Policy (2), box 2, Subj. Subs., Randall S., CFEP, Chair.

67. Wagner, *U.S. Policy toward Latin America,* 145; and Reynold E. Carlson, "The Economic Picture," in *The United States and Latin America,* 2nd ed., ed. Herbert R. Matthews, (Englewood Cliffs, N.J.: Prentice-Hall, 1963), 112.

68. Samuel C. Waugh to J. W. Fulbright, letter, 7 January 1959 and Export-Import Bank of Washington Press Release No. 541, 1 January 1959, F58, Latin America (6), BCN 140, J. W. Fulbright Papers, University of Arkansas Library.

69. U.S. Congress, Joint Economic Committee on Foreign Economic Policy, *Hearings before the Subcommittee on Foreign Economic Policy of the Joint Committee,* 87th Cong., 1st sess., December 4–14, 1961, especially 481; and William Benton, *The Voice of Latin America* (New York: Harper, 1961), 46–49.

70. Dulles, memorandum of conversation with the president, 10:45 a.m., 17 May 1957, Meetings with the President—1957 (5), box 6, Chron. Subs., W.H. Memo. S., JFDP; and R. R. Rubottom, memorandum of conversation between Eisenhower, Dr. Manuel Cisneros, Fernando B. Berchemeyer, Theodore Achilles, and Rubottom, 14 October 1957, State Department—1957 (August–October) (6), box 2, State Department Subseries, Subject Subseries, WHO, Staff Sec.

71. Ruiz Cortines to Eisenhower, letter, 17 February 1958, Cortines, Mexico 1952–57 (2); and Eisenhower's response of 7 March 1958 in Cortines, Mexico 1952–57 (4), both in box 35, International Series (hereafter Inter. S.) (AWF).

72. Eisenhower to Ruiz Cortines, letter, 17 July 1958, Cortines, Mexico 1952–57 (2), Ibid.

73. Eisenhower to Ruiz Cortines, letter, 20 September 1958, Cortines, Mexico 1952–57 (3), box 35, Ibid. The quote is from Staff Notes No. 439, 15 October 1958, Staff Notes—October 1958, box 36, DDE Diary S., Ibid.

74. Randall to Thomas Mann, letter, 16 December 1957; and Randall to James S. Lay, memorandum, "U.S. Policy on International Commodity Agreements," 23 May 1958, both in CFEP 531 U.S. Policy with Respect to International Commodity Agreements (hereafter CFEP 531) (3), box 6, Policy Papers Series, U.S. Council on Foreign Economic Policy: Records, 1954–61 (hereafter PPS, CFEP).

75. See handwritten notes of CFEP minutes on 23 October 1958, and undated (probably 30 October 1958), both in Follow-up (1), box 5, Staff S., CFEP; Joseph Rand to Randall, memorandum, "Rand European Trip—November 5–16, 1958," 19 November 1958, Lead and Zinc—Rand (2), box 6, Records of Joseph Rand, 1954–61 (hereafter JRR); and Christian A. Herter for the president, memorandum, "Your Appointment with the Mexican Ambassador," 30 June, 1960, Mexico—Pres. Mateos 1958 through 1960 (3), box 35, Inter. S. (AWF).

76. For instance, Eisenhower to Henry C. Alexander (chairman, J.P. Morgan & Co.), letter and memorandum, 22 April 1958, Soviet Economic Penetration (2), box 7, WHO, Cab. Sec.

77. Report of the Committee on World Economic Practices, 22 January 1959, Committee on World Economic Practices #1 (hereafter CWEP 1) (1); and Clarence B. Randall to Robert B. Anderson, et al., memorandum, "Major Recommendations of the Committee on World Economic Practices," 2 February 1959, CWEP 1 (4), both in box 3, Subj. Subs., Randall Series, CFEP, Chair.

78. For example, Camilo Ponce Enriquez (president of Ecuador) to Eisenhower, letter, 13 May 1958, Ecuador (2), box 8, Christian A. Herter Papers.

79. L. Arthur Minnich, Jr., minutes of Cabinet meeting, 16 May 1958, 9:05 a.m.–9:50 a.m., May 1958—Staff Notes (1), box 32, DDE Diary S. The list of post-trip programs for Latin America is presented in Robert Gray, Cabinet Paper, Action Status Report, CI—58-7/6, 3 October 1958, Cabinet—Action Status Reports (2), box 1, Cabinet Series, both in (AWF).

80. Dulles to Dwight Eisenhower, letter, 7 January 1958, Dulles, John Foster January 1958 (2), box 7, Dulles-Herter S. (AWF); and Eisenhower, *Wine Is Bitter*, 205–21, 10, 3–4.

81. See "United States-Latin American Relations, 1953–1958," *DSB*, 40 (19 January 1959), 89–105. Quotes are from the president's letter to Milton Eisenhower with attached comments on the report, 26 November 1958, DDE Dictation—November 1958, box 37, DDE Diary S. (AWF).

82. Kubitschek's letter to Eisenhower delivered by Ambassador Peixoto on 28 May 1958, Brazil (8); and Dulles to Eisenhower, memorandum, "President Kubitschek's Proposal to Strengthen Pan-Americanism," 20 June 1958, Brazil (7), both in Inter. S. (AWF).

83. For example, Eisenhower to Kubitschek, letter 5 June 1958, Brazil (8), box 4, Inter. S.; and Dulles to the president, telegram DULTE 2, 5 August 1958, Dulles, August 1958, box 8, Dulles-Herter S., both in (AWF).

84. For example, Alfredo Stroessner (president of Paraguay) to Eisenhower, letter, 24 September 1958, Paraguay (2), box 39, Inter. S. (AWF).

85. Dulles, memorandum of conversation with the president, 23 September 1958, White House—Gen. Correspondence 1958 (2), box 6, Chron. Subs., W.H. Memo. S., JFDP.

86. DOS, Staff Summary Supplement No. 586, "Inter-American Financial Institution Proposed," 30 December 1958; and No. 7, "US Position on American Development Institution," 6 January 1959, both in State Department 467–542 (2), box 19, WHO, Staff Research Group (hereafter Staff Res. Gp.).

87. Don Paarlberg for Mrs. Whitman, memorandum and attachment, "Final Proposal by the United States with Respect to the Inter-American Development Banking Institution," 5 March 1959, Staff Notes March 1–15, 1959 (2), box 59, DDE Diary S. (AWF).

88. Quoted from author unknown, memorandum sent to Eisenhower by Herter, 22 April 1959, Cuba (1), box 8, Inter. S. (AWF).

89. DOS, Staff Summary Supplements No. 263, "Crucial Months Ahead for

Castro," 4 August 1959; and No. 309, "Raul Castro Expresses Zealot's View of Revolution," 17 September 1959, both in State Department 543–638 (1), box 19, WHO, Staff Res. Gp.; A. J. Goodpaster, memorandum of conferences with the president on 23 January and 26 January 1960, dated 25 and 26 January 1960 Staff Notes—January 1960 (1), box 47, DDE Diary S. (AWF). One prediction of spreading revolutionary activity by the Colombian president is presented in Staff Notes No. 555, 26 May 1959, Toner Notes May 1959, box 41, Ibid.

90. R. R. Rubottom, memorandum of conversation between the president, secretary of state, and National Advisory Committee on Inter-American Affairs, 3 December 1959, Staff Notes—December 1959, box 46, Ibid.

91. Quoted from Eisenhower, *Waging Peace,* 530 and 532; and Eisenhower, *Wine Is Bitter,* 11, 239–48.

92. Aldolfo Lopez Mateos (president of Mexico) to Eisenhower, letter, 7 March 1960, Mexico Pres. Mateos 1958 through 1960 (6), box 35, Inter. S.; and Milton Eisenhower to Dwight Eisenhower, letter, undated, Eisenhower, Milton 1958 (2), box 13, Name S., both in (AWF).

93. See Eisenhower to C. Douglas Dillon, memorandum, 10 May 1960, Herter, Christian May 1960 (3); Dillon for the president, memorandum, "Inter-American Development Bank," 17 May 1960; A. J. Goodpaster for Dillon, memorandum, 24 May 1960, the last two are from Herter, Christian May 1960 (2), all in box 10, Dulles-Herter S. (AWF); and Joseph S. Toner (DLF secretary), Minutes of 38th DLF Board of Directors Meeting, DLF-LC/M-60, 20 March 1960, Encouraging Private Home Ownership Abroad (3), box 4, JRR.

94. *PPPUS: Dwight D. Eisenhower, 1960–61* (Washington, D.C.: Government Printing Office, 1961), 570.

95. Peter Lyon, *Eisenhower: Portrait of the Hero* (Boston: Little, Brown, 1974), 818.

96. See U.S. Embassy Rio to Secretary of State, Telegram No. 91, 12 July 1960, Brazil (3) March–December 1960, box 2, Inter. S., WHO, Staff Sec.; and Kubitschek to Eisenhower, letter, 19 July 1960, Brazil (2), box 4, Inter. S. (AWF).

97. Douglas Dillon for the president, memorandum, "Latin American Program," 1 August 1960, Herter, Christian August 1960 (2), box 11, Dulles-Herter S. (AWF).

98. See Christian Herter telephone conversations with Douglas Dillon and Representative Sam Rayburn (majority leader from Texas), 30 August 1960, CAH Telephone Calls 7/1/60 to 8/31/60 (1), box 13, CAHP; and Kaufman, *Trade and Aid,* 200.

99. C. Douglas Dillon, address, "Promoting Economic and Social Advancement in the Americas," 6 September 1960, in Robert Burr, *The Dynamics of World Power: A Documentary History of United States Foreign Policy, 1945–1973,* vol. 3, *Latin America* (New York: Chelsea House, 1973), 452–58, quote is on 455. The Act of Bogotá is discussed on pages 458–63.

100. Joseph Rand to Clarence B. Randall, memorandum, Briefing Paper of CFEP Meeting on Act of Bogotá, 10 October 1960, CFEP Briefing Papers (1), July–December 1960, Office Series, CFEP.

Eisenhower and the Middle East

William Stivers

The Eisenhower years witnessed heightened U.S. activism in the Middle East. For example,

- The United States orchestrated the 1953 overthrow of Iranian Prime Minister Mohammed Mossadegh, an ardent nationalist who had expropriated British oil holdings and had undermined the power of the pro-Western Shah.
- The cornerstone was laid on February 24, 1955, for a "Northern Tier" defense organization by the signing in Baghdad of a Turko-Iraqi pact. The organization was joined by Great Britain (April 5), Pakistan (September 23), and Iran (October 23). While the United States never joined the alliance, Washington sponsored its creation and immediately established military liaison with the pact organization. On February 1, 1958, the United States formalized this liaison by becoming a full member of the pact's military planning committee.
- The United States forced Britain, France, and Israel to withdraw from Egypt following the 1956 Sinai-Suez war. Eisenhower succeeded through a tough diplomacy—denying emergency oil shipments to Britain and France (Nasser had blocked all traffic through the Suez Canal in response to the Israeli and Anglo-French attack) and threatening Israel with U.S. participation in UN economic sanctions.
- The need to compensate for declining British and French influence compelled the administration to secure congressional passage on March 9, 1957, of the Middle East Resolution, a two-pronged program comprising $200 million a year in economic and military assistance to be granted to Middle Eastern countries at the president's discretion, and blanket authorization "to use armed forces to assist any nation or group of such nations requesting assistance against armed aggression from any country controlled by international communism. . . ."[1] The president had requested this authority to implement the "Eisenhower Doctrine," a call to action in the Middle East articulated in his speech to Congress on January 5.
- The civil war in Lebanon, combined with the July 1958 revolution in

Iraq, prompted Eisenhower to order U.S. Marines to Lebanon. The first Marines arrived on July 15. Reinforcements brought the force to an ultimate strength of just over fourteen thousand men. They withdrew in October, after a U.S.-sponsored settlement of Lebanon's internal political crisis had been negotiated and set in place.

In light of these initiatives, it would seem incongruous to contend that Washington asserted such a strong presence in the Middle East without much concern for the region itself and with no clear concept of U.S. objectives. Yet this is the case. U.S. interests in the Middle East subserved a larger interest in Europe; and Washington's objectives in the area were contradictory and delusive.

Eisenhower had Eurocentric priorities. He believed that the United States had paramount economic and military interests in Europe. Europe, however, depended on Middle Eastern oil for its economic health and its military power. Thus, because of American interests in Europe, the United States had important stakes in the Middle East. Events in the Middle East would be considered not in their own right—least of all in regard to how they affected local populations—but with reference to Europe.

U.S. strategy was also Eurocentric. Britain and France were powers in decline, but still enjoyed substantial positions of political and military influence in the Middle East. Eisenhower wanted to retain this "stabilizing" influence—particularly British influence, because he greatly appreciated what the British had done. Cooperation was an administration watchword: Heavy U.S. commitments elsewhere severely restrained America's ability to become a sole, dominating power, even had that been her desire—which it was not. The United States and Europe—primarily Britain—were tied together in a mutual strategic dependence.

Such reliance on formerly colonial powers produced an acute contradiction in U.S. policy. Eisenhower and the men around him fully understood the power of modern nationalism. They understood as well that their association with detested, colonial powers embarrassed American relations with the Arab world—a problem exacerbated by U.S. support of Israel. Fearful of Soviet attempts to gain influence in the Middle East by supporting antiimperialist causes, Eisenhower wanted to break the identity Arabs had established between Washington and the European powers. Rather than support (or try to restore) the old imperial order, the United States would back genuine Arab nationalism and create an identity as the Arabs' true friend. But this happened only in theory: Despite its intellectual understanding of Arab nationalism, in practice the administration's Eurocentrism implied a defense of European interests and power. Ultimately, the United States had no choice but to oppose nationalism in the interests of pro-Western stability. The practical dilemma of supporting any nationalist "excess" that threatened the position of the ex-imperialist powers was particularly acute where Great Britain was concerned, because insofar as nationalism undermined British strength in the region, it weakened the Western posture as a whole.

The Soviet Union vastly complicated an already complex picture. Eisenhower officials were never clear in their thoughts on the link between nationalism and the Soviet Union. The administration knew that nationalism and communism were not identical. Accommodation with nationalist movements was not, therefore, ruled out. But Soviet and nationalist objectives—especially the objectives of radical pan-Arab movements—might coincide. The Soviet Union could then manipulate these movements to eliminate Western influence and replace it with its own. In such instances, Arab nationalism was inimical to Western interests. Thus, because of the possible coincidence of Soviet and "radical" objectives, the United States was led to a defense of the conservative status quo.

Eisenhower's Eurocentrism

The personal origins of Eisenhower's Eurocentrism are well known. During World War II he served as commander-in-chief of Allied forces in Western Europe. In late 1950 he accepted President Truman's offer to assume supreme command of NATO, a post in which he remained until entering politics in 1952. Because of this military experience, he became acquainted, in many cases on intimate terms, with the most important European leaders of the day. Also, as NATO commander, he became firmly convinced of the need for a "United States of Europe." If Europe did not federate, he felt, her economic recovery would be retarded, and she would be unable to rebuild her military strength.[2] Thus, Eisenhower supported not only the functional integration represented by the European coal and steel community and the proposed European army, but he also desired political integration as well.

Eisenhower's opinions on Europe put him squarely in the mainstream of the bipartisan consensus on foreign policy. Internationalists in both Democratic and Republican parties viewed European and American interests as inseparable, not only for economic and strategic reasons but also by virtue of a shared heritage and kindred institutions. The painful lessons of the interwar period had taught them that America could not prosper in an integrated world economy unless the whole world was prosperous—and economically, Europe was a huge part of the world. Economic factors and strategic factors were so tightly linked that they were indistinguishable. Security was multifaceted. Productive and fully employed economies, stable social structures, international freedom of trade, and enhanced military power all were parts of the same whole. If, for example, U.S. tariffs prevented European nations from paying for the goods that they received from the United States, the eventual decline in American export markets might prove the least of many ill effects. Depressed living standards would undermine efforts to re-arm and would increase the domestic appeals of communism. NATO might collapse, leaving America an isolated democracy in a hostile world.[3]

It was because of America's economic interdependence with Europe that Eisenhower and his advisors attached supreme importance to Middle Eastern oil. America's own oil needs were met almost entirely from Western Hemisphere production. But as Eisenhower remarked in his diary on March 13, 1956: "The oil of the Arab world has grown increasingly important to all of Europe. The economy of Europe would collapse if those oil supplies were cut off. If the economy of Europe would collapse, the United States would be in a situation of which the difficulty could scarcely be exaggerated."[4]

These facts, he stated in a subsequent letter to Winston Churchill, should provide "a clear guidepost for all our policies, actions, efforts, and propaganda in the region. . . ."[5]

The same facts would lie at the core of U.S. policy throughout Eisenhower's term. But at no time did they serve as such a "clear guidepost" for action as during the Suez crisis of 1956.

On July 26, 1956 Egyptian President Gamal Abdul Nasser nationalized the Suez Canal Company. The British government, which had in 1875 purchased 44 percent of the company's stock from the Khedive Ismail,[6] was the largest single stockholder; most of the remaining shares were held by private French investors and were traded on the Paris Bourse. Nasser's nationalization decree came one week after the United States reneged on an earlier offer to help finance the Aswan Dam—a giant hydroelectric and irrigation project on the upper Nile to which Nasser had accorded the highest priority. Egypt, Nasser said in a public address announcing the canal expropriation, would apply profits from the tolls toward building the dam.

From the outset, the Anglo-French impulse was to reverse Nasser's move through force. In Prime Minister Anthony Eden's judgment, in which the French concurred, "the economic life of Western Europe was threatened with disruption by seizure of the Canal."[7] The canal was an international asset, recognized as such by the Convention of 1888. "In recent years its importance had been greatly increased by the Middle Eastern oil fields and by the dependence of Western Europe upon them for a large part of its oil supplies."[8] Egypt, as Eden cabled Eisenhower on the evening of July 27, could not be allowed to exploit this asset, "which is vital to the free world . . . by using the revenues for her own internal purposes irrespective of the interests of the Canal and of the Canal users. . . ." Maximum political pressure should be put on Egypt, he said, and if that did not work, "we must be ready, in the last resort, to use force to bring Nasser to his senses."[9] Earlier in the day, U.S. Ambassador Douglas Dillon reported much the same message from French Foreign Minister Christian Pineau.[10]

The Joint Chiefs of Staff shared the Anglo-French assessment. The canal nationalization, they declared in a July 31 memorandum to the secretary of defense, was "militarily detrimental to the United States and its allies." The issue was of such gravity "as to require action by the United States and its allies" that would place the Suez Canal "under a friendly and responsible authority at the earliest practicable date." If action short of force would not suffice to achieve this result, "the United States should consider . . . taking military action in support of the U.K., France and others as appropriate."[11]

Eisenhower and Dulles opposed the use of force, but, employing the guideposts referred to in the president's letter to Churchill, they took a grave view of Nasser's demarche. They stated their positions most clearly during a bipartisan leadership meeting on August 12, 1956. Dulles opined that the United States could not be unsympathetic toward the British and French. If Nasser fulfilled his ambitions, Western Europe would be reduced to a state of literal dependency, and Europe as a whole "would become insignificant." In the words of the rapporteur, Dulles "explained this in terms of the availability of oil and in terms of the far reaching interests of the French and British in Africa. He said that Britain and France cannot let Nasser have a stranglehold on the Canal." Dulles stressed the point once more in the meeting. It would be intolerable, he said, for Western Europe to feel it could not rely on Middle Eastern oil. The issue was one of "life and death" for Britain and France. Two-thirds of Western Europe's oil went through the canal, and the other third through pipelines. Simultaneous closure of the pipelines and the canal could bring a total cutoff of Europe's oil.

Eisenhower added to Dulles's points. He underscored the "heavy investment the United States has made in strenghtening Western Europe, a big stake . . . beyond the immediate considerations involving oil." In the president's eyes, "the main thing was the economy of

Western Europe." Even though Cairo had made no move toward closing the canal, Nasser's "aggressive statements," which reminded Eisenhower of those of Hitler in *Mein Kampf*, showed malign intent. The United States, the president said, did "not intend to stand by helplessly and let this one man get away with what he was trying to do."[12]

The United States, however, showed itself willing to stand by longer than its allies. Disdaining American efforts to stave off armed conflict, Britain and France began as early as July 28 to lay plans and muster forces for an attack on Egypt. The attack was delayed at first because of simple unpreparedness, and then because of Eden's desire to find a suitable pretext on which to act. But by the last week of October, the stops were off. On October 22 and 23, Israel, Britain, and France agreed on a scheme—hatched in Paris—to bring Nasser down. Israeli forces would drive into the Sinai peninsula. Acting under the pretext of protecting the canal, Britain and France would issue an ultimatum demanding that within twelve hours both Egypt and Israel distance their forces at least ten miles from the waterway. When Egypt inevitably refused—an Egyptian withdrawal would have conceded Israel occupation of nearly the whole of the Sinai—the British and French would seize the canal, purportedly to insure free passage.

The Israeli attack came on October 29. The Anglo-French ultimatum followed the next day, and on October 31, British and French war planes started bombing Egyptian bases. An Anglo-French paratroop drop on November 5 preceded a naval bombardment and amphibious assault on the sixth.

The affair was an unmitigated disaster for the Anglo-French allies. Their use of force to keep the canal open on their terms pushed Nasser to block it with scuttled ships. On November 3 the Syrian army closed the Iraq-Syria-Lebanon oil pipeline by blowing up pumping stations. The prospect of a crippling oil squeeze confronted Europe. The pound came under intense pressure as a financial panic set in. On November 7 the British and French forces ceased fire, as they had been called on to do by a UN General Assembly resolution of November 1.

Eisenhower was furious over the attack on Egypt; he felt that the Allies had betrayed trust by their unilateral action. When the pound came under pressure, he had the United States exercise its position in the International Monetary Fund to refuse Britain access to IMF facilities. After the cease-fire, he delayed activating a plan drawn up in August by a government-sponsored committee of oil companies, to fill Europe's essential petroleum needs by diverting Persian Gulf shipments and augmenting Western Hemisphere production. The purpose of his delay was to guarantee that the cease-fire was followed by prompt Anglo-French withdrawal from Egyptian territory. It was only on November 30, after he had extracted such assurances, that he ordered the oil plan put into effect.[13]

Yet throughout the whole affair, Eisenhower maintained Eurocentric priorities. Meeting with his top advisors on October 29, he tempered his anger over the Anglo-French action with the recognition that "much is on their side in the dispute. . . ."[14] In his radio and television address on the Suez crisis delivered on October 31, he complained of the Israeli and Anglo-French resort to force per se without questioning the cause in which they acted. Indeed, he called attention to "the grave anxieties of Israel, of France and of Britain," adding, "we know they have been subjected to grave and repeated provocations."[15] The dispute with Britain and France, as he affirmed to the congressional leadership on November 9, was a "family fight."[16]

One of the main reasons that Eisenhower originally opposed using force was his belief that, although the Allies could seize and operate the canal, such an action would not be conducive to enduring stability.[17] Events proved the president too optimistic on the chances for Allied success. Anglo-French forces were not able to seize and operate the canal; it was closed before they could get to it, confirming Dulles's estimate, made some four hours after he had learned of the Israeli attack, that the canal was likely to be disrupted and the pipelines broken. The administration's diplomacy during the remainder of the crisis was aimed at saving Britain and France from the consequences of their folly. As Under Secretary of State Herbert Hoover, Jr., explained November 9, the United States would "concentrate efforts on preventing a new outbreak of fighting and . . . on providing oil to Europe by getting the Canal repaired and the pipelines open."[18] The rationale for these priorities was asserted by both the president and the secretary of the treasury at the end of a November 21 discussion on the relative importance of Western Europe and the Middle East. The two regions had to be considered together, they said, "and are together the most strategic area in the world—Western Europe requires Middle Eastern oil, and Middle Eastern oil is of importance mainly through its contribution to the Western Europe economy."[19]

Eisenhower knew that there would be no chance of stabilizing the Middle East and of resuming oil flows to Europe unless the British, French, and Israeli occupying forces withdrew from Egyptian territory. Britain and France succumbed to U.S. pressure. The first Anglo-French troops left on December 22, 1956, but Israel resisted. Although the Israelis evacuated most of the Sinai in November, in early 1957 they continued to hold the Gaza Strip and Sharm el Sheik. Egypt, which had started to clear the canal, threatened to halt clearing operations as long as Israel refused to leave. But the Israelis demanded a price for military withdrawal: continued administrative and police presence in the Gaza Strip and assured free passage through the Strait of Tiran.

Failure to reopen the canal would have tightened Europe's economic bind; the American oil lift still left Europe 15 to 20 percent short of its normal supply. After a last representation to Israel—delivered as an *aide-mémoire* to Ambassador Abba Eban on February 11 and rejected by Ben Gurion four days later—Eisenhower and Dulles decided stronger measures were needed. In the *aide-mémoire*, the United States had proposed to guarantee Israel against commando infiltrations by sponsoring movement of the United Nations Emergency Force onto the boundary between Israel and the Gaza Strip as already contemplated in a UN resolution of February 2, 1957.[20] Furthermore, the United States itself would act to establish the principle of "free and innocent passage" through the Strait of Tiran. First, however, Israel would have to withdraw promptly and without conditions. As Dulles argued, this was as far as the United States could go toward accommodating Israel without leading the Arabs to "conclude that U.S. policy was, in the last analysis, controlled by Jewish influence in the United States." Eisenhower responded to the Ben Gurion rejection by resolving to support UN sanctions cutting off aid to Israel—not just government aid, but private aid as well.[21]

In explaining his position to a gathering of congressional leaders on February 20, the president stressed once again the importance of the issue for Western Europe. If Israel persisted in occupying Egyptian territory, "economic stagnation would increase, and . . . the U.N. would be forced to some action. Such a situation could lead to increased influence of Russia in Arab states, interruption of oil through the remaining pipeline and continued blocking of the Canal, the threat of a serious crash in the French and United Kingdom economies, and finally an increased possibility of general war." Dulles seconded the president's remarks with a view that "if Israel should not withdraw there would be increased guerrilla warfare, stoppage of oil supplies, and a growth of Russian influence."[22]

Not all the leaders were convinced. Senators William Knowland and Lyndon Johnson argued vociferously on Israel's behalf, but Eisenhower rebuffed their appeals. In a broadcast on the evening of the twentieth, he promised U.S. cooperation with the UN actions "to exert pressure on Israel to comply with the withdrawal resolutions."[23] Ben Gurion had to give way. On March 1, Golda Meir announced to the United Nations

General Assembly that Israel troops would leave Egyptian territory. This paved the way for the opening of the canal on March 29, re-establishing the main oil link between Western Europe and the Persian Gulf.

The Strategic Nexus

At the same time that Eisenhower acted in service of European inter-ests, he sought to avail himself of European power. Under the circum-stances, this meant entering into a close, collaborative relationship with Great Britain, the nation Eisenhower had long considered as America's "greatest natural friend,"[24] who had done "far more than we to support countries that want to remain free."[25]

In the president's view, Great Britain "should continue to carry a major responsibility" for safeguarding security in the Middle East. "The British were intimately familiar with the history, traditions, and peoples of the Middle East; we, on the other hand, were heavily in-volved in Korea, Formosa, Vietnam, Iran, and in this hemisphere. At the same time, France had heavy commitments in North Africa west of Tripoli."[26] Thus, even as Eisenhower expanded the direct U.S. com-mitment in the region, he did so not with the aim of diminishing British influence, but rather with the aim of concerting Anglo-American actions toward common ends. The expanded U.S. role was to compensate for British decline rather than to further American ambition.

The Baghdad Pact illustrates the collaborative policy at its best. During the Truman administration, Anglo-American strategists first hatched plans for a Middle Eastern command (MEC) and then, for a Middle Eastern Defense Organization (MEDO). Both schemes were predicated on strong British leadership, exercised with U.S. backing, and a key role for Egypt. But Arab hostility killed them, leading policy-makers to concentrate on building a Northern Tier alignment comprising Turkey, Iraq, Iran, and Pakistan—the basis of the Baghdad Pact.

Britain was the main Western partner in the pact, but the United States was involved at the outset in a sponsoring and supporting capac-ity. Before the signing of the Turko-Iraqi Treaty on February 24, 1955, American, British, and Turkish military planners held talks in London, where they completed a comprehensive study of military objectives, strategy, operational concepts, and other matters related to Middle Eastern defense. This study was accepted by the Joint Chiefs of Staff as a point of departure for elaborating an "allied politico-military con-cept" for the region. Further Anglo-American conversations took place in Washington over the summer. A U.S. observer sat in on the military planning sessions in Baghdad, and that observer (the U.S. military attache in Iraq) submitted pact defense studies for comment to the JCS. This tight liasion was formalized on February 1, 1958, when the United States joined the military planning committee without, nevertheless, adhering to the treaty.[27]

U.S. objectives were well served by the Northern Tier alliance. The United States participated in the development of joint strategic plans and allocated aid according to a collective, regional design. Militarily, the United States bolstered indigenous capacities by providing nuclear shield (called "atomic support forces" in the parlance of the times) and helping to improve logistical infrastructure.[28] At the same time, the United States spared itself the burdens of *de jure* membership. The British wanted Washington to shed the veil of pretense and join the pact. But as the secretary of state argued, it made sense to stay out. By keeping distance, the United States would steer clear of intra-Arab conflicts. Formal association could impair U.S. efforts to mediate the Arab-Israeli conflict, and the pro-Israeli lobby would make U.S. membership politically impossible unless, as Dulles explained, "we were able to offer a comparable security arrangement for Israel." Eventual U.S. adherence, therefore, was contingent on Arab-Israeli conciliation.[29]

The "family fight" over Suez did nothing to change the U.S. relationship with Britain. One of the prime goals of post-Suez U.S. policy was to compose Anglo-American differences and to restore the alliance to its former strength. Major progress was made toward that end in 1957, when Eisenhower and Prime Minister Harold Macmillan (Eden's successor) met in Bermuda for three days of highly cordial discussion. U.S. policymakers went into the conference well aware of the need to respect "special British interests" in the Middle East—an easy charge because Anglo-American objectives there were "mutually compatible."[30]

This latter view remained constant. It was on account of such compatibility that, in an NSC document Eisenhower approved on November 4, 1958, the administration reaffirmed its "support for a continued substantial British position in the Persian Gulf and Arabian peninsula" and directed U.S. planners to prepare for possible combined Anglo-American military action to protect European oil supplies from the Middle East.[31]

The Lebanon crisis provided a clear, practical example of Anglo-American collaboration. Civil war erupted in Lebanon in May 1958. The June 1957 parliamentary elections had gone too well for the United States and the pro-American Lebanese president, Camille Chamoun.

A Maronite Catholic, Chamoun had employed CIA election monies and dubious practices to defeat not only radical candidates but also a number of Moslem notables.[32] In the spring of 1958 well-substantiated rumors began to circulate that Chamoun would exploit his strong parliamentary position to change the constitution, which limited him to one term in office, in order to secure reelection. Deprived of political participation, aggrieved Moslems turned to armed revolt.

At the onset of the rebellion, Chamoun made an initial, veiled request for American intervention, inquiring euphemistically what the United States would do if he asked for help. The JCS reaction was to consider a U.S. move into Lebanon as a possible joint action with the British. Military discussions took place, and by the middle of June, an Anglo-American intervention plan—"Operation Blue Bat"—had been drawn up.[33] Although the ultimate decision was to intervene unilaterally, Harold Macmillan was one of the first to learn of it, just after a congressional "consultation" on the afternoon of July 14. As soon as the congressmen had left, the president, in the presence of the secretary of state, telephoned the prime minister to inform him of the impending action. Macmillan accepted Eisenhower's view that instead of participating in the landing, British forces should be held in reserve. The prime minister added that Jordan's King Hussein had sent a request for British support. The president should realize, therefore, how much the situation might expand. The two men vowed that they "were in this together, all the way."[34]

On July 17, the situation did expand as Macmillan warned. London decided to prop up Hussein's shaky regime with 2,200 British paratroopers from Cyprus. Foreign Minister Selwyn Lloyd flew to Washington to confer with Eisenhower and Dulles. Eisenhower assured him that aside from combat troops, "we could and we would support the British in every feasible way, including the provision of logistical support. . . ." He pledged, furthermore, that if the British got into trouble, he "would take all necessary measures to make the operation a success." He quickly made good on his word. Fifty U.S. fighters flew cover for the airlift of British troops to Amman. The operation was accompanied by a U.S. announcement that it would begin air shipment of petroleum supplies to British forces in Jordan. Israeli reluctance to permit overflight privileges for U.S. and British supply flights was overcome at Washington's behest.[35] Thus, the interventions in Lebanon and Jordan became two interlinked parts of a single, jointly managed operation to stabilize pro-Western regimes in the Middle East. In this operation, as in the situation as a whole, Great Britain was an important element of U.S. power.

The Enigma of Nationalism

At the same time that Washington saw its chief concern in Europe, administration policymakers had full awareness of the strength and vitality of Arab nationalism. They knew, moreover, that Arab nationalists identified America with European colonialism, and that so long as Washington was besmirched by that association, the Soviet Union would gain credit in the Arab world. Writing in his diary two weeks before his inauguration, Eisenhower could not have put the problem more clearly. "Nationalism is on the march," he wrote,

> and world communism is taking advantage of that spirit of nationalism to cause dissension in the free world. Moscow leads many misguided people to believe that they can count on Communist help to achieve and sustain nationalist ambitions. . . . The free world's hope of defeating the Communist aims does not include objecting to national aspirations. We must show the wickedness of purpose in the Communist promises and convince dependent peoples that their only hope of maintaining independence, once attained, is through cooperation with the free world.[36]

But in the Middle East, "cooperation with the free world" meant acquiescing in Western hegemony. Eisenhower could do nothing to change this meaning. As long as U.S. priorities were Eurocentric, there were strict limits to Washington's ability to tolerate Arab nationalists, who by virtue of being nationalists desired the diminution of European influence in the region. NSC 5820/1, a comprehensive review of U.S. Middle Eastern policy approved by the president on November 4, 1958, illustrates the difficulty that Eisenhower administration officials had in grasping this nettle.

The document painted a grim picture. Political trends in the Middle East, it said, "are inimical to U.S. and other Western interests." Since 1956, "the West and the radical pan-Arab nationalist movement have been arrayed against each other," as the West supported conservative regimes opposed to radical nationalism. In 1958, the conservative resistance collapsed, "leaving the radical nationalist regimes almost without opposition in the area. . . ."

The most dangerous challenge, however, arose "not from Arab nationalism *per se*, but from the coincidence of many of its objectives with many of those of the U.S.S.R. and the resultant way in which it can be manipulated to serve Soviet ends." These ends consisted of the weakening and ultimate elimination of Western influence, "using Arab nationalism as an instrument, and substituting Soviet influence for that of the West." Washington's ability to keep the Russians from achieving their goals depended upon how closely the United States could work "with Arab nationalism and associate itself . . . with such aims and aspirations of the Arab people as are not contrary to the basic interests of the United States."

But the United States could not go too far in getting closer to nationalist regimes. "We face the fact that certain aspects of the drive toward Arab unity, particularly as led by Nasser, are strongly inimical to our interests." Any U.S. approaches toward Nasser, therefore, had to be undertaken in such a way as to maintain freedom of action in dealing with other Arab leaders, who would be given discreet encouragement whenever "we see signs of independent [anti-Nasser] views. . . ."

Thus, the United States would "endeavor to establish an effective working relationship with Arab nationalism while at the same time seeking constructively to influence and stabilize the movement and to contain its outward thrust. . . ." When the "essentially neutralist character of pan-Arab nationalism" precluded "maintenance of the special political, military and economic interests comprising the Western position in the area," the United States would be prepared "if necessary" to make "appropriate revisions in the existing Western strategic position." But Washington would try to keep such revisions at a minimum, retaining as much of the special Western interests as it could. Moreover, all such policy guidelines subserved the two "*primary* objectives" that it was "essential" Washington achieve: "Denial of the area to Soviet domination," and "continued availability of sufficient Near Eastern oil to meet vital Western European requirements on reasonable terms."[37]

To a point, there was considerable wisdom in this curious potpourri. Unlike the British and French at the time of Suez, Eisenhower policymakers knew that it would be counterproductive to launch a frontal attack on pan-Arab nationalism, hence, their advocacy of ostensible accommodation conjoined with discreet encouragement of "independent" leaders. But beyond that point, the study was an exercise in delusion. The idea that the United States could move closer to something called "Arab nationalism *per se*," distinct from a nationalism whose objectives coincided with the Soviet Union's, was absurd almost by definition, because it is hard to conceive of an Arab nationalism that did not seek diminished Western influence. It is also hard to conceive of how the administration could reconcile its fundamental Eurocentricism with a policy of accommodating nationalist demands.

The Eisenhower advisors hoped to square the circle through tactical finesse—getting closer to Arab nationalists, but not too close; giving up some privileged positions, but only to the minimum extent required; supporting pro-Western, anti-Nasser regimes, but not so obviously as to let the Soviets pose as sole champion of Arab unity. Yet no amount of finesse could spare U.S. policymakers the ultimate burden of hard choice, and when hard choices were made, they invariably followed the logic maintaining conservative, pro-Western "stability" in the region.

Eisenhower encountered his first test before his inauguration. Following the nationalization of the Anglo-Iranian Oil Company (AIOC) holdings on April 30, 1951, the British company (in which the government owned a majority share) was joined by the other six major world oil companies in a devastating boycott of Iranian oil. Denied access to world oil markets, Iran suffered progressive economic deterioration and resultant political disorder. In an appeal sent to the president-elect on January 9, 1953, Prime Minister Mossadegh evoked the two years of misery and distress that Iran had suffered at British hands. He expressed gratitude for the sympathy that many Americans had shown toward Iran, noting, however, that although the U.S. government had been friendly on occasion, it had still given financial aid to Britain while withholding it from Iran. Mossadegh closed the communication expressing the hope that when Eisenhower took power he would give "careful consideration" to the Iranian case.

Mossadegh was clearly angling to cut a deal with the United States at Britain's expense. Eisenhower's first response, dated January 10, offered asssurances that he would study Mossadegh's views "with care and sympathetic concern." In a subsequent dispatch sent at the end of May, Mossadegh addressed a more explicit plea for aid, asking Eisenhower either to help in removing the obstacles to Iranian oil sales or to give economic assistance enabling Iran to use other resources. This time Eisenhower responded with a more explicit refusal. After waiting more than a month before sending his reply, the president asserted that Iran's economic problems were because of its failure to reach agreement with the AIOC on compensation. It would be inappropriate, therefore, for the United States to extend aid to Iran to make up for revenues that could have been earned from the sale of oil; nor would the United States government step in as a purchaser. Eisenhower also indicated that British ideas on a fair settlement approximated his own.[38]

Leaked by Mossadegh's political enemies, the news of Eisenhower's rejection further weakened the prime minister's tenuous grip on power.[39] This was in fact what the administration desired. On July 22, approval had been given to a CIA scheme—in the works since November 1952—to stage a coup against Mossadegh. CIA operative Kermit Roosevelt went to Iran in mid-July. He made contact with the Shah, with retired General Fazlollah Zahedi (whom the Shah would appoint prime minister in place of Mossadegh), and with dissident army and police officers. Two Iranian agents were given $100,000 to recruit a mob. A false start on August 15 forced the Shah into a brief exile in Rome. On the 18th and 19th, however, the mob and anti-Mossadegh army elements took to the streets, terrorizing the prime minister's supporters. Zahedi took power on August 19; Mossadegh surrendered, and several days later the Shah returned. U.S. aid followed quickly— first $900,000 directly out of the CIA safe, and then a $45 million emergency grant announced on September 5. In October, 1954, the Iranian parliament ratified an oil settlement. In place of the AIOC monopoly, an international consortium would purchase and distribute Iranian production; 40 percent of the shares in this new enterprise would be held equally by five large American oil firms.[40] The first CIA-sponsored overthrow of a foreign government seemed a thoroughgoing success.

Intervention in Lebanon

Eisenhower's decision to intervene in Lebanon was by contrast much more difficult than the decision to topple Mossadegh, but the reason behind it was largely the same. The administration was determined to maintain a conservative status quo against the pressures of radical nationalism.

In his memoirs, Eisenhower asserts, "behind everything was our deep-seated conviction that the Communists were principally responsible for the trouble" in Lebanon.[41] It is doubtful that Eisenhower really thought this at the time. Although Washington policymakers always worried about Soviet *exploitation* of local instabilities, the evidence clearly demonstrates their awareness that Communists did not cause the civil war. As Robert Murphy, under secretary of state for political affairs at the time, later recorded, "Much of the conflict concerned personalities and rivalries of a domestic nature. . . . Communism was playing no direct or substantial part in the insurrection, although Communists no doubt hoped to profit from the disorders. . . . The outside influences came mostly from Egypt and Syria."[42] In a White House meeting held on June 15, CIA Director Allen Dulles said much the same. The Soviets, he stated (with Eisenhower present), "have not entered the Lebanese situation at all except by radio."[43]

Eisenhower's determination to safeguard the status quo in Lebanon, despite the lack of an appreciable Communist role in the rebellion, was reinforced by the conjuncture of events. President Chamoun had established firm pro-Western credentials by refusing to sever diplomatic relations with Britain and France during the Suez crisis and by later accepting the Eisenhower Doctrine. He had, in consequence, exposed himself to intensified political attack by advocates of Arab unity. In Syria, pan-Arab tendencies steadily gathered strength, culminating in the United Arab Republic (UAR), a union between Egypt and Syria proclaimed on February 1, 1958. Pan-Arab pressures also mounted in Saudi Arabia. On March 23, King Saud succumbed to them, yielding effective power to Crown Prince Faisal, a man Eisenhower deemed "pro-Nasserite."[44] In such a context it was extremely important to back Chamoun, because if a pro-Western leader like Chamoun called for help and the United States did not respond, as Dulles warned on June 15, "that will be the end of every pro-Western government in the area." Eisenhower agreed, noting that "in such circumstances we would have to fulfill our commitments." He said this even though he knew that Chamoun had precipitated the rebellion by seeking a second term, and despite the fact that the Eisenhower Doctrine, which promised support to friendly states threatened with external aggression from countries controlled by international communism, did not strictly apply to the Lebanon conflict.[45]

But the ambiguities were mere quibbles. Although the domestic political situation presented a "confusing picture," the civil war would not have been prolonged and might not have started without foreign intervention[46] in the form of "vicious" pan-Arab propaganda and UAR aid (both weapons and Syrian personnel) to insurgent forces.[47] Civil strife fomented from without could destroy national independence just as effectively as direct aggression over a border. The Lebanon crisis was a test case of repelling "indirect aggression."[48]

Still, notwithstanding their desire to end the rebellion, policymakers approached the idea of an intervention in Lebanon with some misgiving. In May, Eisenhower had informed Chamoun that U.S. troops would not be sent to Lebanon to secure him a second term and that a second Arab nation would have to concur in the action. Eisenhower understood the pitfalls of intervention. He knew that a "substantial part of the population" would actively or passively oppose a U.S. armed presence. The problem reminded him of British efforts in the early 1950s to hold their Suez military base "with the entire population against them, and the impossible situation that resulted." He wondered where things would lead, and where they would end. Rather than solving Lebanon's problems, an intervention by Western forces might have the opposite effect, inflaming confessional strife and leading to territorial partition. Arab resentment over such an action would turn to Nasser's favor and overwhelm pro-Western leaders in other countries. Moreover, Chamoun himself had on May 22 referred the matter to the United Nations Security Council, and on June 12 the advance party of a UN observer team arrived in Lebanon. An American military move into Lebanon would be extremely awkward before it could be determined whether the UN action would succeed. If it failed, Western intervention would still be a last resort: other possibilities—such as use of Pakistan, Turkey and Iraq[49]—would be looked into first.

By early July the crisis had calmed. Washington officials were now hopeful that they could avoid intervention, however, these hopes were soon dashed. At daybreak on July 14, 1958, a military coup overthrew the Hashemite monarchy of Iraq. The administration was not certain whether Nasser had a direct hand in the coup, but in Washington's estimate the revolutionaries were clearly Nasser sympathizers. There was now no doubt in Eisenhower's mind that the United States— Chamoun had made a frantic request for help to the U.S. ambassador in Beirut—would have to intervene in Lebanon. The Iraqi revolution increased the danger of hostile infiltration and the likelihood of Lebanon going under as a sovereign state. King Saud professed fear for his own neck. Given the upheaval in Iraq, the United States had no choice in the matter: failure to respond to Chamoun's appeal would "set up a chain reaction which will doom the pro-West governments of Lebanon and Jordan and Saudi Arabia and raise grave problems for Turkey and Iran."[50] The time had come, Eisenhower believed, "to stop the trend toward chaos."[51]

When Eisenhower announced the Marine landings on July 15, he did not claim, in the lexicon of his Middle East Doctrine, that he was responding to an armed aggression by countries controlled by "international communism." He instead parsed words, stating in a radio and television address that Lebanon had been victimized by an "internal aggression" that *followed the pattern* of Communist "aggression" in Greece, Czechoslovakia, China, Korea, and Indochina.[52] He thereby spared himself the burden of asserting that Syria and Egypt were Soviet controlled, while still invoking the Communist threat. In private, however, there was no need to blur the fact that pan-Arab radicalism was the immediate concern. Meeting with the president on July 23, Secretary Dulles likened Arab nationalism to a "flood which is running strongly." "We cannot," he said, "successfully oppose it, but we can put up sandbags around positions we must protect—the first group being Israel and Lebanon and the second being the oil positions around the Persian Gulf." The president proceeded to expand on the secretary's assessment. Ultimately, the Western positions could not be held "against the underlying and often unthinking convictions of the Arab world. . . ." The United States, he said, had to find some way to change those convictions, in order to "get ourselves to the point where the Arabs will not be hostile to us."[53]

The Lebanon affair ended on a note of irony. In early June, President Nasser had contacted the United States with a three-part formula for pacifying Lebanon: Chamoun would serve out his term (which expired on September 28); Lebanese army commander General Fuad Chehab would become president; and the opposition would be granted amnesty. Washington forwarded the proposal to Chamoun without endorsement, for as Dulles explained in a cable to Beirut, the United States would not "become accomplice with Nasser" in anything the Lebanese government did not want. Chamoun obliged by ignoring Nasser's initiative. Now, after the intervention in July, U.S. envoy Robert Murphy brokered a settlement remarkably similar to the Nasser plan: Chamoun would finish out his term; the Chamber of Deputies would elect General Chehab to succeed him; and the new regime would pursue a policy of conciliation. So with respect to Lebanese internal politics, the outcome of the intervention was a solution that might have been achieved five or six weeks earlier with the cooperation of the archenemy, Nasser. Moreover, Eisenhower had never fully appreciated the moderating role played by General Chehab. A Christian like Chamoun, Chehab had refused to order the army into offensive action against the Moslem rebels for fear of splitting his troops on religious lines and igniting full-scale confessional war. For Eisenhower, however, Chehab was derelict in his duty and should have been fired. Had the firing occurred and a more aggressive commander put in Chehab's place, Murphy might not have achieved such success in sponsoring the political settlement that Nasser had largely devised.[54]

Arab Nationalism and the Suez

In view of the antinationalist sentiment that seemed to motivate his feelings toward Egypt, Iraq, Syria, Lebanon, and Iran, Eisenhower's behavior during the Suez crisis presents a stark anomaly. Instead of siding with his European allies to strike Nasser down, he opposed their use of force and thereby doomed the Suez Campaign.

The anomaly, however, was only apparent. The extremity of U.S. solicitude for the Anglo-French position has already been noted. There was no similar solicitude displayed toward Egypt. In Dulles's mind, Nasser had employed "bullying tactics" over the canal. In the bipartisan leadership meeting of August 12, the president declared that he could not accept "an inconclusive outcome that left Nasser in control."[55]

Clearly, neither Eisenhower nor Dulles was prepared to assert categorical support of Nasser's sovereign right to expropriate the canal. Far from it, their first impulse was to reverse the nationalization by putting the waterway under international control. Dulles prevailed on Great Britain and France to convene a twenty-two-nation conference in London to work out a plan giving user states a say in running the canal. On August 23, the conference approved a formula vesting full operational control of the canal in an internationally constituted board.[56]

Nasser would never have accepted such a severe derogation of sovereignty. On September 4, one day after meeting with a committee of conference representatives, the Egyptian leader rejected the scheme. Anticipating failure, Eisenhower and Dulles had already prepared a fallback position—the so-called Users Association. The user governments would together create an organization that would handle the technical aspects of canal operations—piloting vessels, organizing traffic through the canal, and collecting tolls. Such an organization would make it possible to send convoys through the canal without any Egyptians at all, unless Egypt chose physically to block passage. If the Egyptians cooperated, they would receive a share of the tolls to compensate them for the cost of canal maintenance, and Egyptian technical experts would be consulted on operational matters.[57]

The users idea was no more acceptable to Nasser than the scheme for international control. He branded it "an association to usurp rights, to usurp sovereignty, to declare war."[58] Both schemes had the effect, moreover, of diluting U.S. admonitions against resort to force. For at the same time as Eisenhower opposed military action, the measures he proposed could only be obtained by military means. If that were not enough to confuse Anglo-French leaders, Eisenhower did not, in his correspondence with Eden, rule out the use of force in extreme circumstances. What he demanded, rather, was that every peaceful approach to a settlement be explored and exhausted first. He was not referring just to negotiations. Writing Eden on September 8, he suggested ways to squeeze Egypt harder: a users' association, economic pressures "which, if continued, will cause distress," exploiting intra-Arab rivalries, and developing alternatives to the canal and existing pipelines. He did not "want any capitulation to Nasser."[59]

Eisenhower's opposition to military action stemmed almost entirely from tactical considerations. He did not like the nationalization, but conceded that "world public opinion was largely on [Nasser's] side." The British and the French would have to make a very good case to justify attacking Egypt. Indiscriminate military action without proper justification would be counterproductive. Afro-Asian countries would unite against the West, providing an opening for sure Soviet gains. There might, of course, be instances that called for military action, but Suez was "the wrong issue about which to be tough."[60]

U.S. appraisal of the political consequences of the Suez attack confirmed Eisenhower's fears. The Anglo-French "case" had in no way improved since July, prompting the president's acid remark that the British might have improved the case "if the Egyptians had not simply nationalized the canal and then operated it effectively afterward."[61] Because of the seeming injustice of the Allies' cause, third-world reaction was vehement, "one of unanimous revulsion," in the estimate of CIA Director Allen Dulles. "Earlier doubts as to Nasser's ambitions, and outrage over the tragic events in Hungary, have been drowned out by a wave of revived age-old hatred of Western imperialism and colonialism"—a hatred that the Soviets had just begun to exploit.[62]

None of these considerations implied an affinity for Nasser. Even after the attack, Eisenhower stated that "he did not fancy helping Egypt. . . ," but he had to nonetheless. The United States had been signatory (along with Britain and France) to the Triparite Declaration of May 25, 1950. It had pledged in the declaration to take immediate action to stop any violation of frontiers or armistice lines. If the United States did not fulfill its pledge, U.S. prestige would decline in Arab eyes, and the Soviets would enter the picture.[63] Eisenhower could not afford, moreover, to stand behind Israel, Britain, and France against the opinion of most of the world. America was already sufficiently embarrassed at being identified with British and French "colonial policies not compatible" with her own.[64]

Yet he still shared his allies' view on the Egyptian leader. He regarded him as an "evil influence." His complaint with the British and French was that "they chose a bad time and incident on which to launch corrective measures." Preferring a flanking action to a frontal assault, Eisenhower stressed the advisability of building up an Arab rival to Nasser (King Saud was his candidate): "if we could build him up as the individual who captured the imagination of the Arab world, Nasser would not last long."[65]

Eisenhower had come to a hostile view of Nasser months before Egypt nationalized the Suez Canal. When Nasser assumed the premiership of Egypt in April 1954, Washington hoped to win him to a pro-Western alignment. CIA agents Kermit Roosevelt and Miles Copeland became good friends with Nasser, meeting with him on almost a daily basis. But U.S. hopes of winning Nasser over were soon dashed.

On April 28, 1955 Israel launched a fierce reprisal raid into the Gaza Strip, revealing Egypt's military impotence. The Egyptians were further humiliated when Israeli war planes flew over Cairo with impunity. Nasser began looking for arms. When Western countries turned him down, he looked to the Soviet bloc. In July he concluded an arms agreement with Czechoslavakia, which he announced on September 27, 1955, much to Washington's dismay.

Nasser had already started to slip from U.S. favor with his opposition to the Baghdad Pact and his espousal of neutralism at the Bandung Conference of Afro-Asian leaders in April 1955. But rather than confront him, the administration tried now to purchase friendship. Spurred by the Czech arms deal, the United States offered in December 1955 to grant $56,000,000 for the first stage of Aswan Dam construction. The American offer was accompanied by commitments for a $14 million grant from Britain and a $200 million loan from the World Bank.

But the aid had strings: Egypt would have to submit herself to an anti-inflationary domestic policy supervised by the World Bank. Resentful over such conditions, Nasser stalled for better terms. In the meantime the Egyptian press waged a bitter propaganda campaign against the Baghdad Pact, the West's refusal to sell Egypt arms, and Western support for Israel. Rumors circulated that Nasser was talking with the Soviets about financing the dam.

Eisenhower was coming to the position that Nasser was largely responsible for the ills of the region. The failure of the super-secret Anderson mission in early 1956 etched this impression indelibly in Eisenhower's mind.

In mid-January Eisenhower sent former Deputy Secretary of Defense Robert Anderson to the Middle East, armed with authority to give magnanimous promises of economic aid to Israel in return for an Egyptian-Israel peace. In small military aircraft, Anderson shuttled between Cairo and Tel Aviv via Rome or Athens. He met on numerous occasions with Nasser and Ben-Gurion in an effort that lasted until the middle of March.

The initiative foundered because there were few grounds on which Nasser and Ben-Gurion could bridge differences. Ben-Gurion refused to accept Anderson as an intermediary and demanded to negotiate with Nasser personally. For domestic political reasons, however, it was out of the question for Nasser to conduct face-to-face negotiations with the Israeli prime minister. Ben-Gurion had no concessions to offer, to say nothing of what he would have to concede to make a peace treaty palatable to Nasser. Without Israeli willingness to bargain over territory and Palestinian repatriation, no amounts of American largesse would induce Nasser to conclude an Egyptian-Israeli peace.

The Anderson mission failed, therefore, because of the mutual incompatability of the Israeli and Egyptian positions. But when the failure of the mission had become patent in early March, Eisenhower put almost the entire burden of blame on Nasser. "We have reached the point," he noted in his diary entry for March 8, "where it looks as if Egypt under Nasser is going to make no move whatsoever to meet the Israelites in an effort to settle outstanding differences." Because of Soviet arms, the Arabs were becoming more arrogant by the day, "and disregarding the interests of Western Europe and the United States in the Middle East. . . ."

Five days later Eisenhower repeated the refrain: "Nasser proved to be a complete stumbling block." He said this even though he also felt that Israel had an "attitude of making no concessions whatsoever in order to obtain a peace."[67] His response was to approve a multifaceted action program drawn up by Dulles on March 28 to punish and isolate Egypt. The program comprised continued denial of arms export licenses; delay in concluding the Aswan Dam negotiations; delay in granting oil and grain to Egypt under the PL 480 program; holding in abeyance decisions on the CARE program for Egypt; increased aid to pro-Western regimes and political forces in Libya, Ethiopia, Lebanon, and Saudi Arabia; and stepped-up support to the Baghdad Pact. These measures, as Dulles put it, would "let Colonel Nasser realize that he cannot cooperate as he is doing with the Soviet Union and at the same time enjoy most-favored nation treatment from the United States."[68] The subsequent U.S. withdrawal from the Aswan project—announced to Egypt in a meeting on July 19 between Dulles and Egyptian Ambassador Ahmed Hussein—was consistent with the anti-Nasser offensive that Eisenhower envisioned in March. Thus, as of early 1956, Washington and Cairo were antagonists. They would never during the Eisenhower presidency put their relationship on a firm, positive footing.[69]

Eisenhower Assessed

As a short-run proposition, Eisenhower's Middle Eastern policy was a remarkable success. The success, however, involved many hidden, future costs that we are paying now.

In the short run, Eisenhower achieved what he desired. Pro-Western regimes in the area remained pro-Western, and, with the exception of the damage inflicted by the British and French at Suez, European oil supplies remained secure.

In the last two years of his presidency, moreover, the pan-Arab movement lost steam, although not through Eisenhower's doing. Iraq's Premier Kassem rejected union with the U.A.R.; Nasser's support of Kassem's pro-union opposition incited a virulent Iraqi-Egyptian propaganda struggle. In the meantime, disaffection mounted in Syria over Egyptian domination of the U.A.R.; Syria would withdraw from the union in September 1961 after an army-led revolt. Finally, the Soviet Union found itself in a house of mirrors, aiding two regimes that hated each other (Egypt and Iraq), and in a quandary over whether to aid local Communists at the risk of alienating the noncommunist, Nationalist leaders who held power.

Still, despite the apparently favorable situation he left to his successor, Eisenhower must ultimately be judged—unfavorably—on the basis of opportunities that he lost. The United States had never before enjoyed such leverage in the Middle East and would probably never again. This leverage was put to little constructive use.

The success in overthrowing Mossadegh delegitimized the Shah's regime and ultimately brought on a revolution steeped in anti-Americanism. Eisenhower thus threw away an opportunity to help consolidate a noncommunist nationalism that, if allowed to develop, would have provided a far more solid bulwark of stability in the region than a personalized monarchy that never overcame the discredit of having been installed by Washington.

Eisenhower's hostility toward Mossadegh was bred in his Eurocentrism. He was intellectually incapable of adopting imaginative approaches toward dealing with the problems that did not fall into the confines of a pre-ordered world view. Despite his occasional musings over the need to work with nationalist forces in the Middle East, in the ultimate reckoning his real interest never ranged beyond the threefold task of maintaining pro-Western stability, safeguarding oil supplies, and halting the spread of Soviet influence in the region—all subsets of the overriding U.S. interest in Europe.

His Eurocentrism was particularly disabling when Eisenhower confronted the question of Nasser. He failed to follow through on initial friendly relations with Nasser because he perceived Nasser's aggressive neutralism, expressed most strongly in Cairo's opposition to the Baghdad Pact, as a menace to the Western position in the Middle East. He considered the failure of the Anderson mission entirely Nasser's fault. He was pained over having to side with Egypt over Suez. The president gained esteem in the Arab world by forcing the allied invaders out of

Suez, but did not then choose to work with Nasser toward resolving the underlying political and economic problems of the region. Instead, he hastened to ensure that neither Nasser nor the Soviets reaped too much advantage from Suez; he declared the Eisenhower Doctrine and committed the United States to propping up the status quo.

The Soviet Union was part of the reason that Eisenhower devised his policies in a confined universe. Arab nationalism presented a great unknown and threatened to upset the established order of things. The Soviet Union could exploit this disorder in a variety of ways that could not be strictly foretold. Inasmuch as the Soviet Union threatened Western interests in the region, it did so in proportion to opportunities— afforded by circumstance—for political, economic, and military penetration, either in league with local Communists or with progressive Nationalists who threw Communists in jail. To stop the Soviets, the United States had to close the openings Moscow might slip through. Anti-Sovietism in such a context translated into a general opposition to internal dissidence (as in Lebanon) and to destabilizing radical nationalisms that imperiled pro-Western regimes. In this way, it was easy to concoct an anticommunist rationale for anything the United States did in the region, whatever the Soviet involvement, or lack of it.

The chief problem that Eisenhower never dealt with remains at the core of violent conflict in the Middle East today. The plight of the seven to nine hundred thousand Palestinian refugees, victims of the 1948–49 Arab-Israeli War, has been mentioned only once in passing in this essay. The omission is quite fitting, because it amply reflects the level of Washington's concern with the issue. On August 26, 1955, Secretary of State Dulles proposed a peace settlement linking the formal fixing and guarantee of borders with the "resettlement and, to such an extent as may be feasible, repatriation" of the homeless Palestinians, whom Israel would compensate from the proceeds of an international loan subscribed to by the United States. The proposal got nowhere, and Washington never put any real political weight behind it. By the time of the President's "Eisenhower Doctrine" address of January 5, 1957, he felt comfortable in brushing the whole business off. The legislation that he was proposing did not deal with "the Arab refugee," he said. The UN was taking care of that, and the United States was willing to assist the UN.

Such cavalier treatment of an issue that comprised at once a grievous human tragedy and the greatest single threat to enduring stability in the region contrasts sharply with the political strongarm tactics Eisenhower used with telling effect to push Israel out of the Gaza Strip and Sharm el Sheikh. The events of the immediate post-Suez period suggest what

216 *Reevaluating Eisenhower*

might have been accomplished if Eisenhower had used his leverage on behalf of the Palestinians. But there was a difference between using U.S. leverage for the immediate sake of Europe's oil and using it to fulfill the long-term requirements of regional stability. Ensuring Europe's oil demanded nothing more than a narrow realism. Coping with the Palestinian question demanded sensitivity toward the fate of an Arab people. But Eisenhower was concerned with problems only to the extent they affected direct Western interests. His Eurocentric tunnel vision brought long-run dangers that might have been avoided with a broader view.

Notes

I wish to thank the president of the Carnegie Endowment for International Peace, Thomas L. Hughes, for providing the domicile where this project was completed. A special debt is owed the Endowment librarian, Jane Lowenthal, whose aid was indispensable. The essay was read by Wilma Liebman and Monica Yin, who made it intelligible. Portions of this essay appear in *America's Confrontation with Revolutionary Change in the Middle East, 1948–1983* (New York: Macmillan Publishing, 1986).

1. "The Middle East Resolution, approved March 9, 1957," in U.S., Congress, Senate Committee on Foreign Relations, *A Select Chronology and Background Documents Relating to the Middle East,* 94th Cong., 1st sess., 1975, 216–18 (217, quote).

2. Eisenhower diary entries for June 11, 1951, November 24, 1951, and January 6, 1953, in *The Eisenhower Diaries,* ed. Robert H. Ferrell (New York: W.W. Norton, 1981), 194–95, 206, 222.

3. In his diary entry for December 1, 1947, Eisenhower wrote: "Unless broken economies are restored they will almost certainly fall prey to communism, and if the progress of this disease is not checked, we will find ourselves an isolated democracy in a world elsewhere controlled by enemies." Ferrell, *The Eisenhower Diaries,* 144.

4. Ibid., 319.

5. Eisenhower to Churchill, 29 March 1956, quoted in Donald Neff, *Warriors at Suez: Eisenhower Takes America into the Middle East* (New York: Simon & Schuster, 1981), 282.

6. Ruler of Egypt from 1863 to 1869, Ismail Pasha's profligate expenditure ran him deeply into debt, necessitating sale of his Suez Canal shares. In 1876 he had to relinquish control of Egyptian finances to an international debt commission.

7. Anthony Eden, *Full Circle* (London: Cassell, 1960), 424.

8. Ibid., 426.

9. Ibid., 427–28.

10. Dwight D. Eisenhower, *The White House Years: Waging Peace 1956–1961* (Garden City, N.Y.: Doubleday, 1965), 36.

11. Joint Chiefs of Staff memorandum, "Nationalization of the Suez Maritime Canal Company by the Egyptian Government," 31 July 1956, JCS. 2105/38, Declassified Documents Reference System (hereafter DDRS), (78) 370A.

12. Minutes, Bipartisan Leadership Meeting, 12 August 1956, DDRS, (76) 217B. In relating the figures on Europe's petroleum interest in Suez, Dulles really meant that two-thirds of Europe's *Middle Eastern* oil went through Suez. Europe drew around 75 percent of its petroleum supply from the Middle East, not 100 percent as Dulles implies in his remarks.

13. Eisenhower, *Waging Peace,* 98; memorandum of conference with the president, 20 November 1956, DDRS, (78) 451B; minutes, Bipartisan Leadership Meeting, 12 August 1956, DDRS, (76) 217B; minutes, Bipartisan Legislative Meeting, 9 November 1956, DDRS, (76) 217C.

14. Memorandum of conference with the president, 29 October 1956, DDRS, (78) 449D.

15. *Public Papers of the Presidents of the United States: Dwight D. Eisenhower, 1956* (Washington, D.C.: Government Printing Office, 1958), 1064.

16. Minutes, Bipartisan Legislative Meeting, 9 November 1956, DDRS, (76) 217C.

17. Eisenhower, *Waging Peace,* 37.

18. Minutes, Bipartisan Legislative Meeting, 9 November 1956, DDRS, (76) 217C.

19. Memorandum of conversation with the president, 21 November 1956, DDRS, (78) 451A.

20. The communication is reproduced in Eisenhower, *Waging Peace,* 684–85.

21. Eisenhower, *Waging Peace,* 185.

22. Minutes, Bipartisan Legislative Meeting, 20 February 1957, DDRS, (76) 218A.

23. *Public Papers of the Presidents: Eisenhower, 1957:* 154.

24. Eisenhower diary entry for 15 May 1947, in Ferrell, *The Eisenhower Diaries,* 141–42.

25. Ibid., entry for 26 May 1946, 136–37.

26. Eisenhower, *Waging Peace,* 22–23.

27. [State Department?] memorandum to Eisenhower, "Defense of the Middle East," [July?] 1955, DDRS, (78) 283A; report by the Joint Strategic Plans Committee to the Joint Chiefs of Staff, "U.K. Views Regarding the Middle East," J.S.P.C. 883/78, 11 August 1955, DDRS, (78) 366A; memorandum by Office of Foreign Military Affairs (Department of Defense) to Eisenhower, "Middle East Areas," 5 May 1955, DDRS, (81) 37A (quote); note by JCS Secretariat to holders of JCS 1887/117, 7 December 1955, DDRS, (78) 367A; report by the Joint Middle East Planning Committee to the Joint Chiefs of Staff, "Baghdad Pact Planning Staff Study. . . .", JCS 1887/302, DDRS, (78) 367A.

28. J.S.P.C. 883/78, see note 27; Joint Chiefs of Staff memorandum, "Logistic Support of Our Strategy in the Middle East," 12 August 1955, DDRS, (78) 367B.

29. [State Department?] memorandum to Eisenhower, DDRS, 1978, 283A,

see note 27; Eden talks, Washington, 30 January–1 February 1956, memorandum of conversation, 30 January 1956, DDRS, (78) 283B (quote); memorandum of conversation with the president, 20 December 1956, DDRS, (81) 391B.

30. Summary Briefing Paper, Bermuda Conference, 20–24 March 1957, DDRS, (78) 207C.

31. National Security Council memorandum, "U.S. Policy Toward the Near East," 4 November 1958, NSC 5820/1. Military action to protect European oil supplies was suggested only as a last resort and with the recognition that "this course . . . could not be indefinitely pursued."

32. CIA activities in the 1957 Lebanese elections are described in Wilbur Crane Eveland, *Ropes of Sand* (New York: W.W. Norton, 1980), 248–53.

33. Eisenhower, *Waging Peace,* 266, 273; Townsend Hoopes, *The Devil and John Foster Dulles* (Boston: Little, Brown, 1973), 434–35; report by the Joint Middle East Planning Group to the Joint Chiefs of Staff, "Study of the Long Range Military Implications of U.S./UK Intervention in Lebanon," 23 June 1958, DDRS, (81) 311A.

34. Eisenhower, *Waging Peace,* 273.

35. Ibid., 279 (quote), 280–82.

36. Eisenhower diary entry for 6 January 1953 in Ferrell, *The Eisenhower Diaries,* 223.

37. NSC 5820/1.

38. The correspondence is printed in *Department of State Bulletin,* 29 (20 July 1953): 74–77.

39. The exchange was officially released, along with the January messages, on July 9, in both Tehran and Washington.

40. Barry Rubin, *Paved with Good Intentions: The American Experience and Iran* (New York: Oxford University Press, 1980), 54–90, 94–96; *Public Papers of the Presidents: Eisenhower, 1953:* 579–81.

41. Eisenhower, *Waging Peace,* 266.

42. Robert Murphy, *Diplomat Among Warriors* (Garden City, N.Y.: Doubleday, 1964), 404.

43. Department of State memorandum of conversation with the president, 15 June 1958, DDRS, (81) 371B.

44. Eisenhower, *Waging Peace,* 264.

45. Murphy, *Diplomat Among Warriors* (quotes); Eisenhower, *Waging Peace,* 265.

46. Department of State to U.S. Embassies in Paris, Beirut, and London, 24 June 1958, DDRS, (77) 64C.

47. Department of State memorandum of conversation between the secretary of state and the ambassador of Italy, 25 June 1958, DDRS (76) 101A.

48. Murphy, *Diplomat Among Warriors;* Eisenhower, *Waging Peace.*

49. Eisenhower, *Waging Peace,* 267; Department of State to U.S. Embassy, Beirut, 19 June 1958, DDRS, (77) 134C; see notes 43 (quotes) and 47.

50. Briefing notes by Allen Dulles, meeting at the White House with congressional leaders, 14 July 1958, DDRS, (79) 12D Department of State to all U.S. Diplomatic Posts, 14 July 1958, DDRS, (77) 134G; Department of State to U.S. Embassy, Paris, 14 July 1958, DDRS, (76) 101H.

51. Eisenhower, *Waging Peace,* 270.

52. *Public Papers of the Presidents: Eisenhower, 1958:* 555.

53. Memorandum of conference with the president, 24 July 1958, DDRS, (77) 355A.

54. Department of State to U.S. Embassy, Beirut, 11 June 1958, DDRS, (81) 371A; State Department report of the history of the Lebanon crisis before 25 June 1958, DDRS (76) 100J; meeting at the White House with congressional leaders, 14 July 1958, see note 50.

55. Bipartisan Leadership Meeting, 12 August 1956, DDRS (76) 217B.

56. Under Dulles's original proposal twenty-four nations would attend: the top sixteen users of the canal plus the signatories of the 1888 Convention of Constantinople, which provided for free use of the waterway by all nations. Egypt and Greece did not attend. The final formula was approved by an 18–4 vote, with Ceylon, India, Indonesia, and the Soviet Union dissenting. India had proposed another formula by which the board would have consultative functions only. The formula that was passed was one Dulles had worked out with Britain and France.

57. Eisenhower, *Waging Peace,* 46–51, 669–75.

58. Quoted in Neff, *Warriors at Suez,* 318.

59. The president's correspondence is reproduced in Eisenhower, *Waging Peace,* 664–71 (670, quote).

60. Ibid., 50.

61. Memorandum of conference with the president, 30 October 1956, DDRS, (78) 450B.

62. "Status Report on the Near East given by the Director [Allen Dulles] at the White House to a Bi-Partisan Congressional Group, 9 November 1956," DDRS, (78) 18A.

63. Memorandum of conference with the president, 29 October 1956, 7:15 p.m., DDRS, (78) 449D (quote); memorandum of conference with the president, 29 October 1956, 8:15 p.m., DDRS, (78) 450A.

64. Conference with the president, 30 October 1956.

65. Eisenhower to Dulles (in Paris), 12 December 1956, DDRS, (76) 217D.

66. Eisenhower diary entries for 11 January and 8 March 1956, in Ferrell, *The Eisenhower Diaries,* 307–08, 318–19 (quote).

67. Ibid., entry for 13 March 1956, 319.

68. Ibid., entry for 28 March 1956, 323–24; memorandum by Dulles to the president, "Near Eastern Policies," 28 March 1956, DDRS, (80) 302B (quote).

69. This statement must be qualified by the fact that in late 1958 the United States restored surplus food aid to Egypt under the P.L. 480 program. This action followed Nasser's harsh repression of Egyptian Communists, which continued throughout 1959. Nevertheless, in his memoirs Eisenhower still asserted in retrospect that if Nasser "was not a Communist, he certainly succeeded in making us very suspicious of him." Eisenhower, *Waging Peace,* 265.

Restoration and Reunification
Eisenhower's German Policy

Anne-Marie Burley

The Federal Republic of Germany came into being on May 23, 1949. Comprised of the three postwar zones administered by the U.S., Great Britain, and France, the new republic boasted a parliamentary government headed by Chancellor Konrad Adenauer. Despite this new respectability, however, the scars of defeat remained fresh. The Allied occupation continued in the form of a High Commission whose members, one from each of the three Western Allies, supervised Adenauer's activities. Moreover, the supposedly temporary division of prewar German territory was becoming increasingly formalized as the Soviet Union engineered the transformation of the Soviet zone into the German Democratic Republic (GDR). The new East German government was installed in October.

When General Eisenhower was elected president in November 1952, he was anxious to erase these continuing reminders of Germany's wartime status. New lines of battle were being drawn in the cold war, and Germany was needed in the Western ranks. In this respect, the timing of his election might have been considered auspicious: in the spring of 1952 Stalin had sent a note to the Western powers proposing a conference to discuss a German peace treaty and the formation of a unified German government. However, from 1953 to 1955 the central question occupying the Eisenhower administration was not reunification, but restoration—a question characterized in the rhetoric of the era as how to "bring Germany back into the free world."[1]

As he assessed the global nature of U.S.-Soviet rivalry, Eisenhower became increasingly convinced that the rearmament of the Federal Republic had to take priority over the settlement of any other aspect of the future status of Germany. The policy that Eisenhower and Secretary of State John Foster Dulles mapped out envisioned rearmament and the concomitant restoration of West German sovereignty within a framework that would ensure the integration of the Federal Republic into the Western Alliance. If this goal could be attained, reunification would somehow follow. In the meantime, all Soviet initiatives on the subject were to be regarded as duplicitous attempts to prevent the strengthening of Western defenses.

On the surface, Eisenhower's determination to rearm the Federal Republic can be directly traced to the impact on American strategic thinking of the Korean War and the growing conflict in Vietnam. However, in addition to the need to strengthen NATO's military capabilities, Eisenhower and Dulles were also motivated by the belief that there could be no middle ground anywhere in the world between the United States and the Soviet Union. From this perspective, failure to carve out a secure place for the Federal Republic in the Western Alliance would be practically to invite further expansion from the East. Thus, Eisenhower's choice of priorities must be understood not only in terms of short-term defensive strategy, but also in the context of pre-emptive diplomacy.

Although the internal logic of Eisenhower's policy dictated that restoration would lead to reunification, in reality the two objectives proved to be fatally inconsistent. The combination of motives that led to U.S. support for West German rearmament led also to a demand for reunification strictly on Western terms. Unfortunately, after 1955 the Soviet Union perceived that acquiescence to those terms would result in NATO membership for Germany as a whole, and consequently declared that reunification was no longer an issue. Moreover, after working hard to facilitate the integration of the Federal Republic into the Western Alliance, Eisenhower and Dulles meant to ensure that their work would not be undone by an adverse shift in West German domestic politics. This meant backing Adenauer against the Social Democratic party (SPD), whose leaders had asserted ever since 1949 that Adenauer's choice of the West would effectively preclude any possibility of reunification.

Largely as a result of the factors mentioned above, and also because of more pressing domestic and foreign policy concerns, Eisenhower's policy toward Germany in the second half of his presidency was designed above all to maintain the status quo. He and Dulles necessarily responded to major Soviet challenges to the status of Berlin in the late 1950s, and to Adenauer's concerns on a number of smaller matters as they arose. They encouraged West German participation in the negotiations leading to the creation of the European Economic Community in 1957. Otherwise, they left it to Adenauer to make the next move on reunification and the more general question of improving relations with the GDR. From the perspective of those, including many West Germans, who saw reunification as a top priority, Eisenhower's policy toward Germany was ultimately self-defeating. From the vantage point of policymakers who saw the world only in terms of how best to safeguard U.S. interests, however, it was eminently successful.

When Eisenhower took office in January 1953, the drive for West German rearmament was well underway. The treaty creating the European Defense Community (EDC) had been signed between France, West Germany, Italy, and the Benelux countries in May 1952, and Eisenhower had been a strong supporter of the concept in his year as commander of NATO just before his presidential campaign. To Eisenhower, the EDC represented the ideal dual solution that would turn German power to American advantage. As he described it: "most NATO nations believed that establishment of an effective collective security for Western Europe was not feasible without a strong West German contribution. Not only did I agree; I also believed that an organization of NATO forces under the EDC plan would minimize or make impossible the resurgence of an independent German military machine that could again threaten her Western neighbours."[2]

In addition to those advantages, there was a growing perception among American backers of the EDC that this solution would also forestall any possibility of West German gravitation toward the Eastern bloc. As the memories of the World War were displaced by the urgency of the cold war, the underlying fear of "losing Germany" played an increasingly important role in motivating U.S. support for the EDC.

U.S. plans for strengthening the Western Alliance included a nascent vision of a strong European community; thus the EDC offered a particularly satisfactory method of achieving American goals. The unification of Western Europe through common institutions fitted in neatly with Dulles's policy of "getting tough" with the Western European nations.[3] This policy was designed to replace the one-way dependence of the Marshall Plan years with an interdependence based on a trans-Atlantic partnership in which the Western Europeans would pull their own weight. In addition to easing the financial burden on the United States, this configuration held the potential of transforming the U.S.-Soviet rivalry from a stand-off between two superpowers and their dependents into a two-against-one deterrent. Accordingly, the United States lobbied hard for the EDC, doing everything possible to convince the recalcitrant French. In a telephone conversation between Dulles and Deputy Secretary of Defense Roger M. Kyes in February 1954, Dulles discussed the EDC game plan—American and British assurances to the

French of their intentions of keeping troops in Europe and continuing the North Atlantic Treaty, combined with positive hints from Adenauer concerning his willingness to settle the nagging dispute over the Saar Valley.[4]

The State Department waited anxiously in August 1954 for news of the fate of the EDC treaty in the French Assembly. Once its rejection was final, however, Dulles went to work immediately to accomplish the same ends by different means. He succeeded within two months. A conference of the foreign ministers of nine interested countries, the six original EDC countries plus the United States, Great Britain, and Canada, convened in London at the end of September and laid the groundwork for a foreign ministers' conference of all the NATO powers, which met in October in Paris. This second conference produced a network of treaties and agreements whereby the Western European Union Treaty of 1948 was expanded to include the Federal Republic as a full member of NATO, West German sovereignty was restored, and procedures for determining the future national status of the Saar Valley established.

Dulles did not hesitate to use pressure tactics at the Nine Power Conference in London. In a televised cabinet meeting held on October 25, 1954, he recounted his policy statement on September 29, the second day of the conference:

> I pointed out to our colleagues there, the history of the United States' action in relation to Europe—both our positive action and our negative action. And I said that whenever Europe was really working to get together in unity and strength, then American help was outgiving, and we were very generous when we did.
>
> But, I said that when Europe goes in the other direction, intends to be divisive and quarrelsome and to recreate the current cycle of war, then we pull away. And I said, at the moment, there was a great wave of disillusionment that had swept all over the United States. But, I said, if it is possible to find a new pattern of unity and strength so that the hopes which we had all placed into EDC could honorably and honestly be transferred to a new organization, then, I said, I would recommend to you, Mr. President, that you would renew the same statement of policy which you had made last April in relation to EDC, namely under those circumstances that we would continue to bear fair share [*sic*] of the burden of the defense of Europe so long as the danger persisted.[5]

This passage echoes Dulles's celebrated threat, in a speech given on December 14, 1953, of an "agonizing reappraisal" of U.S. defense commitments should the EDC fail. On both occasions Dulles demonstrated the overriding importance that he and Eisenhower attached to the question of West German rearmament. Yet this essential aim was inevitably couched in terms of U.S. devotion to the cause of European unity.

Dulles's language also foreshadowed the terms that both he and Eisenhower would use to describe the success of the London and Paris conferences. In a special message to the Senate on the new treaty arrangements resulting from the conference, Eisenhower reasserted the advantages of simultaneously contributing to Western defense needs and preventing Germany from ever again posing a military threat to the rest of Europe. He added: "their fundamental significance goes far beyond the combining of strength to deter aggression. Ultimately, we hope that they will produce new understanding among the free peoples of Europe and a new spirit of friendship which will inspire greater cooperation in many fields of human activity."[6] Nevertheless, much of the rhetoric about European unification obscured a more specific goal: ensuring West German allegiance to the West.

Eisenhower and Dulles feared that unless half of Germany were securely anchored to the West, all of Germany would drift toward the East. In his memoirs, Eisenhower recounts a conversation he had in 1956 with Indian Prime Minister Jawaharlal Nehru, in which Eisenhower expressed "grave doubts that a people as dynamic as the Germans could ever be successfully treated as neutrals. . . ."[7] This assertion does not imply that the German people could never be content with a neutral status, but rather reflects the president's conviction that Germany was too lucrative a prize for either superpower to ignore. Accordingly, he constantly rebuffed Soviet proposals for a disarmed, neutral Germany as nothing more than veiled attempts to clear the way for Communist subjugation of the entire country.[8] Yet as Eisenhower well knew, many West Germans believed that neutrality would provide the quickest and perhaps the only road to reunification. To undermine political support for that position, it was vital to demonstrate that Adenauer's unwavering advocacy of the EDC as a step toward European integration was justified. Moreover, the strong ties between the Federal Republic and the Western Alliance that the EDC symbolized could be presented as a *fait accompli* to the Soviet Union.

Although Eisenhower and Dulles often presented the EDC debate as the product of a voluntary Western European move toward integration, the United States was involved in a great deal of the backstage maneuvering. In fact, the United States often acted as the Federal Republic's silent partner, working to assuage West German fears and to present West German interests in the best light possible to the French and British. Shortly before the French Assembly was due to vote on the

EDC treaty, Dulles was confronted with West German suspicions that the United States was withdrawing its support for the EDC in order to force Adenauer into a separate settlement with French Prime Minister Pierre Mendes-France.[9] A month later Dulles was informed that some members of the West German government were convinced that France had decided to exchange an alliance with the Federal Republic for a guarantee of peaceful coexistence with the Soviet Union. In the meantime, Dulles suspected the French and the British of secretly conspiring to defeat the treaty.[10]

Adenauer's worries about a U.S.-French deal were entirely misplaced. On the contrary, Dulles contemplated the necessity of sacrificing ties with France for the sake of securing the Federal Republic. As early as March 1954 Dulles held a gloomy conversation with Admiral Arthur W. Radford, chairman of the Joint Chiefs of Staff, in which they discussed the question of the EDC and Germany. According to the minutes of this conversation, Dulles characterized the French situation as "deplorable," and alluded to the possibility of "cutting loose on our treaties with France." He added, "We could lose Europe, Asia and Africa all at once if we don't watch out." He was referring partly to the worsening French military situation in Southeast Asia, but was equally worried that French recalcitrance on the EDC would open a dangerous hole in the Western defense system.[11]

The necessity of contingency planning in the event of French rejection of the EDC treaty became increasingly obvious as the summer of 1954 progressed. Dulles discussed the problem with the British and ensured that the resolution passed by the Senate on July 30 authorized Eisenhower to take any steps necessary to "restore sovereignty to Germany and to enable her to continue to the maintenance of peace and security."[12] A week after the final French vote on August 30, Dulles informed Eisenhower that the State Department was considering the possibility of allowing the Federal Republic to join NATO directly. Should the French reject this scheme, an alternative plan contemplated bypassing the French completely and entering into a defense agreement solely with Great Britain and the Federal Republic. Despite his deep desire for European integration, Adenauer was prepared to rebuild a West German national army in conjunction with whatever alternative the United States chose to support.[13]

In line with the NATO option, Dulles went to London on September 14 to enlist British support. Partially as a result of his visit, the British announced two weeks later at the Nine Power Conference that they would be willing to keep their current forces on the Continent. This guarantee helped quiet French fears of yet another German attack, and thus was largely responsible for the success of the Paris Conference in October. From the U.S. standpoint, the solution reached at the Paris conference was clearly preferable to abandoning the French. This would have been an extreme step; nevertheless, the very possibility indicates that the United States was less interested in European unity than in achieving the twin strategic objectives of strengthening NATO by a West German defense contribution and assuring the Federal Republic's loyalty to the West. Further, in the more general context of a worldview that saw American failure as inevitably leading to Soviet success, the induction of the Federal Republic into NATO was a vital preemptive move. Once taken, it was a position that needed only to be protected.

According to the American plan, the restoration of West German sovereignty logically should have been followed by reunification on the basis of free elections throughout Germany. The logic of this sequence derived from a policy rationale designed to rebut charges that the integration of the Federal Republic into the Western alliance would destroy any chance of German unity. Adenauer faced these charges from the Social Democrats daily within the Federal Republic and had long since developed the concept of negotiation from strength. According to this view, building a strong West Germany within a strong Western Alliance would bolster the Western negotiating position to the point where the Soviet Union would be forced to cave in and accede to Western demands.

The United States quickly adopted the negotiation from strength rationale during the struggle to rearm the Federal Republic. The agreements resulting from the Paris Conference were publicized as a settlement designed to create "a position of solidity and strength for Western Europe" that could lead to "a new basis for discussion."[14] Nevertheless, U.S. policymakers were fully aware of Soviet attempts to thwart the EDC, and Dulles even attributed the lack of diplomatic progress on the German question, an Austrian peace treaty, and the status of the satellite countries to Soviet preoccupation with this goal.[15] He would have been more candid had he acknowledged his own unwillingness to bargain. Between the Berlin Conference of Foreign Ministers in January 1954 and the Geneva Summit Conference in July 1955, with a follow-up conference of Foreign Ministers in Geneva that October, the leaders of the Big Four powers saw the chance of a formal peace settlement with a reunified Germany glimmer on the horizon and then disappear completely. In light of the stance adopted by U.S. leaders during this period, it is questionable whether the doctrine of negotiation from strength was an unexpectedly fruitless policy or a deliberately manipulated rationalization.

The Soviet Union gave plenty of indication that the formation of the EDC or its equivalent would be regarded as an irrevocably hostile step. About a month before the British Conference of Foreign Ministers, the First Secretary at the Soviet Embassy in Washington asked *New York Times* reporter James Reston to lunch with one of the embassy's counselors. Reston immediately called Dulles to advise him of what Reston regarded as a highly unusual event, and then called back later that afternoon to report the conversation. According to Reston, the Soviets were truly worried about the "fatalistic" American view of the upcoming Berlin Conference and wanted to sound out the possibility of trading a German settlement for U.S. recognition of Communist China.

The Soviet counselor, Konstantin F. Fedoseev, asserted that the successful conclusion of a German settlement required above all a "climate of good will," but that such good will on the part of the United States could never be reconciled with the EDC, which, like NATO, was a "hostile operation." Dulles made no comment on the China proposal—the State Department had already rejected a similar suggestion contained in a Soviet note sent in November 1953. Concerning EDC, NATO, and general good will, Dulles simply stated that the lack of U.S. optimism about the conference stemmed from the difficulty of bridging the fundamental gap caused by Soviet nonacceptance of the U.S. theory of collective security.[16]

The position presented by the Soviet counselor in December 1953 was echoed precisely by Marshal Bulganin at the Geneva Summit Conference in July 1955, two months after the Federal Republic's formal entry into NATO. Bulganin said: "It must be admitted that the remilitarization of Western Germany and its integration into military groupings of the Western powers now represent the main obstacles to its unification."[17] Bulganin then proposed the creation of a collective security system that would ultimately involve the dissolution of both the Warsaw Pact and NATO. Given the steadfastness of the Soviet position, Dulles and Eisenhower could not have been very surprised when, despite the promising communique issued from the Geneva Summit Conference, the ensuing conference of foreign ministers failed to agree even on preliminary steps toward reunification and left the matter at a permanent impasse. They must have foreseen that this would be the price of including the Federal Republic in the Western collective security system, for how could they rationally have expected the Soviet Union, after actively trying to prevent the absorption of half of Germany into the Western Alliance, to do anything more than hold more tightly to the other half?

There is another interpretation of Soviet moves during this period, however—one that lends more credence to the concept of negotiation from strength. To begin with, James Reston told Dulles that his policies "really had the Russians worried."[18] Before leaving for the Berlin Conference, Dulles explained to Eisenhower that he expected the Soviet negotiators to make a final attempt to break up the Western Alliance, and thus that any discussion of German reunification would be out of the question.[19] From this perspective, the Soviet Union could be expected to behave more reasonably once the uselessness of her present course of action had become evident in the face of Western unity and resolve.

The Soviet leadership's sudden willingness to sign the Austrian peace treaty in the spring of 1955 and its desire for a summit conference could have been interpreted as concessions in the wake of the demonstrated Western determination to establish the equivalent of the EDC by other means. Further evidence for the likelihood of this interpretation is provided by the minutes of a Cabinet meeting held during the Geneva Conference. Under Secretary of State Herbert Hoover, Jr. described the results of this conference to date and reported that the Soviet Union had apparently accepted West German participation in NATO. As a result, U.S. officials in Geneva saw a possibility of a genuine shift in the Soviet position.[20]

Although U.S. policymakers may have been able to marshal the preceding evidence in defense of the policy of negotiation from strength, the implementation of that policy was nevertheless fundamentally flawed. To use his newly acquired strength effectively in negotiation, Dulles would have had to be willing to bargain part of it away. Thus, he could have strengthened his negotiating position by proposing the EDC and demonstrating his determination to go through with it, then trading his potential success for a present German settlement. If he felt that it was necessary to demonstrate that the Western Alliance possessed unity of purpose and the ability to act cohesively by actually establishing the EDC or its equivalent, he might have accomplished these objectives as well as reunification had he been willing to dismantle part of his newly constructed edifice in exchange. As it was, however, the strength of the Western Alliance was augmented by the inclusion of the Federal Republic, but that augmentation was presented to the Soviet Union as part of the new status quo. Eisenhower and Dulles did not allow themselves enough room to trade on the strength they created, thereby ensuring round after round of fruitless negotiation. Given their choice of priorities, there was no other alternative.

The method by which the United States achieved the sovereign restoration of the Federal Republic effectively foreclosed any immediate possibility of reunification. Whether or not the architects of the doctrine of negotiation from strength foresaw its flaws from the outset is less important than the fact that if restoration and reunification were meant to be the two complementary halves of U.S. policy toward Germany, this policy was self-defeating. On the other hand, if the underside of the American drive to integrate the Federal Republic into the Western Alliance was the desire to prevent Soviet encroachment on the whole of Germany, then it is not surprising that reunification should have secretly been regarded as something of a pipe dream. The latter assumption further leads to the conclusion that the key task for the rest of the Eisenhower era was to ensure that the accomplishments of the first part of the administration did not unravel—that the Federal Republic remained secure and satisfied in the arms of the Western Alliance. The attainment of this goal depended on Adenauer's continuing political credibility within the Federal Republic.

The effect of the cold war on West German domestic politics was largely determined by Adenauer's belief that reunification on Eastern terms could only mean a Communist Germany, and correspondingly that the Federal Republic's national interests must be identified with the military strength of NATO and the politics of Western European integration. Adenauer explained his rationale in the conclusion to the first volume of his memoirs. "In this world situation there was only one possibility that made sense for Germany: to make common cause with the West and to take her place in a free Europe, economically, militarily, and politically. It was a policy of pure self-preservation. . . . If we did not align ourselves with the West, with Europe, we would not thereby approach by a single step the reunification of Germany in freedom."[21] Eisenhower and Dulles shared Adenauer's philosophy, and fully recognized that his political career depended on the speed and success of its implementation.

As congenial as Adenauer's outlook was, U.S. policymakers were all too aware that the opposition Social Democrats vigorously opposed his choice of the West. Thus, in 1951 when Eisenhower was supreme commander of NATO, he and High Commissioner John J. McCloy sought to persuade SPD chief Dr. Kurt Schumacher of the merits of the EDC.[22] They failed, and although Schumacher died in 1952, the SPD did not change its party line on the folly of integration with the West until 1960. Thus, throughout his presidency Eisenhower necessarily realized that if Adenauer's tenure in office depended on the restoration of West German sovereignty as a full-fledged member of the Western family of nations, so too did the success of U.S. policy toward Germany require a constant awareness of the impact of every move on Adenauer's political fortunes. Dulles's similar realization of this necessity was sharpened by a close personal friendship with the chancellor, based on liking and strong mutual respect.[23]

Adenauer faced a federal election in September 1953, and Eisenhower and Dulles were understandably anxious that he should win. Shortly after the appointment in January 1953 of James B. Conant to replace McCloy as the American high commissioner, Dulles called Conant to discuss the coordination of Conant's arrival in Bonn with a trip that Dulles was planning to make. Dulles emphasized that although he would pay a courtesy call on Adenauer, the real purpose of his trip was to gather firsthand information on the major currents in West German domestic politics.[24] Two months later Adenauer took a much publicized twelve-day tour of the United States, which served to provide West German voters with visual evidence of the warm U.S.-West German relations fostered by Adenauer.

The administration continued to express its support for Adenauer directly and indirectly through the summer months. Eisenhower sent Adenauer a public letter after the East German uprising on June 17, affirming U.S. support for German reunification and stressing the importance of the EDC to the Western strategy of negotiation from strength. Dulles also stated publicly in early September that Adenauer's defeat could be disastrous.[25] The size of the CDU-CSU victory exceeded American expectations; nevertheless, Adenauer was reelected chancellor of the Bundestag by an absolute majority of only one vote.[26]

This latter fact was not lost on either Eisenhower or Dulles in the days following the French rejection of the EDC, almost exactly one year after the election.[27] Thus, when Adenauer reacted to the French rebuff by an unequivocal demand for West German sovereignty and limited rearmament, the United States recognized the domestic pressures motivating his action and continued with preparations for the Paris Conference.[28] Further, even in the happy aftermath of the Paris Agreements, Dulles worried about how the United States could help Adenauer sell his concessions on the status of the Saar Valley to the West German public.[29]

The solicitude displayed by U.S. policymakers for Adenauer's political welfare did not cease after the ratification of the Paris Agreements in May 1955. On the contrary, thereafter it became necessary to ensure that Adenauer himself remained satisfied with his choice of the West, as well as his constituents. The NATO powers formally welcomed the Federal Republic as one of their number at a ministerial meeting held in Paris in early May. In preparing the agenda for this meeting, Dulles debated whether or not to schedule a discussion of the forces' effectiveness—a subject that showed up many of the weaknesses of the French defense system. He decided instead to relegate the matter to a prior meeting of defense ministers on the grounds that if presented with such a gloomy picture at their first NATO meeting, the West Germans "[might] think they joined the wrong club."[30] Behind the jocularity lay the constant awareness of Germany's swing status between East and West and a determination to maintain the strength of the Western attraction.

Despite Dulles's best intentions, the administration ran into difficulties with its German policy on a matter much closer to home than reunification or the status of Berlin. Considerable ill feeling was generated by Adenauer's request for the return of German assets seized by the United States during the war. Senator Everett M. Dirksen sponsored a congressional bill proposing such a step in 1954 but was unable to garner enough support. The issue was set for discussion between American and West German representatives on January 20, 1955. Several weeks earlier, Dulles and Livingston Merchant discussed the question of how to bolster Adenauer in the matter.[31] In a Cabinet meeting on January 7, Dulles argued for the West German position on the grounds of its political importance to Adenauer and the long American tradition of preservation of property rights. He was supported by the president and the secretary of defense but was opposed by the attorney general and the secretary of the treasury.[32] No further action was taken for the next few years despite repeated requests from Adenauer. Eisenhower finally pledged to put the matter before Congress in July 1957, but after a year of waiting the West German Bundestag passed a resolution protesting his inaction.[33]

On the international scene, the Geneva Summit Conference in July 1955 presented the first major test of the newly forged bonds between the United States and the Federal Republic. As a nonparticipant whose country's fate was a priority topic of discussion, Adenauer was understandably worried. He need not have been. Not only did Eisenhower mistrust the motives behind the Soviet desire for a disarmed and neutral Germany, but he also refused even to discuss preliminary steps in that direction, because "we had obligations to Adenauer and the Federal Republic of Germany. No matter how harmless a Soviet proposal might appear, we were determined to do nothing that might injure the Chancellor or weaken Western resolution to sustain freedom in the German Republic."[34]

Eisenhower's awareness of these obligations may have been heightened by the fact that in June the Soviets had invited Adenauer to come to Moscow to discuss mutual problems. Adenauer was slated to make this trip after the Geneva Conference, and despite their confidence in him, U.S. policymakers worried that the Soviet leaders would try to damage his domestic political standing by making him an offer on reunification that he would be forced to reject.[35] Thus, it was doubly important that the United States present a unified front with the Federal Republic at Geneva.

The Geneva Summit confirmed the U.S. decision to allow Adenauer to dictate the policy line on any matters concerning reunification or the treatment of the East German regime. Eisenhower's policy toward the Federal Republic from 1955 to 1958 consisted largely of avoiding any action that might undermine Adenauer in any way, bolstering him when possible, and mollifying or reassuring him when necessary. The U.S. government did its best to help Adenauer during the West German election in 1957, and was highly gratified when Adenauer's party obtained an absolute majority for the first time, absolving it of the need to form a coalition government with the Free Democratic party.[36]

Only two significant incidents disturbed the smooth course of U.S.-West German relations during this period: a report of Dulles's approval of a plan devised by Admiral Radford to replace American troops in the Federal Republic with increased reliance on nuclear weapons in 1956, and the use of West German bases by American planes carrying American troops to Lebanon in the summer of 1958. The Radford Plan in particular horrified Adenauer, because he felt that without its own troops in the Federal Republic, the U.S. would be less motivated to defend the West Germans against Soviet attack. In both cases Adenauer's strenuous protests were speedily answered by long letters from Dulles, and after the Radford Plan debacle, a visit by Allen Dulles. U.S. relations with the Federal Republic also deteriorated somewhat at the end of the decade when the Berlin Crisis had given way to a mild detente, and Adenauer worried that Eisenhower's firm stance against Soviet expansionism might be wavering. During this period Adenauer drew closer to France under DeGaulle, but the full implications of this relationship did not surface to trouble the United States until after 1960.

In November 1958, Khrushchev announced that the Soviet Union was transferring control of East Berlin to the GDR, and that the three Western allies had six months to negotiate an agreement with the East Germans over access rights to West Berlin. If the West refused to negotiate with the GDR, the Soviet Union threatened to sign a separate Soviet-East German peace treaty. The ensuing Berlin Crisis should be viewed above all as marking a watershed in U.S.-Soviet relations—a six-month period in which Eisenhower convincingly demonstrated the futility of such tactics. Khrushchev backed down and began to emphasize the importance of peaceful coexistence, initiating a thaw that ultimately led to his visit to the United States in September 1959. However, to the extent that the crisis focused U.S. attention on the necessary decision to be made about Allied relations with the Federal Republic, concern for Adenauer and the justification of the political priorities with which he had identified himself remained uppermost.

Eisenhower read Khrushchev's challenge as an attempt to force Western recognition of the GDR, a crucial step toward the acknowledgment of the permanent division of Germany. Such a step would have also spelled political disaster for Adenauer. When the storm first broke in November, there were differences of opinion among the three allies over "the degree with which the Western powers could deal with the East German government without loss of prestige or undue damage to Adenauer."[37] At one end of this spectrum of opinion was Adenauer himself, who stood adamant against any dealings whatsoever with the East German regime; at the other end, the British favored exploring a range of options rather than risk another blockade. Eisenhower found himself in the position of mediator, particularly when Khrushchev moderated his stance somewhat in March 1959, and the three Allies began to try to develop a unified position on the advisability of another summit conference.

In a diary entry on May 27, 1959, the day of Dulles's funeral, Eisenhower recorded a meeting with Adenauer and observed that the chancellor seemed "to have developed an almost psychopathic fear of what he considers the 'British weakness.' "[38] Although he sought to explain the British position to Adenauer in terms of Prime Minister Harold Macmillan's domestic political difficulties, Eisenhower remained acutely aware of the potential impact of the crisis on party politics within the Federal Republic. He never accused the chancellor of pure political opportunism; on the other hand, he certainly recognized that Adenauer was often motivated by a keen survival instinct. Analyzing the difficulties of establishing a unified Western policy on Berlin, Eisenhower noted, "It was possible that Adenauer's party could be defeated if elections were one day held throughout East and West Germany, a possibility that did nothing to bring the two majority political parties in Germany together in developing a solid German position on unification."[39]

Adenauer was well aware of how best to exploit his political leverage in the United States. On Allen Dulles's visit to close the rift caused by the Radford Plan, Adenauer told him: "My policy was based on firm confidence in the United States, and . . . if this was disappointed, it would have grave political effects for my government."[40] Alternatively scolding and importuning, Adenauer did his best to ensure that West German concerns remained uppermost in the minds of selected Washington policymakers. He sought assurances of continued U.S. support primarily for his personal peace of mind, rather than as backing for any specific objectives. Left to himself, he seemed content to leave his reunification policy in the holding pattern initiated by his enunciation of the doctrine of negotiation from strength.

In the election year of 1957 Adenauer broached the possibility of using liberalization of the East German regime's domestic policies as a prerequisite to opening relations between the two states. Further, at the height of the Berlin Crisis when he may have been unsure of how far the United States was willing to push the British, he intimated to Macmillan that he might be willing to deal with the East Germans in ways which could not be interpreted as de facto recognition.[41] However, after the Soviet six-month deadline on Berlin had safely passed and U.S.-Soviet relations had begun to settle back into normal channels, Adenauer rebuffed Eisenhower's suggestion that the Federal Republic move to develop better relations with the GDR. Adenauer asserted that the United States did not understand the extent of the domestic repression of East Germans that was triggered by such West German advances.[42] Eisenhower did not expect such a pessimistic reaction. He might have been less surprised had he remembered the further connection between the publicity accorded East German repression in the Federal Republic and the resulting bad press for Adenauer's policies.

Although Eisenhower's choice of priorities necessitated his acceptance of the existence of two German states, he could not afford to be complacent on the subject. He inevitably included German reunification when listing the major foreign policy objectives of his administration. At the same time, he tried to turn the situation to advantage by exploiting the propaganda value of the German division. In addition to reminding both American and foreign audiences of the Soviet determination to maintain a division that forcibly separated German families and friends, he and Dulles also used this issue as a springboard for denunciations of Soviet policies in the Eastern Europe satellite countries.

The U.S. insistence on free elections throughout Germany led naturally to an emphasis on the universal right to self-determination, which in turn served to spotlight the Soviet denial of this right to the peoples of Eastern Europe. Eisenhower neatly demonstrated this technique in his opening statement at the Geneva Summit Conference of 1955, first addressing the problem of German reunification and then moving to the following assertion: "The American people feel strongly that certain peoples of Eastern Europe, many with a long and proud record of national existence, have not yet been given the benefit of this pledge [of self-determination] of our United Nations wartime declaration . . . ."[43] In succeeding years, he rarely mentioned German reunification without simultaneously drawing attention to the plight of the satellite peoples.

Although it may have seemed perfectly natural for German reunification and the satellite countries to be linked together in a catalogue of American grievances against the Soviet Union, this emphasis made little sense in the context of a policy that purportedly envisaged reunification as a realizable goal. At the close of the Geneva Summit Conference Dulles told his brother that the biggest obstacle to German reunification from the Soviet point of view was the effect that permitting free elections in the GDR would have on the other satellite countries.[44] Yet despite this conjecture and the further observation that the Soviets were stopping in Berlin on their way home from the Geneva Conference because they were nervous, Dulles agreed in the same conversation to suggest to the president that he mention the satellites in his speech summarizing the results of the conference.

Eisenhower was also certainly aware of the importance of allowing the Soviet Union to maintain its prestige in any situation—he later attributed the success of U.S. policy during the Berlin Crisis to the fact that Khrushchev had been allowed to retreat without losing face.[45] Judging by these criteria, a policy that sought reunification while intimating that it would be only the first desirable step toward self-determination throughout Eastern Europe seemed clearly calculated to fail. On the other hand, the very exploitation of this connection as propaganda illuminates a much larger dimension of Eisenhower's policy toward Germany—a dimension that reflects a discrete and cohesive world-view.

From Eisenhower's perspective, the division of Germany was inextricably linked with the division of China, Korea, and, most recently, Vietnam. It was a symbol of the boundary between capitalism and communism being drawn all over the world—a boundary all the more horrifying when drawn through a country rather than between countries. U.S. policymakers saw these nations as interconnected fronts in the struggle against the Soviet Union and articulated the same policy toward them all. As stated by General Walter Bedell Smith, "In the case of nations now divided against their will we shall continue to seek to achieve unity through free elections supervised by the United Nations to insure that they are conducted fairly."[46]

Smith made this statement referring specifically to the situation in Vietnam. Several months earlier, Dulles had characterized the Communist program for the reunification of Korea as " 'Chinese copy' of the Soviet scheme for the unification of Germany. Their idea is to have elections so set up that the Communists can dictate the outcome and thus impose their rule upon the whole country."[47] Further, as noted previously, the Soviet Union had already tried unsuccessfully to interest the State Department in a deal exchanging German reunification for U.S. recognition of Communist China. Eisenhower and Dulles felt that to give way on one front was to lose them all; by the same token, although German reunification might remain unattainable, discrediting the Soviet role in the GDR and the satellite countries could benefit U.S. standing elsewhere.

In a world that was at once both interconnected and polarized, the United States derived part of its self-image from its negative identity with regard to the Soviet Union. International politics was a zero-sum game; accordingly, Soviet wrongdoing threw U.S. policies into shining relief. Thus, although most of the goals that Eisenhower sought to accomplish at the 1955 Geneva Summit Conference came to naught at the Foreign Ministers Conference three months later, he still pronounced the conference "a limited success." He added, "The record was now established: All could now see the nature of Soviet diplomatic tactics as contrasted with those of the Free World."[48] This kind of reasoning meant that as long as the Soviet Union retained a stranglehold on the GDR, both Eisenhower and Adenauer had a ready justification for their policies, regardless of the specific motives behind them.

The U.S. unquestionably saw itself in a positive role as well—a role largely conditioned on the concept of "world responsibility."[49] In addition to shouldering the leadership of the fight against "International Communism," Eisenhower and Dulles felt particularly responsible for the growth and direction of Western Europe. As early as 1947 Dulles testified before the Senate Foreign Relations Committee that Marshall Plan aid should fund "not the rebuilding of the prewar Europe but the building of a new Europe, which, more unified, will be a better Europe."[50] Eisenhower had also long harbored the notion of a Europe strong enough and united enough to take its place in a trans-Atlantic partnership with the United States. It was perhaps inevitable that in fostering such a development U.S. policymakers should adopt a "what was good for the U.S. will be good for Europe" attitude. Thus, Eisenhower dreamed of a "United States of Europe," and set out at the beginning of his presidency to demonstrate to the French that the EDC represented "the path of enlightened self-interest."[51]

The United States under Eisenhower assumed special responsibility for the Federal Republic, strongly flavored with the paternalism underlying U.S. dealings with Western Europe as a whole. This special relationship stemmed partly from Eisenhower's vision of himself as a peacemaker and partly from the pattern of West German reconstruction under Adenauer. Eisenhower first pondered the future of Germany as a conquering general whose main concern was not only to attain peace through military victory but also to preserve it by avoiding a repetition of the mistakes of the interwar period. The victors should not attempt to crush Germany permanently, but rather to root out the seeds of militarism and allow her to take her place in the international community as a peaceful nation.

In a speech given in Frankfurt on October 1, 1945, Eisenhower said, "The success or failure of this occupation will be judged by the character of the Germans 50 years from now. Proof will come when they begin to run a democracy of their own and we are going to give the Germans a chance to do that, in time."[52]

Four years later the time had arrived, and a mere six years after that, in October 1954, Eisenhower agreed with Dulles that the Federal Republic's transformation from a conquered and ravaged land to a "rehabilitated and equal member of the Western Alliance" was a "near miracle—a shining chapter in history."[53] This transformation was also evidently a tribute to the wisdom and forebearance of American peacemaking.

The Federal Republic gratified American political sensibilities by adjusting well to a system of parliamentary democracy designed specifically to avoid the instability of the Weimar era. The West German people also proved that the influx of Marshall Plan funds had been a sound investment, demonstrating hard work and thrift as their economy began to thrive. Eisenhower noted this achievement with great satisfaction, and in a debate within the Cabinet on whether or not to return confiscated German assets he suggested that it was time that more U.S. funds be used to "crown success," rather than to prop up weak allies who had not apparently benefited from previous aid.[54]

To some degree, U.S. policymakers must have felt that they were watching the remaking of the Federal Republic in the image of their own political, social, and economic principles. This sensation could only have been intensified by the increasing evidence that West Germans were becoming Europe's most enthusiastic imitators of every aspect of American culture. Driving from the airport to Bonn on a visit in August 1959, Eisenhower was astonished "at the extent to which American styles and American products had influenced the country in dress, manners and even billboards. . . ."[55] It is impossible to quantify the degree to which such factors influenced the evolution of Eisenhower's policy toward Germany, but they must have reinforced his overriding desire to integrate the Federal Republic into the Western Alliance.

In retrospect, Eisenhower's policy toward Germany appears to have addressed a wide range of political, economic, and strategic concerns—all except the fundamental desire of the German people to be reunited as one nation. This desire was inscribed in the West German Basic Law, the equivalent of a constitution, in the form of a binding directive to all present and future German leaders. Eisenhower often spoke about the inhumanity of the German division, the suffering it imposed on separated families and friends. In light of Nazi atrocities and the tremendous human cost of both world wars, he could not afford to harp on this subject; nevertheless, he implied that reunification was a moral imperative as well as a political right. Yet despite the rhetoric, his policy decisions clearly demonstrated that the all-important business of choosing sides in the U.S.-Soviet rivalry took precedence over such specific moral and humanitarian concerns.

The U.S. stance on reunification was publicly justified in terms of allowing the leaders of the Federal Republic to make the first move. However, Eisenhower and Dulles did everything possible to ensure that Adenauer remained in office. They did so precisely to avoid having to contend with West German leaders who were willing to take such an initiative. The rationalization for intervening in the domestic politics of a nation whose sovereignty had just been proclaimed with such fanfare was that those West Germans who were willing to accept neutrality in exchange for reunification simply did not perceive the danger posed by the Soviet Union.[56] As a result, Eisenhower did not feel that he was merely "playing politics," but rather that he was doing "the right thing."[57]

Notes

1. Dulles used this expression in a telephone conversation with Senator William Knowland on July 17, 1954, in which he discussed policy options should plans for the European Defense Community fail. John Foster Dulles, *Minutes of Telephone Conversations of John Foster Dulles and Christian Herter, 1953–1961* (Washington, D.C.: University Publications of America, Film A-327, 1980) (hereafter cited as Dulles, *Telephone Conversations*).

2. Dwight D. Eisenhower, *The White House Years: Mandate for Change, 1953–1956* (Garden City, N.Y.: Doubleday, 1963), 398–99.

3. U.S., President, *Minutes and Documents of the Cabinet Meetings of President Eisenhower, 1953–61* (Washington, D.C.: University Publications of America, Film A-326, 1980), (hereafter cited as *Cabinet Minutes*). For a more detailed explanation of the objectives that this policy was designed to achieve, see the cable sent by Dulles to Douglas Dillon, U.S. ambassador to France, on October 4, 1957, quoted in Dwight D. Eisenhower, *The White House Years: Waging Peace, 1956–1961* (Garden City, N.Y.: Doubleday, 1965), 352.

4. Dulles, *Telephone Conversations*, 23 February 1954.

5. *Cabinet Minutes*, 25 October 1954.

6. Robert L. Branyan and Lawrence H. Larsen, eds., *The Eisenhower Admin-*

istration, 1953–1961: A Documentary History (New York: Random House, 1971), 184–88.

7. Eisenhower, *Waging Peace,* 112.

8. Eisenhower, *Mandate for Change,* 523.

9. Dulles, *Telephone Conversations,* call to Livingston Merchant, assistant secretary of state for European affairs, 20 August 1954.

10. Dulles discussed West German fears regarding a French-Soviet deal in a telephone call to General Walter Bedell Smith, under secretary of state, on September 21, 1954. He mentioned his own suspicions concerning collusion between the French and the British in a conversation with Bernard Baruch on August 31, 1954—the day after the French rejection of the EDC treaty. Dulles, *Telephone Conversations.*

11. Dulles, *Telephone Conversations,* 24 March 1954.

12. Dulles, *Telephone Conversations,* call from Senator Alexander Smith, 7 August 1954.

13. Eisenhower, *Mandate for Change,* 404–5.

14. *Cabinet Minutes,* 24 October 1954.

15. Ibid.

16. Dulles, *Telephone Conversations,* 30 December 1953.

17. Eisenhower, *Mandate for Change,* 517.

18. Dulles, *Telephone Conversations,* 30 December 1953.

19. Eisenhower, *Mandate for Change,* 342.

20. *Cabinet Minutes,* 22 July 1955.

21. Konrad Adenauer, *Memoirs, 1945–1953* (London: Weidenfeld and Nicolson, 1966), 431.

22. Blanche Weisen Cooke, *The Declassified Eisenhower* (Garden City, N.Y.: Doubleday, 1981), 199-20.

23. Dulles's close personal relations with Adenauer gave rise to some procedural irregularities in communication between Washington and Bonn, compounded by the fact that U.S. high commissioner, and later ambassador, James B. Conant did not get along particularly well with the chancellor. On a number of occasions Adenauer apparently bypassed regular State Department channels and sent messages to Dulles through his brother, Allen Dulles, director of the CIA, and through John J. McCloy. Dulles discussed this problem with McCloy in a telephone conversation on March 27, 1953, and with his brother in a conversation on November 13, 1953.

24. Dulles, *Telephone Conversation,* 28 January 1953.

25. Roger Morgan gives a full account of U.S. maneuvering before the 1953 West German election in *The United States and West Germany, 1945–1973* (London: Oxford University Press, 1974), 41–42.

26. Dulles, *Telephone Conversations,* 11 September 1953.

27. Eisenhower, *Mandate for Change,* 402–3.

28. Ibid.

29. Dulles discussed this problem with his brother in the course of a congratulatory telephone call from Allen Dulles on October 25, 1954.

30. Dulles, *Telephone Conversations,* call to Mr. Hensen, 8, April 1955.

31. Dulles, *Telephone Conversations,* 4 January 1955.

32. *Cabinet Minutes,* 7 January 1955.

33. Morgan, *United States and West Germany,* 62.

34. Eisenhower, *Mandate for Change,* 523.

35. *Cabinet Meetings,* 10 June 1955.

36. Gerald Freund, *Germany Between Two Worlds* (New York: Harcourt, Brace, 1961), 86.

37. Eisenhower, *Waging Peace,* 332–33.

38. Robert H. Ferrell, ed., *The Eisenhower Diaries* (New York: W. W. Norton, 1981), 363.

39. Eisenhower, *Waging Peace,* 351, n. 12.

40. Konrad Adenauer, *Erinnerungen, 1955–1959,* 206–13, quoted in Morgan, *United States and West Germany,* 65.

41. Eisenhower, *Waging Peace,* 353–54.

42. Ibid., 418.

43. Branyan and Larsen, *Eisenhower Administration,* 640–44.

44. Dulles, *Telephone Conversations,* 25 July 1955.

45. Eisenhower, *Waging Peace,* 338.

46. Address on the Geneva Accord, Geneva, 21 July 1954, Branyan and Larsen, *Eisenhower Administration,* 354–55.

47. Ibid., 336–41, address on the Geneva Conference, Geneva, 7 May 1954. Dulles attributed the phrase "a Chinese copy" to President Eisenhower.

48. Eisenhower, *Mandate for Change,* 528.

49. Dulles suggested that this phrase be substituted for the term "world leadership" in commenting on a draft of the 1956 State of the Union Address. He felt that it would be less likely to offend nations inclined to resent the evident U.S. position of preeminence in world affairs. *Cabinet Minutes,* 12 December 1955.

50. Address on European Unity, 12 February 1953, Branyan and Larsen, *Eisenhower Administration,* 174–78.

51. Eisenhower, *Waging Peace,* 125; *Mandate for Change,* 400.

52. H. S. Bagger, ed., *Eisenhower Speaks* (New York: Inter-Allied Publications, 1946), 28.

53. Eisenhower, *Mandate for Change,* 409.

54. *Cabinet Minutes,* 7 January 1955.

55. Eisenhower, *Waging Peace,* 418.

56. In his public letter to Adenauer, Eisenhower said: "Those who in Germany believe they can suggest an easy, safe solution through defenseless neutralization should carefully ponder the true wisdom and safety of such a course." Branyan and Larsen, *Eisenhower Administration,* 180.

57. In a Cabinet meeting on November 12, 1953, Eisenhower explained his belief that the best way to gain domestic support is to do "the right thing" abroad. He contrasted this philosophy with an episode during the Truman administration when foreign policymakers had frankly characterized their activities as simply "playing politics."

Eisenhower and Arms Control

Robert A. Strong

The Eisenhower legacy in arms control is full of apparent contradictions. The administration that gave us "massive retaliation" also gave us Atoms for Peace; and the presidency that began by promising "more bang for the buck," ended with a solemn warning about the "military-industrial complex." Such contradictions are no doubt inherent in the political paradoxes of the nuclear age that have led every postwar president to build arms while seeking arms control. But in Eisenhower's case the tensions between the preparations for nuclear war and the gestures toward nuclear peace seem more extreme. In part this may be a reflection of Eisenhower's misunderstood leadership style, which has made his administration the subject of recent revisionist scholarship.[1] But a more important explanation of the contradictory arms control policies of the Eisenhower years is the fact that our thirty-fourth president served at a time when thinking about nuclear strategy and the control of nuclear weapons went through its intellectual and political adolescence.

Confusion about how nuclear weapons would be incorporated into military planning, bureaucratic confrontations over early arms control proposals, and rapid technological changes that forced constant reevaluation of defense and national security decisions made it difficult to pursue a consistent set of policies in the 1950s. Moreover, translating presidential decisions into popularly supported programs was complicated by the erratic education of the American people regarding nuclear issues. Public ignorance and indifference to the dangers of nuclear war in the early years of the decade gave way to periods of near hysteria when the nature of fallout and meaning of Sputnik became important items on the national agenda.

These delayed popular reactions to the realities of the nuclear age tended to produce two very different kinds of proposals. Some citizens and observers, particularly at the end of the decade, advocated a massive American arms buildup to guarantee permanent superiority over the Soviet Union. Others saw in the dangers of fallout and the hideous consequences of thermonuclear war good reasons to renounce nuclear testing, ban the bomb, and pursue fundamental changes in the international system.

Eisenhower did not agree with either of these conclusions and tried to steer a moderate course between them. He consistently sought to provide an adequate defense without bankrupting the national treasury, and he frequently counseled those around him about the revolutionary changes wrought by nuclear weapons without offering revolutionary ways to bring them under control. In the process of formulating a moderate national security policy, he made concessions to both the advocates of nuclear strength and the predictors of nuclear doom and, as a result, left a record of inconsistent and incomplete efforts.

Massive Retaliation and Atoms For Peace

> Of the various presidential tasks to which I early determined to devote my energies, none transcended in importance that of trying to devise practical and acceptable means to lighten the burdens of armaments and to lessen the likelihood of war.[2]

Dwight D. Eisenhower was inaugurated almost three months after the first American test of a hydrogen bomb and nearly six months before the first Soviet thermonuclear explosion. In many respects the end of 1952 and the beginning of 1953, rather than 1945, mark the beginning of the nuclear age. The first hydrogen bomb tested by the United States was more than eight hundred times more powerful than the one used on Hiroshima,[3] and there was no theoretical limit to how large these new weapons could be made and no long-term shortage of the raw materials used in their construction. What is more, the arrival of the hydrogen bomb coincided with the perfection of smaller tactical nuclear weapons that the Army began to deploy in 1953.[4] During the Eisenhower presidency, nuclear weapons would, for the first time, be available to American armed forces in large numbers, at low costs, and in a wide variety of configurations. By the end of his presidency they would be equally available to the Soviet Union.

The new tactical nuclear weapons were quickly assimilated into existing plans for the defense of Europe, prompting Eisenhower to observe at the end of his first year in office that "atomic weapons have virtually achieved conventional status with our armed forces."[5] Assimilation of the hydrogen bomb was not so easy. Its enormous destructive capacity was hard to imagine, even for those who had seen the horrors of World War II and the consequences of Hiroshima and Nagasaki. For Churchill, "the entire foundation of human affairs was revolutionized" by the development of the hydrogen bomb.[6] Eisenhower was fully aware of the revolution and cautious about how he informed the American people about the realities connected with these new and awesome weapons. After a joint press conference with Lewis Strauss, the chairman of the Atomic Energy Commission, where Strauss freely admitted that hydrogen bombs could be made to completely destroy any city, even New York, Eisenhower chided his commission chairman and expressed concern about how the American public would learn about the hydrogen bomb.[7] Revolutions are not easily announced. Nor are they easily incorporated into existing policies. The changes in nuclear technology in 1953 pushed the Eisenhower administration in two different directions. They led, at the same time, to a greater dependence on nuclear weapons, both tactical and strategic, as the basis for the nation's defense, and to a serious search for some first step towards arms control.

In 1952, the implications of thermonuclear warfare were being considered by a relatively small number of scientists, strategists, and senior government officials. Public concerns in that election year were more immediate—getting out of Korea and reducing the swollen defense budget. Eisenhower promised to do both and used the new generation of nuclear weapons to get control of defense spending and progress at the Korean armistice negotiations.

Eisenhower's fiscal conservatism, which was both a strong personal conviction and an important campaign issue in 1952, shaped the early defense decisions of his administration. Eisenhower was convinced, as he later wrote in his memoirs, "that the relationship . . . between military and economic strength is intimate and indivisible,"[8] and that a reduction in defense spending would actually enhance American strength in competition with the Soviet Union. Early in his administration he added the secretary of the treasury and the director of the bureau of the budget to the National Security Council and insisted that all military planning be evaluated in terms of strict budgetary realities. He told his Cabinet that, "We cannot defend the nation in a way which will exhaust our economy,"[9] and, against considerable opposition from the military services, introduced his "New Look" in defense. The New Look involved a reduction in overall military expenditures, in part facilitated by a winding down of the Korean War and a redistribution of priorities giving emphasis to the Air Force and strategic weapons.[10] Between fiscal years 1954 and 1955, defense expenditures were reduced by $4.8 billion, while the Air Force budget was increased by nearly $1 billion.[11] In a National Security Council document dated October 30, 1953, and titled "Basic National Security Policy," the administration made its first military priority the development of "a strong military posture, with emphasis on the capacity for inflicting massive retaliatory damage by offensive striking power."[12] The New Look was, in simplest terms, an explicitly nuclear defense.

When one of Eisenhower's Cabinet officers reduced this policy to the alliterative slogan, "more bang for the buck," he summarized not only the essence of Eisenhower's defense budget, but also the connection between that budget and traditional American attitudes concerning peace and war. Americans at mid-century still believed that defense spending in time of peace should be kept to a minimum, and that the weapons and strategies used in time of war should produce the rapid and complete defeat of our enemies. Swings from isolationism to total war had characterized American behavior in the decades before Eisenhower came to power and were still possible in the 1950s. Eisenhower's own party had within its ranks both isolationists and rabid anticommunists. The isolationists approved of administration plans to save "bucks," while the enemies of the Soviet Union took comfort in the size of the "bang" available to American armed forces. The hydrogen bomb, in its first year of existence, had not yet to frighten the American public or to challenge American thinking about war; in some ways it reinforced the conclusions that the nation had learned from the first half of the twentieth century.[13]

The arrival of the thermonuclear age did more than permit reduced defense spending; it also gave the new administration a powerful diplomatic instrument that both Eisenhower and Dulles were willing to use. When negotiations for the Korean armistice bogged down, signals were sent to China and the Soviet Union suggesting that in the absence of progress at the peace table, the new administration would "move decisively without inhibition in our use of weapons, and would no longer be responsible for confining casualties to the Korean Peninsula."[14] The decision to emphasize nuclear weapons in the military budget was accompanied by a willingness to be vague about when these powerful weapons might be used. Vague threats enhanced the deterrent effect and the diplomatic leverage that nuclear weapons clearly possessed. The essence of Eisenhower's doctrine was this vagueness. In John Foster Dulles's famous explanation of the policy he said only that the United States would, if provoked, be prepared "to retaliate, instantly, by means and at places of our choosing."[15]

Although massive retaliation became the official doctrine associated with the Eisenhower administration, and although Eisenhower was willing to threaten nuclear attacks in Asia, in private he was much more ambivalent about using the new weapons of mass destruction. In 1945, when consulted in Europe by Secretary of War Henry L. Stimson about plans to drop the first atomic bomb on Japan, Eisenhower recommended that it not be used because Japan was already close to surrender, and because it would be a severe shock to world opinion if the United States were to use atomic weapons without sufficient cause.[16] In a Cabinet meeting in March of 1953, he surprised his advisors with an outburst about the futility of actually carrying out a nuclear defense of Europe: "Any notion that 'the bomb' is a cheap way to solve things is awfully wrong. It ignores all facts of world politics—and the basic realities for our allies. It is cold comfort for any citizen of Western Europe to be assured that—after his country is overrun and he is pushing up daisies— someone still alive will drop a bomb on the Kremlin."[17]

In public Eisenhower counseled against any notion of preventive nuclear war. "It is an impossibility in this age of the hydrogen bomb. . . . Many thousands of persons would be dead and injured and mangled, the transportation system destroyed, and sanitation systems all gone. That is not preventive war—that is war."[18] Speaking to a group of military officers in June 1954, the president questioned the wisdom of ever carrying out a massive nuclear attack on our Communist enemies:

> No matter how well prepared for war we may be, no matter how certain we are that within 24 hours we could destroy Kuibyshev and Moscow and Leningrad and Baku and all the other places that would allow the Soviets to carry on war, I want you to carry this question home with you: Gain such a victory, and what do you do with it? Here would be a great area from the Elbe to Vladivostok and down through Southeast Asia torn up and destroyed without government, without its communications, just an area of starvation and disaster. I ask you what would the civilized world do about it? I repeat, there is no victory in any war except through our imaginations, through our dedication, and through our work to avoid it."[19]

While Eisenhower approved a defense plan explicitly based on nuclear weapons and a diplomacy that practiced nuclear blackmail, he did not regard deterrence and massive retaliation as permanent or desirable solutions to the nation's security problems. In the long run, disarmament would be necessary.

In his first major foreign policy address as president, Eisenhower told the American Society of Newspaper Editors in April 1953 that "we had come down a dread road with no turning, where the worst threat was atomic war and the best hope was a life of perpetual terror and tension with the cost of arms draining the wealth and energies of all peoples."[20] Those costs were high not only in terms of strained domestic economies, but also in terms of deferred world development. In a global equivalent of his domestic budget decisions, he pledged to devote "a substantial percentage of the savings achieved by disarmament to a fund for world aid and reconstruction."[21] The specific disarmament proposals in the "Chance for Peace" speech were not new, but because they came from a new president and were addressed to a new group of Soviet leaders, they were well received by the press and public. Unfortunately, arms control in the first year of the Eisenhower presidency did not get past the speechmaking stage.

The early drafts of what eventually became the "Atoms for Peace" speech were prepared throughout 1953, and were intended to be an explanation to the American people of the dangers and consequences of the hydrogen bomb.[22] Such a speech had been proposed by Robert Oppenheimer in 1952, but his suggestion, contained in a document called the "Candor Report," had been ignored by the Truman administration.[23] Eisenhower saw merit in Oppenheimer's suggestion, ordered the creation of his own Operation Candor, and directed C. D. Jackson, his advisor on psychological warfare, to write a major presidential address about nuclear weapons. The first dozen drafts of the speech were all rejected. Apparently they were too candid, and Eisenhower complained that they "left the listener with only a new terror, not a new hope."[24] The hope that was later inserted into the speech was a proposal for the creation of an international agency to administer a limited amount of enriched uranium for scientific research and energy production. In what must be one of the rare occasions of a postwar president actually making policy by himself, the idea for an "atom bank" originated with Eisenhower shortly after the announcement of the Soviet thermonuclear test.[25] The idea was simple. Both the United States and the Soviet Union, and perhaps Great Britain, would divert nuclear material currently destined for defense projects to an international agency that would use the materials for peaceful endeavors. At the beginning the amounts of fissionable material would be small, but if the agency grew, it might eventually slow the growth of nuclear arsenals. More important, if the United States and the Soviet Union could cooperate in this project it would, Eisenhower wrote to his brother, Milton, get the atomic armaments problem off "dead center."[26]

Atoms for Peace was not popular in the Eisenhower Cabinet. The secretaries of defense and state raised questions about the wisdom of announcing such a program in a public speech and speculated about the impact that it would have in Europe, where our allies were still debating the European Defense Community.[27] The whole idea of sharing atomic materials and presumably atomic technology with developing countries was also controversial with those congressmen and bureaucrats who had a stake in the administration of atomic energy and the strict secrecy that surrounded it. Critics of the proposal would later refer to it as "Watts for Hottentots."[28] With persistent presidential pressure these objections were either resolved or postponed until detailed negotiations on the bank could begin. After consulting with Churchill in Bermuda, a final draft of Atoms for Peace was rapidly prepared while the president flew to New York to address the United Nations.

In a long diary entry Eisenhower explains the purposes that he tried to achieve through the speech. First and foremost, he regarded Atoms for Peace as a serious arms control endeavor. Because it was a modest program that would divert small amounts of fissionable material and would not require any inspection of the Soviet Union, it would avoid the obstacles that were preventing progress in all other disarmament discussions. And, if we could "get the Soviet Union working with us in some phase of this whole atomic field that would have only peace and the good of mankind as a goal . . . [it] might expand into something broader." The "world is racing toward catastrophe," Eisenhower wrote in his diary, and "something must be done to put a brake on this movement."[29] This sincere hope for a beginning to Soviet-American cooperation in halting the arms race was tempered by the recognition that the "U.S. could unquestionably afford to reduce its stockpile by two or three times the amounts that the Russians might contribute to the United Nations agency, and still improve our relative position in the cold war and even in the event of the outbreak of war."[30] Atoms for Peace was modest in its objective, but even more modest in the risks it posed for the United States. In fairness, it must be noted that Eisenhower was willing to make a much larger American commitment of fissionable material to the program than would have been expected from the Soviet Union or Great Britain.[31] But such a concession would not have changed the essence of Atoms for Peace, which as arms control was always more important for its symbolism than its substance.

The United Nations' speech succeeded in combining a candid explanation of the power of hydrogen bombs with a hopeful description of the peaceful uses of atomic energy and, like the Chance for Peace speech earlier in the year, won immediate public praise. But the negotiations that eventually created the International Atomic Energy Agency (IAEA) were extremely slow. The Soviets raised legitimate questions about the dangers of proliferation that Eisenhower had seriously underestimated, saying only that "the ingenuity of our scientists will provide special safe conditions under which such a bank of fissionable material can be made essentially immune to surprise seizure."[32] By the time the

IAEA was finally in operation nearly four years after the speech was given, the stockpiles of weapons and fissionable material on both sides were so large that no commitment to the international development of atomic energy could be regarded as an arms control measure. Throughout Eisenhower's eight years in the White House, both the fears of the nuclear age, which Atoms for Peace tried to alleviate, and the search for a first step in arms control, which Atoms for Peace tried to provide, would continue to be presidential preoccupations.

Open and Poisonous Skies

> That failure (of arms control) can be explained in one sentence. It was the adamant insistence of the communists on maintaining a closed society.[33]

The lack of progress on Atoms for Peace throughout the mid-1950s and the inconclusive negotiations on comprehensive disarmament that were conducted in various United Nations' committees, left the administration without a realistic arms control proposal at a time when the president was conscious of the growing dangers of the arms race and under pressure to explore the diplomatic opportunities created by the change in Soviet leadership. A new starting point was needed.

The "Open Skies" initiative emerged from a conference between academics and administration officials arranged by Nelson Rockefeller, C. D. Jackson's successor in the peculiarly cold-war position of psychological warfare advisor.[34] The conference met at the Marine base in Quantico, Virginia, to consider, among other things, proposals for the scheduled Geneva Summit, the first meeting of Soviet and American heads of state since World War II. One of the proposals that members of the conference favored was the possibility of exchanging blueprints of military bases with the Soviet Union and permitting each superpower to photograph each other's installations from the air. Eisenhower read the conference report despite efforts by Dulles to prevent him from seeing it,[35] and was particularly enthusiastic about the suggestion for mutual aerial inspection. Calling Dulles immediately, he urged the secretary to study the idea carefully because "it might open a tiny gate in the disarmament fence."[36] Dulles continued to oppose any suggestions that Geneva should be more than an exploratory meeting of heads of state and expressed his reservations about Open Skies. He was afraid that in serious negotiations the Allies would be unable to remain united, and that the president's good nature would lead him to accept some ill-considered Soviet offer.[37] For a time Dulles's caution prevailed.

Throughout the mid-summer of 1955, and even after the president had arrived in Geneva, bureaucratic maneuvering among Eisenhower's advisors kept Open Skies alive. Rockefeller enlisted support from the Chairman of the Joint Chiefs of Staff, Admiral Radford, and from Andrew Goodpaster, the president's trusted staff secretary; and he made sure that drafts of the proposal and some of the experts who had worked on it were close at hand during the Geneva meetings. Members of the administration who were aware of the U-2 plane, which had been tested for the first time shortly before the Geneva summit,[38] would have had special reasons to be interested in Open Skies. Even if the proposal was rejected, the fact that it had been made before the United States began its U-2 flights over the Soviet Union might have been expected to blunt some of the criticism that those flights were bound to attract. On the eve of the conference session in which disarmament was the scheduled topic, Eisenhower met with his leading foreign policy advisors. He decided to insert into a formal statement on the problem of inspection, which he would deliver the next day, a personal proposal that the two superpowers exchange information about the location of military establishments and the right to conduct aerial reconnaissance. The president's introduction of Open Skies was brief and general, and he expressed a willingness to consider any Soviet suggestions regarding details. His proposal was also dramatic: "As I finished [Geneva remarks on Open Skies], a most extraordinary natural phenomenon took place. Without warning, and simultaneous with my closing words, the loudest clap of thunder I have ever heard roared into the room, and the conference was plunged into Stygian darkness. Our astonishment was all the greater because in our air-conditioned and well-lighted room there had been no inkling of an approaching storm. For the moment there was stunned silence. Then I remarked that I had not dreamed I was so eloquent as to put the lights out."[39]

Although some members of the Soviet delegation expressed interest in Eisenhower's remarks, Khrushchev immediately announced his opposition. During the Geneva Conference Khrushchev displayed his emerging dominance of the Soviet collective leadership, and the president spent the remaining conference sessions trying "to persuade Mr. Khrushchev of the merits of the Open Skies plan, but to no avail.[40] The Soviets criticized Open Skies as inspection without disarmament, and they were justified in doing so. Like Atoms for Peace, Open Skies was only a first step in the disarmament process, and a step that would have been more painful for a secretive society like the Soviet Union than for an American government that regularly announces its defense plans in official reports and newspaper leaks. Unfortunately, the Soviet alternative to inspection without disarmament was disarmament without inspection—an even more unacceptable proposition.

The stalemate in Soviet-American arms control negotiations in the mid-1950s that kept the skies closed to legal surveilance also ensured that the skies would be increasingly contaminated with radioactive particles. Both superpowers conducted extensive tests of hydrogen weapons between 1953 and 1958, and as public awareness of the immediate and long-term consequences of fallout became known, fears not anticipated in Operation Candor gripped the nation. Late in 1954 media reports described the sickness and suffering of Japanese fishermen who were inadvertently exposed to high levels of radiation when their ship, the Lucky Dragon, sailed too close to a South Pacific test site.[41] A slightly different wind pattern would have produced hundreds of additional casualties among American service personnel and the inhabitants of nearby islands. The story of the unlucky Japanese fishermen was the first evidence of fallout to reach a broad public audience. With photographs in *Life* and major stories in daily newspapers and weekly news magazines, fallout, nine years after Hiroshima, was becoming a major public concern.

The detailed stories about radiation frightened the American people for a number of reasons. Radioactive particles carried for hundreds of miles vastly increased the numbers of likely casualties in a nuclear war; but more important, they produced those casualties in an uncontrolled and indiscriminate fashion. Moral principles about how wars should be conducted had already been eroded by events in World War II. In the thermonuclear age, those principles were swept away. At the mercy of weather patterns, fallout could not distinguish between soldiers and civilians; carried long distances, it could not distinguish between friendly and enemy territory. Worst of all, its full effects would not be felt for several generations; strontium 90 could not even distinguish between the living and the as-yet unborn. "The atomic weapon," Eisenhower observed in a White House meeting about Atoms for Peace, "is the first weapon which ever really scared America."[42]

The fear that Americans experienced was exacerbated by government secrecy about the details of test results and test accidents, and by an inconclusive scientific debate concerning the extent of radiation hazards. Controversy and uncertainty increased anxiety about fallout and helped to make it a political issue in the 1956 presidential campaign. Adlai Stevenson, running against Eisenhower for a second time, was advised by his staff not to challenge the president on national security issues. He chose to ignore that advice. Throughout the campaign he somewhat inconsistently called for an end to the draft and unilateral American suspension of nuclear weapon testing. The latter, he argued, would slow the arms race that "threatens mankind with stark, merciless, bleak catastrophe."[43] During the primaries he spoke to the same American Society of Newspaper Editors that had heard Eisenhower's Chance for Peace speech three years earlier, pointing out that very little progress toward peace had been achieved. "I believe we should give prompt and earnest consideration to stopping further tests of the hydrogen bomb . . . deeply believe that if we are to make progress toward the effective reduction and control of armaments, it will probably come a step at a time. And this is a step which, it seems to me, we might now take."[44] More than any other issue in his unsuccessful campaign, the test ban proposal touched a nerve in Stevenson's audiences. For a time in October it gave his campaign the only momentum that it ever enjoyed.[45]

Eisenhower was slow to respond to the testing issue, but eventually succeeded in portraying Stevenson's idea as irresponsible. In speeches and press conferences at the end of the campaign, Eisenhower objected to the unilateral aspect of the Stevenson test suspension arguing that the Soviets could gain a significant advantage during the period of self-imposed American restraint. Any progress Stevenson was making on the testing issue ended when the White House released a letter from Bulganin praising the concept of an uninspected test ban currently being advocated by "certain prominent public figures in the United States."[46] Endorsement from a Soviet leader was not likely to win votes in a cold-war presidential election, and the whole episode helped to set back any prospects for serious negotiations on the testing question.

Eisenhower resented Stevenson's H-bomb speeches and his claims that the administration was doing nothing about the arms race. He felt that the testing issue was too complicated and technical for electioneering, and he felt that the Democrats were exploiting exaggerated public fears of limited radiation hazards. He may also have been preempted. Robert Divine argues that the Eisenhower administration was considering its own test ban proposal in the fall of 1956 just before Stevenson began to give the issue a prominent place in his campaign speeches.[47] Whether administration plans were shelved for political or other reasons is not yet known, but the political debates in 1956 did little to accelerate movement toward testing restrictions.

From 1956 until the fall of 1958 when a moratorium was finally announced, the administration debated various plans for banning nuclear tests. The issue raised a number of complicated technical and political questions. How would a test ban be verified? Would it be connected to broader disarmament measures? What effect would it have on the possibilities of reduced radiation weapons, antiballistic missile systems, and peaceful applications for nuclear explosions, all of which were under development at the end of the decade? How would our British and French allies be able to proceed with their independent nuclear programs if both the United States and the Soviet Union were demanding a suspension of testing? The administration was deeply divided on these questions and Eisenhower was, to some extent, "the prisoner of his technical consultants on such issues as testing and fallout."[48] Edward Teller, the father of the H-bomb, was particularly effective in lobbying the president against test suspensions,[49] and only the appointment of a presidential science advisor in 1957 gave Eisenhower independent success to authoritative interpretations of the technical issues.

In 1957 and 1958 Soviet scientists met with their Western counterparts to discuss verification procedures for a possible test ban agreement. Although it was easy for them to agree that the inspection of a test ban was theoretically feasible, the details of a mutually acceptable inspection system were complicated and controversial. Large tests could always be detected, but smaller tests and underground tests, and particularly tests in specially prepared underground caverns, might be difficult to distinguish from earthquakes. A politicized scientific debate raged throughout the late 1950s over exactly what sorts of tests could be reliably identified and how many inspection stations and visits would be needed to do the job. The Soviets, who regarded numbers of inspection sites as a central political issue, were frustrated by American negotiators, who saw it as a scientific problem and constantly revised inspection proposals to conform with the results of rapidly changing technical research. The moratorium on testing that began at the end of 1958 was preceded by an orgy of nuclear explosions by both superpowers. There were a total of ninety-eight atmospheric tests in 1958, more than twice the number in any previous year.[50] Once these tests were complete, both the United States and the Soviet Union exercised some restraint and entered into official negotiations in Geneva for a permanent test ban. No nuclear weapons were tested in 1959, and only three were exploded by the French in 1960. A limited test ban treaty was eventually negotiated and was the first step in serious East-West arms negotiations that both Eisenhower and Stevenson had advocated. It was, however, a step not taken until 1963. The last few years of the Eisenhower presidency, which were characterized by growing fears of Soviet military power, did not produce a domestic or international climate conducive to arms control.

Sputnik and Strategic Vulnerability

I have pondered, on occasion, the evolution of the military art during the mid-fifties. The Army in which I was commissioned a second lieutenant in 1915 underwent phenomenal changes in the thirty years from then until the German surrender in 1945 . . . But those changes, startling as they were, faded into insignificance when compared to those of the postwar period.[51]

The nuclear revolution in 1945 and the thermonuclear revolution in 1952 and 1953 were followed by a series of revolutionary changes in the systems designed to deliver nuclear explosives. Propeller-driven bombers stationed in Europe gave way to jets capable of flying intercontinental distances. And as new aircraft were being deployed, intensive research was conducted on improved versions of the German V-2 rocket that would make all aircraft increasingly vulnerable to preemptive attack. The first generation of missiles, under active development by the middle of the decade, were liquid-fueled and had to go through an elaborate fueling procedure before they could be fired. Like bombers, it was possible that these missiles would be destroyed in a surprise attack before orders could be given for their fueling. Within a few years of their deployment these early missiles were replaced by more reliable and instantly available solid-fueled rockets deployed on nuclear-powered submarines and in hardened silos. Eisenhower presided over the transition from propeller bombers to Polaris missiles, and because the Soviet Union was engaged in similar research and development projects he also presided over the growing vulnerability of the United States to Soviet attack. That vulnerability would contribute to new domestic fears and to a climate of international tension that would hinder East-West negotiations on arms and other issues.

Throughout the second half of Eisenhower's presidency a series of studies by members of the administration, by blue ribbon commissions, by social scientists at the RAND corporation, and by prospective Democratic presidential candidates and the congressional committees on which they served challenged the wisdom of massive retaliation and the ability of the United States to defend itself against an uncertain Soviet threat. Although these studies varied in their estimates of Soviet capabilities and in their policy recommendations, they contained a common theme: The day would come, sooner or later, when American military targets and American cities would be vulnerable to Soviet attack. When that day came, threats of massive retaliation would lack credibility, and more important, the means for carrying out that retaliation would be seriously threatened.

As early as the summer of 1953, Albert Wohlstetter, an economist working at the Air Force's RAND Corporation, was briefing Pentagon officials on the vulnerability of our overseas bomber bases.[52] Even before the development of hydrogen bombs, atomic weapons were enormously destructive, and because American bombers were parked on runways in the open or in lightly constructed hangars, the possibility existed that an atomic attack on our European bases would disable nearly all of our planes. Wohlstetter, speaking to a generation that vividly remembered Pearl Harbor, warned that unless action was taken to protect our planes and diversify our arsenal, the Soviet Union could defeat the United States in a devastating surprise attack. The Air Force paid little attention to Wohlstetter's proposals for building expensive concrete hangars, but used the vulnerability problem to justify larger deployments of SAC bombers. The number of bombers needed by the United States was, of course, a function of the number we suspected the Soviet Union of having, and so long as the latter figure was unknown, the need for more American planes was difficult to argue against. In 1955, inaccurate intelligence reports led to complaints from congressional Democrats about a dangerous "bomber gap."[53] The gap did not exist, but there would be real gaps to come.

Although Eisenhower emphasized strategic weapons and Air Force procurements in his New Look, and although he responded to the bomber vulnerability problem by approving substantial funding for missile development, he resisted exaggerated projections of the Soviet threat and resented Democratic charges that he was not doing enough to provide for the nation's defense. He pushed forward with the U-2 program, despite its considerable political risks, in order to minimize uncertainty about Soviet military capabilities, and he authorized a number of high-level internal studies of the strategic balance between the United States and the Soviet Union.

In February 1955, the National Security Council received a report from a group headed by James Killian, president of MIT and later Eisenhower's first science advisor. The Killian Report described the United States as having a temporary strategic superiority over the Soviet Union, but warned that the Soviets were catching up and that the first country to develop ICBMs would enjoy an important relative advantage.[54] The report recommended both increased attention to missile development and the protection of existing strategic bases. It also predicted that once both sides had developed missiles, the resulting strategic stalemate could prove to be long-lasting and relatively immune to sudden technological changes. In the long-run the Killian Report would turn out to be correct, but in the volatile years of Eisenhower's second term, few Americans believed that they were witnessing the arrival of stability in the superpower strategic relationship.

A second report to the NSC was commissioned in 1957 and supervised by H. Rowan Gaither.[55] The Gaither Report warned that the Soviet Union was leading in the race to develop ICBMs and that in the period between 1959 and 1962 there would be a critical imbalance in the strategic capabilities of the two superpowers. The report recommended increased funding for the deployment of first-generation missiles and accelerated development of a variety of strategic weapons. It also called for more spending on civil defense and on research that might lead to effective missile defense systems. Unlike the authors of the Killian Report, the members of the Gaither panel predicted a dynamic arms race in which breakthroughs in offensive or defensive weaponry would create periods of instability, threats to national security and dangers of preemptive attack. In the words of Albert Wohlstetter, who briefed the Gaither committee and later wrote an influential article on nuclear strategy for the journal *Foreign Affairs,* the balance of terror was a "delicate" one subject to changes in technology that could give one of the superpowers a meaningful military advantage.[56]

Eisenhower rejected this conclusion. His response after being briefed on the findings of the Gaither committee was a general observation on the feasibility of fighting nuclear wars. "You can't have this kind of war," he reportedly said. "There just aren't enough bulldozers to scrape the bodies off the streets."[57] Eisenhower's revulsion at the thought of nuclear war and his conviction that even small numbers of such weapons would provide an effective deterrent may have been sound judgments, but in the fall of 1957 they were judgments that were not widely shared. The highly classified final report of the Gaither committee was received by the president a month after the launching of Sputnik, amidst growing public anxiety over the obvious Soviet successes in missile development. The contents of the Gaither Report quickly leaked[58] and gave political ammunition to the prospective Democratic presidential candidates who would make the "missile gap" and the space program important issues in their maneuvering for the 1960 election.

The missile gap, like the bomber gap before it, did not exist. Eisenhower, who had access to the intelligence generated by the U-2 flights over the Soviet Union, had confidence that the Soviet missile program was not progressing as rapidly or successfully as his political opponents feared or the Russians claimed, but he was obviously constrained in how much of that intelligence he could share with Congress or the public. Surprised by the extent of the public anxiety brought on by Sputnik and the Soviet space program, Eisenhower was unable to alleviate public fears or the political pressures created by those fears. Sputnik became the compelling symbol of Soviet technological progress and American vulnerability, and the focus of criticisms of Eisenhower's defense policies.

Throughout the late 1950s those policies endured a wide range of attacks. Advocates of limited nuclear war, including Henry Kissinger, criticized the administration for having no nuclear options other than massive retaliation.[59] Army generals who had suffered the budget cuts of the New Look called for increased spending on conventional forces to handle crisis situations where nuclear threats were inappropriate or no longer credible.[60] And nuclear strategists, who had been little known consultants to the federal government for most of the decade, began to speak to public audiences and write popular books about the grisly details of planning nuclear war.[61] Even when these strategists spoke in support of existing policies, their manner and message did little to reassure the American public. The end of the decade saw the fictional creation of Dr. Strangelove and a cultural preoccupation with nuclear nightmares. Michael Mandelbaum characterizes the period from 1957 to 1963 as the "nuclear epoch," the period in the postwar era when Americans fully confronted the grim realities of life on a nuclear armed planet.[62] In such an atmosphere the need for arms control was obvious, but the prospects were bleak. Fear of the Soviet Union, apprehensions about American weaknesses, and debates about the fundamental issues of nuclear strategy made progress in arms control difficult to achieve.

Before Sputnik there had been some hope for a breakthrough in the United Nations disarmament negotiations in Geneva and London. In 1955, Eisenhower had appointed Harold Stassen to take charge of the negotiations that had previously been conducted by the staff of the United Nations ambassador. Stassen brought energy, intelligence, and ambition to his duties, and his appointment signaled increased presidential concern for arms control. When Soviet negotiators showed a willingness to compromise on inspection proposals and on plans to phase in comprehensive disarmament, hope for fruitful negotiations rose. Stassen went to London in 1957 with new instructions on a variety of disarmament problems including an unofficial proposal to combine aerial inspection with assurances that nuclear weapons would be used exclusively for defensive purposes, and a suggestion to devote all production of fissionable material after 1959 to peaceful purposes. Stassen's plan also called for gradual reductions in conventional forces in Europe and significant cutbacks in defense spending and military manpower. In essence, this package was an integration of Open Skies and Atoms for Peace into existing comprehensive disarmament proposals. Stassen was enthusiastic about the possibility for a dramatic breakthrough in the stalled United Nations' negotiations, and he unwisely showed his new instructions to his Soviet counterpart before explaining them to our European allies. The British, who were just beginning to deploy their own nuclear deterrent, objected to the restrictions on future production of fissionable material and the lack of consultation on such an important initiative. Dulles, who had been looking for some way to clip the wings of his latest competitor, objected to Stassen's actions just as vigorously as did the British. Stassen was ordered back to Washington for "consultations," and the prospects for progress on the new Soviet and American UN initiatives were never tested. By the end of the year Sputnik had changed the climate of East-West competition and the likelihood that any comprehensive arms control agreements could be reached.

Eisenhower spent his last years in the presidency searching for a forum for serious negotiations with the Soviet Union. He received Khrushchev at Camp David, accepted an invitation to visit the Soviet Union, and scheduled a second summit. After Dulles's death he took a more visible role in foreign affairs and hoped that personal diplomacy at a summit or in the Soviet Union would produce agreement on the elusive first step in arms control and the reduction of cold-war tensions. When an American U-2 plane was shot down over Soviet territory and its CIA pilot captured, any expectations for substantive diplomacy with the Soviet Union ended. Eisenhower was resigned to finishing his presidency without achieving the chance for peace he had sought from the beginning.

Conclusion

> With both sections of this divided world in possession of unbelievably destructive weapons, mankind approaches a state where mutual annihilation becomes a possibility. No other fact of today's world equals this in importance; it colors everything we say, everything we plan, and everything we do.[63]

Eisenhower clearly regarded arms control as an important subject. He made it the centerpiece for two of the major international initiatives during his first term—Atoms for Peace and Open Skies. He devoted his first and his last foreign policy speeches—the Chance for Peace and the Farewell Address—to the international and domestic consequences of the arms race. He consistently appointed able assistants to work on arms control policy and generally gave them the support they needed to make headway against a cautious State Department and a suspicious Pentagon. He was personally convinced that arms control negotiations were necessary. In a letter Eisenhower wrote in 1956, he stated the central dilemma of the nuclear age about as well as anyone could: "The true security problem . . . is not merely man against man or nation against nation. It is man against war . . . when we get to the point, as we one day will, that both sides know that in any outbreak of general hostilities, regardless of the element of surprise, destruction will be reciprocal and complete, possibly we will have sense enough to meet at the conference table with the understanding that the era of armaments has ended and the human race must conform its action to this truth or die."[64]

Speaking to Bulganin and Molotov at Geneva, he compared the origins of World War I with the situation in 1955. "Whereas once it was said that wars began where diplomacy fails, diplomacy must now begin because war has failed."[65] Despite a strong personal commitment to arms control, Eisenhower was able to achieve very little. Some of the problems that prevented successful negotiations were technological; others were political; many are still with us.

Part of the problem in the 1950s was the level of technological development. In the early decades of strategic competition with the Soviet Union there was real danger that a surprise attack could be decisive. That danger was a function of the vulnerability of early delivery systems, and although fears of a successful first strike persist, they were more legitimate in the 1950s. Eisenhower observed when the first invulnerable missile platform, the Polaris submarine, went into operation that, "It seems a wry and sad commentary on human intelligence that the development of a unique weapons system did more to restore a feeling of Western confidence in a stable future than had all the disarmament talks conducted over a period of years."[66]

The technology of inspection, or rather the lack of it, was also important during Eisenhower's presidency. It delayed test ban negotiations and stood in the way of all comprehensive agreements. During most of the decade inspection of arms control agreements meant permanent observation sites and special visits to sensitive facilities. Eisenhower was skeptical that any such system would ever work. Frustrated by violations of the Korean armistice, he told his advisors that "adequate inspection and control [of nuclear weapons] is impossible. If the Swiss and the Swedes cannot inspect North Korea, how can we inspect the USSR?"[67] The development of U-2 planes, satellites, and sophisticated aerial cameras eventually provided both sides with good intelligence about bomber and missile installations. Ironically, it was Sputnik that set the precedent for satellite overflights and made possible the opening of Soviet society that Open Skies and U-2 flights had attempted to achieve.

Gradual technological improvements on vulnerability and inspection dictated a gradual approach to arms control. Throughout the Eisenhower era, the arms control initiatives of the United States were designed to be first steps in a process that would take time before producing substantial reductions and serious controls. The comprehensive disarmament proposals that were endlessly discussed in the first decade after Hiroshima grew increasingly unrealistic. By the mid-1950s both the United States and the Soviet Union had arsenals so large that no inspection system, no matter how intrusive or sophisticated, could guarantee that all warheads and all nuclear facilities would be discovered and controlled. Complete nuclear disarmament, if ever possible, would require a level of international trust almost unimaginable in the midst of the cold war. In 1955 the Eisenhower administration officially withdrew American support for UN comprehensive disarmament proposals. Throughout the decade Eisenhower sought limited agreements that would help to create sufficient trust to permit subsequent negotiations. Writing to General Alfred Greunther about the importance of Open Skies, Eisenhower emphasized this need for trust: "But if we assume that the kind of inspection to which I referred would eliminate the danger of devastating surprise attack, the agreement for such inspection and this result would yield an immense gain in mutual confidence and trust. This means that we would thus have established a truly realistic basis for studying disarmament."[68]

Virtually all postwar arms control agreements have been defended in this way. They are presented as parts of a larger series which, at a later date, will produce genuine reductions. They are described as political measures that increase confidence and make it possible to proceed to the central issues of disarmament. These kinds of arguments have led some cynics to see arms control as little more than a public relations tool for managing the arms race, and the arms control proposals of the 1950s as nothing more than propaganda.[69] There is little evidence that Eisenhower's commitment to arms control was either cynical or insincere. He was, however, careful to ensure that he did not risk the nation's security. In his statement on disarmament at the Geneva conference, he expressed the dilemma of national leaders in the nuclear age: "The quest for peace is the statesman's most exacting duty. Security of the nation entrusted to his care is his greatest responsibility. Practical progress to lasting peace is his fondest hope. Yet in pursuit of hope he must not betray the trust placed in him as guardian of the people's security."[70] Confronted with the difficult choices between his hopes for peace and his responsibilities to national security, Eisenhower always allowed his responsibilities to circumscribe his hopes. His arms control proposals were cautious. They were also one-sided.

Atoms for Peace and Open Skies would have involved more sacrifices for the Soviet Union than for the United States, and we were not alone in suggesting agreements that offered less than equal terms. Early in the 1950s the Soviets favored proportional conventional disarmament in Europe at a time when Warsaw Pact forces were far larger than their NATO counterparts. Later they gave priority to controlling nuclear weapons before discussing conventional force reductions, even though nuclear weapons were regarded as the West's only defense against the superior Red Army in Europe. In 1958, Khrushchev proposed a temporary test ban after completing a long and apparently successful series of atmospheric explosions. Eisenhower could respond only after the United States had completed its own new set of tests.

Throughout the history of arms control negotiations, initial negotiating positions have been less than generous, and finding formulas for equal limitations has been a slow and painstaking process. Even after negotiations have been completed, finished treaties and agreements have often been so complex that it is usually easy to generate political controversy about which side had come out ahead. Under these circumstances the American statesman seeking peace has to worry not only about his nation's security, but also his own political future.

Ever since Hiroshima, but particularly in the 1950s, public reactions to news of nuclear dangers and predictions of Soviet military advances have been almost schizophrenic. For some there is a powerful temptation to renounce nuclear weapons, and in the late 1950s a large segment of the British population did precisely that. The Ban the Bomb movement attracted a middle-class following and the temporary endorsement of the Labor party. The United States did not experience widespread public protest against nuclear weapons until the 1980s, but even during the Eisenhower years there were many Americans, particularly intellectuals, who called for an end to testing and a serious beginning to disarmament negotiations. For a time, Stevenson was cheered when he proposed a suspension of nuclear testing and warned of the madness of the arms race. This reaction was, however, not the only or the typical response. Many Americans faced with the dangers of the nuclear age demanded the creation and maintenance of military superiority. In 1956 Eisenhower won easy reelection against the test ban proposals of Adlai Stevenson. Four years later the Republicans lost against accusations that they had failed to address a growing missile gap. The political lesson seems clear. Of the two impulses that an anxious public feels in the nuclear age, the one to arm has been more potent than the one to negotiate. This may have been the lesson of 1980 as well as 1960, and it remains to be seen whether the nuclear protest campaigns in Europe and the United States in the early 1980s can generate any long-term policy changes. Eisenhower's own observations on this subject may be of interest. When he met with Macmillan during the height of the British nuclear protest of the late 1950s he warned, "I believe that the people in the long run are going to do more to promote peace than any governments. Indeed, I think that people want peace so much that one of these days governments had better get out of their way and let them have it."[71]

During his years in the White House Eisenhower increasingly came to regard government as an obstacle to effective defense and foreign policymaking. He once praised his science advisors for being "one of the few groups that I encountered in Washington who seemed to be there to help the country and not help themselves."[72] Although a career military officer, or perhaps because he was a career military officer, he doubted the need for large defense budgets and recognized the serious problems of service rivalries, technological excess, and systems salesmanship in military procurement.[73] In 1959, he pushed through Congress a major reorganization of the Department of Defense, the full impact of which would not be felt until the McNamara era, and he ended his presidency by speaking to the American people about the dangers of the military-industrial complex.

In the decade that followed his Farewell Address, the term *military-industrial complex* would come to mean something different than Eisenhower intended. He was not worried by simple economic interest groups that profited from military contracting. He saw a more subtle problem. Defense in the age of nuclear-warhead-guided-missiles was becoming so complex that elected officials deferred too readily to elites whose judgments, whether biased or not, were often unchecked. "The potential for the disastrous rise of misplaced power exists and will persist," and this problem will occur whether "unwarranted influence" is "sought or unsought."[74] In other words, the danger that Eisenhower feared was not that weapons manufacturers would necessarily corrupt the government and usurp power, but that elected officials and citizens might very well abdicate it. Defense issues in the nuclear age were so technical that they were rapidly escaping the realm of effective political discourse.

A related problem was afflicting universities and research institutions. The level of military research and development spending held the potential for overwhelming our educational institutions and compromising the principal source of independent expertise in the society. Along with the dangers of the military-industrial complex, Eisenhower cautioned against the prospect that "public policy could become the captive of a scientific-technological elite."[75] In both cases he was urging citizens and statesmen to keep control of the military issues confronting the nation and to continue the quest for arms control. "Disarmament," he said, "with mutual honor and confidence, is a continuing imperative."[76]

But if Eisenhower left office worried about the inordinate influence of experts in national defense, he was equally concerned that politicians might take demogogic advantage of nuclear questions. He was conscious in 1953 when he read early drafts of the documents produced for Operation Candor that it would be easy to generate volatile public fears of nuclear weapons and war, and he resented both the Stevenson test ban and the Kennedy missile gap issues. Neither Stevenson nor Kennedy, in Eisenhower's view, gave the American people a fair account of radiation hazards and the Soviet missile program. The people may have wanted peace, but experts and politicians were unlikely to provide it. Eisenhower ended his Farewell Address by confessing his own failures: "Because this need (for disarmament) is so sharp and apparent, I confess that I lay down my responsibilities in this field with a definite sense of disappointment. As one who has witnessed the horror and the lingering sadness of war, as one who knows that another war could utterly destroy this civilization which has been so slowly and painfully built over thousands of years, I wish I could say tonight that a lasting peace is in sight."[77]

Eisenhower tried throughout his presidency to moderate the demands of the military-industrial complex without making appeals to the fears of a nation newly threatened with the possibility of annihilation. He tempered his dependence on nuclear weapons and massive retaliation with a sincere commitment to move toward their control. He prepared arms control proposals that were realistic starting points that would permit initial negotiations with a cold-war adversary but without risking national security. He failed to achieve any significant arms control successes, but his efforts, inconsistent as they often were, provide vivid demonstration of how difficult it will always be to make progress toward the elimination of weapons that both guarantee and threaten our national survival.

Notes

1. The most recent and theoretically innovative account of Eisenhower's misunderstood leadership style is that of Fred I. Greenstein, *The Hidden-Hand Presidency* (New York: Basic Books, 1982), In the handling of foreign affairs and national security two recent books praise Eisenhower's effectiveness: Douglas Kinnard, *President Eisenhower and Strategy Management* (Lexington: University Press of Kentucky, 1977) and Robert Divine, *Eisenhower and the Cold War* (New York: Oxford University Press, 1981).

2. Dwight D. Eisenhower, *The White House Years: Waging Peace, 1956-1961* (Garden City, N.Y. Doubleday, 1965), 467.

3. Robert C. Williams and Philip L. Cantelon, eds., *The American Atom* (Philadelphia: University of Pennsylvania Press, 1984), 181.

4. Greg Herken, *Counsels of War* (New York: Knopf, 1985), 103.

5. Ibid.

6. Quoted in Michael Mandelbaum, *The Nuclear Question* (New York: Cambridge University Press, 1979), 49.

7. Stephen Ambrose, *Eisenhower: The President* (New York: Simon & Schuster, 1984), 169.

8. Dwight D. Eisenhower, *The White House Years: Mandate for Change, 1953-1956* (Garden City, N. Y.: Doubleday, 1963), 446.

9. Ambrose, *Eisenhower: The President*, 224.

10. The same policies had been adopted earlier by the British in the year after Churchill returned to power.

11. R. Gordon Hoxie, *Command Decision and the Presidency* (New York: Readers' Digest Press, 1977), 203.

12. Lawrence Freedman, *The Evolution of Nuclear Strategy* (New York: St. Martin's Press, 1983), 81.

13. According to John Spanier, "No policy could have been more typically American than massive retaliation." John Spanier, *American Foreign Policy since World War II*, 9th ed. (New York: Holt, Rinehart & Winston, 1983), 101.

14. Eisenhower, *Mandate for Change*, 181.

15. John Foster Dulles, speech before the Council on Foreign Relations, New York, 12 January 1954. Reprinted in Robert A. Goldwin and Harry M. Clor, eds., *Readings in American Foreign Policy* (New York: Oxford University Press, 1971), 482.

16. Eisenhower, *Mandate for Change*. 312–13.

17. Emmet John Hughes, *The Ordeal of Power* (New York: Atheneum, 1963), 101.

18. Press conference 17 August 1954. Quoted in Henry Cabot Lodge, *As It Was* (New York: W.W. Norton, 1976), 68.

19. Robert H. Ferrell, ed., *The Diary of James C. Hagerty* (Bloomington: Indiana University Press, 1983), 69.

20. This is Eisenhower's summary of the speech given in his memoirs and not an exact quote from the text of the speech. Eisenhower, *Mandate for Change,* 145.

21. *Public Papers of the Presidents of the United States: Dwight D. Eisenhower 1953* (Washington: Government Printing Office, 1960), 186.

22. For a detailed account of the preparation of the speech see John Lear, "Ike and the Peaceful Atom," in *Eisenhower as President,* ed. Dean Alberton. (New York: Hill and Wang, 1963), 87–111.

23. Herken, *Counsels of War,* 67–103.

24. Eisenhower, *Mandate for Change,* 252.

25. Ibid.

26. Ibid., 254.

27. Thomas F. Soapes, "A Cold Warrior Seeks Peace: Eisenhower's Strategy for Nuclear Disarmament," *Diplomatic History* 4 (Winter 1980): 61–62.

28. Herken, *Counsels of War,* 104.

29. Robert H. Ferrell, ed., *The Eisenhower Diaries* (New York: W. W. Norton, 1981), 261.

30. Ibid., 262.

31. Ambrose, *Eisenhower: The President,* 147.

32. *Documents on Disarmament 1945–1959,* vol. 1 (Washington: Government Printing Office, 1960), 399.

33. Eisenhower, *Waging Peace,* 468.

34. There is some dispute over where the idea for Open Skies originated. Both Stassen and Rockefeller claim credit for it. See John E. Eisenhower, *Strictly Personal* (Garden City, N.Y.: Doubleday, 1974), 178. The best source on the development of the Open Skies proposal is Walt W. Rostow, *Open Skies: Eisenhower's Proposal of July 21, 1955* (Austin: University of Texas Press, 1982).

35. Herken, *Counsels of War,* 110.

36. Memo of telephone conversation between Eisenhower and Dulles, 6 July 1955. Quoted in Rostow, *Open Skies,* 46.

37. See Appendix H to Rostow, *Open Skies,* 159–64.

38. Stephen Ambrose, *Ike's Spies* (Garden City, N.Y.: Doubleday, 1981), 270.

39. Eisenhower, *Mandate for Change,* 521.

40. Ibid.

41. For a detailed account of these events and their consequences on administration policy, see Robert Divine, *Blowing on the Wind* (New York: Oxford University Press, 1978).

42. Rostow, *Open Skies,* 62.

43. Divine, *Blowing on the Wind,* 94.

44. John Bartlow Martin, *Adlai Stevenson and the World* (Garden City, N.Y.: Doubleday, 1978), 311–12.

45. Robert Divine notes that during the last two weeks in October Stevenson received overwhelmingly positive mail about his test ban proposal. Robert

Divine, *Foreign Policy and U.S. Presidential Elections 1952–1960* (New York: New Viewpoints, 1974), 160.

46. Divine, *Blowing on the Wind*, 98.

47. Martin, *Adlai Stevenson*, 383; Divine, *Blowing on the Wind*, 91–92.

48. Divine, *Blowing on the Wind*, 152.

49. Ambrose, *Eisenhower: The President*, 399–400.

50. For a complete list of atmospheric tests, see Williams and Cantelon, *The American Atom*, 179–83.

51. Eisenhower, *Mandate for Change*, 457.

52. Fred Kaplan, *The Wizards of Armageddon* (New York: Simon & Schuster, 1983), 85–110.

53. For a complete account of the bomber gap issue, see John Prados, *The Soviet Estimate: U.S. Intelligence Analysis and Russian Military Strength* (New York: Dial Press, 1982), 41–50.

54. Freedman, *Evolution of Nuclear Strategy*, 158–60.

55. Ibid., 160–63. See also, Desmond Ball, *Politics and Force Levels* (Berkeley: University of California Press, 1980), 3–40.

56. Albert Wohlstetter, "The Delicate Balance of Terror," *Foreign Affairs* 37 (January 1959): 2.

57. Herken, *Counsels of War*, 116.

58. For a detailed discussion of the Gaither Committee Report and its unauthorized release, see Morton Halperin, "The Gaither Committee and the Policy Process," *World Politics* 13 (April 1961):3.

59. Henry A. Kissinger, *Nuclear Weapons and Foreign Policy* (New York: Harper, 1957).

60. Maxwell Taylor, *The Uncertain Trumpet* (New York: Harper, 1959).

61. Herman Kahn, *On Thermonuclear War* (Princeton: Princeton University Press, 1960).

62. Michael Mandelbaum, *The Nuclear Revolution* (New York: Cambridge University Press, 1981), 218–19.

63. State of the Union Address, 7 January 1960. *Peace and Justice: Selected Speeches of Dwight D. Eisenhower* (New York: Columbia University Press, 1961), 207.

64. Quoted in Herbert Schoville, Jr., *MX: Prescription for Disaster* (Cambridge, Mass: MIT Press, 1982), 1.

65. Blanche Wiesen Cook, *The Declassified Eisenhower* (Garden City, N.Y.: Doubleday, 1981), 154.

66. Eisenhower, *Waging Peace*, 483.

67. Rostow, *Open Skies*, 63.

68. Soapes, "A Cold Warrior Seeks Peace," 65–66.

69. This is the conclusion of Peter Lyons, *Eisenhower: Portrait of a Hero* (Boston: Little, Brown, 1974), 584–85, 663–64.

70. Eisenhower, *Mandate for Change*, 443.

71. Cook, *The Declassified Eisenhower*, 149.

72. James R. Killian, *Sputnik, Scientists and Eisenhower* (Cambridge, Mass: MIT Press, 1977), 241.

73. For an account of Eisenhower's opinion on these subjects see Ibid., 230.

74. *Public Papers of the Presidents of the United States: Dwight D. Eisenhower 1960-61* (Washington: Government Printing Office, 1961), 1038.

75. Ibid., 1039.

76. Ibid.

77. Ibid., 1039–40.

About the Contributors

ANNE-MARIE BURLEY received a M. Phil. in International Relations from Oxford University in 1982. She is a Ph.D. candidate in the Department of Government at Harvard University.

NORMAN A. GRAEBNER has been Edward R. Stettinius Professor of Modern American History at the University of Virginia since 1967, and in 1982 was named Randolph Compton Professor at the White Burkett Miller Center of Public Affairs. He is the author of several books on American diplomatic history including *The New Isolationism, Manifest Destiny,* and *The Age of Global Power.*

RICHARD H. IMMERMAN is assistant professor of history at the University of Hawaii. His *The CIA in Guatemala: The Foreign Policy of Intervention* received the Stuart Bernath Memorial Book Award from the Society for Historians of American Foreign Relations in 1983. He has also written (with Stephen E. Ambrose) *Milton S. Eisenhower: Educational Statesman.* He is currently involved in a collective study of Eisenhower's and Johnson's decisions concerning Vietnam.

DAVID MAYERS is assistant professor of politics at the University of California, Santa Cruz. He has published articles about George Kennan and about U.S.-Soviet-Chinese relations. His *Cracking the Monolith: US Policy Against the Sino-Soviet Alliance, 1949-1955* is based on his University of Chicago Ph.D. thesis.

RICHARD A. MELANSON is associate professor of political science at Kenyon College. His work has appeared in the *Western Political Quarterly,* the *Human Rights Quarterly,* and the *Political Science Reviewer.* Among his books are *Foreign Policy and Domestic Consensus* (1985), *Writing History and Making Policy: The Cold War, Vietnam, and Revisionism* (1983), and *Neither Cold War Nor Détente? Soviet-American Relations in the 1980s* (1982).

WILLIAM STIVERS is currently Director of the University of Southern California's Graduate Program in Germany. When he wrote the essay in this volume, he was a resident associate at the Carnegie Endowment for International Peace. He has published essays on the Middle East in *Foreign Policy, Diplomatic History,* and *The Business History Review,* and his book *Supremacy and Oil* was published in 1982.

ROBERT A. STRONG is assistant professor of political science at Tulane University. He is currently co-authoring a study of the Carter presidency. He was a director of the Carter Oral History Project at The White Burkett Miller Center, University of Virginia.

KENNETH W. THOMPSON is the Director of the White Burkett Miller Center of Public Affairs at the University of Virginia and a professor in the department of government and foreign affairs. He is the author of more than two dozen books on international relations and American foreign policy including most recently *The President and the Public Philosophy* (1981) and *Winston Churchill's World View* (1982).

THOMAS ZOUMARAS recently completed his Ph.D. in history at the University of Connecticut, where he worked with Thomas G. Paterson. He is currently teaching in the Department of History at Dickinson College.

Index